RE-IMAGINING SEXUAL HARASSMENT

Perspectives from the Nordic Region

Edited by
Maja Lundqvist, Angelica Simonsson and Kajsa Widegren

Foreword by
Ruth Lewis

First published in Great Britain in 2023 by

Policy Press, an imprint of
Bristol University Press
University of Bristol
1–9 Old Park Hill
Bristol
BS2 8BB
UK
t: +44 (0)117 374 6645
e: bup-info@bristol.ac.uk

Details of international sales and distribution partners are available at
policy.bristoluniversitypress.co.uk

British Library Cataloguing in Publication Data
A catalogue record for this book is available from the British Library

ISBN 978-1-4473-6652-2 paperback
ISBN 978-1-4473-6653-9 ePub
ISBN 978-1-4473-6654-6 OA PDF

FSC
www.fsc.org
MIX
Paper | Supporting
responsible forestry
FSC® C013604

This book was initiated and funded by the Swedish Secretariat for Gender Research and Nordic Information on Gender (NIKK).

The Swedish Secretariat for Gender Research is part of the University of Gothenburg, and collaborates with partners in national, Nordic, and international arenas. The Secretariat has many years of experience working with research on sexual harassment and has produced a number of research reviews and reports. This is also where the three editors of the book are affiliated.

Nordic Information on Gender (NIKK) is a cooperation body under the Nordic Council of Ministers, based at the Secretariat. NIKK produces, gathers and strategically disseminates research, policy, knowledge, and practice from a Nordic and cross-sectoral perspective.

The editors would like to express their deepest thanks to all colleagues at the Swedish Secretariat for Gender Research for their help and invaluable input on everything from ideas to texts, and for their support throughout the process.

Also, this project would not have been possible without the contributions from all of the writers. Thank you for your excellent collaboration and all the creative and thought-provoking texts that we have had the privilege of reading and putting together.

Contents

List of figures

Notes on contributors

Sumaya Jirde Ali is a Norwegian-Somali social debater, author, poet and literary critic. Ali has published three collections of poems and a Nynorsk pamphlet. Ali's day job is as a social anthropologist, and she is also a regular critic in *Vinduet*, a columnist in *Morgenbladet* and editor-in-chief of the feminist cultural magazine *Fett*. In the autumn of 2022, Ali made her debut as a playwright on the National Stage in Bergen. Previous publications include: *Ikkje ver redd sånne som meg*, Det Norske Samlaget, 2018; *Melanin hvitere enn blekemiddel*, Aschehoug, 2018; and *Når jeg ser havet, slokner lyse*, Aschehoug, 2021.

Silas Aliki is a lawyer at Folkets Advokatbyrå (The People's Law Firm) and a freelance writer. They have also studied literary composition and warfare studies. Silas is interested in juridical and security policy, the consequences of the class society, and trans issues, and has also written cultural criticism. Publications include: *Sveriges dolda NATO-samarbete*, Tidskriften Bang, 2014; *Transfobins historia*, Glänta, 2019; and *Våra berättelser ska inte avbrytas*, Kontext Press, 2020.

Hildur Fjóla Antonsdóttir, PhD in sociology of law, currently holds a Postdoctoral Fellowship at the EDDA Research Center at the University of Iceland. Her research interests are in the field of sexual violence and justice, including social and legal justice. Her publications include: '"A witness in my own case": Victim–survivors' views on the criminal justice process in Iceland', *Feminist Legal Studies*, 2018; 'Injustice disrupted: Experiences of just spaces by victim-survivors of sexual violence', *Social & Legal Studies*, 2020; and 'Compensation as a means to justice? Sexual violence survivors' views on the tort law option in Iceland', *Feminist Legal Studies*, 2020.

Elin Bjarnegård is Associate Professor in Political Science at the Department of Government, Uppsala University. Her research interests are at the intersection of comparative politics and gender studies. Her articles have appeared in journals such as *American Political Science Review, Journal of Democracy* and *Journal of Peace Research*. She is the author of the book *Gender, Informal Institutions and Political Recruitment*, Palgrave Macmillan, 2013, and editor of the forthcoming book *Gender and Violence against Political Actors*, Temple University Press, 2023. She is currently leading a Swedish Research Council project on sexual corruption and sextortion in Tanzania.

Dolores Calvo holds a PhD in sociology from the University of Gothenburg (2013). She is an independent researcher and consultant based in Stockholm, who is also affiliated with the Department of Government at Uppsala University. Calvo is currently working on a project on the implementation of policies against sextortion in Tanzania, including questions of abuse of power, sexual abuse, gender norms, coercion, and consent. She has conducted research in the following fields: gender, gender mainstreaming, gender-based violence, trafficking, prostitution, feminism, collective action, and grassroots movements. She has worked in Sweden, Latin America, and at EU level.

Paulina de los Reyes is Professor of Economic History at Stockholm University. She has conducted research on postcolonialism and intersectionality with a special focus on global inequalities. Her research areas also include feminist theory, postcolonial feminism, and the political economy of social reproduction. Among her recent publications are: 'Migrant mothers: Work, nation and racialisation in Swedish official discourses 1970–2000', *Scandinavian Economic History Review*, 2022; 'When feminism became gender equality and anti-racism turned into diversity management', in *Challenging the Myth of Gender Equality*, Policy Press, 2016; and 'Hegemonic feminism revisited: On the promises of intersectionality in times of the precarisation of life' (with Diana Mulinari), *NORA - Nordic Journal of Feminist and Gender Research*, 2020. She has also been the editor of an anthology on postcolonial feminism.

Åsa Eldén is a researcher at the Department of Government, Uppsala University and holds a PhD in sociology. She is also an independent consultant and researcher collaborating with agencies and civil society organisations in Sweden, Türkiye, and internationally. Her work focuses on gender-based violence, honour violence, media, the women's movement, gender equality in development, and the shrinking democratic space. In recent years, she has been working on the topic of sextortion in development cooperation and in the Nordic context, together with the research team who co-authored her chapter.

Jeff Hearn is Senior Professor, Human Geography, Örebro University, Sweden; Professor of Sociology, University of Huddersfield, UK; and Professor Emeritus, Hanken School of Economics, Finland. He is co-managing editor of the Routledge *Advances in Feminist Studies and Intersectionality* book series, and co-editor of *NORMA: The International Journal for Masculinity Studies*; and was (co-)chair of RINGS: International Research Association of Institutions of Advanced Gender Studies, 2014–20. His research focuses on gender, sexuality, violence, work, organisations, policy, ICTs, and transnational processes. Recent books include: *Age at Work* (with Wendy Parkin), Sage, 2021; *Knowledge, Power and Young Sexualities* (with Tamara Shefer); and *Digital Gender-Sexual Violations* (with Matthew Hall and Ruth Lewis), both Routledge, 2022.

Anne Hellum is Professor at the Department of Public and International Law at the University of Oslo. Her main areas of teaching and research are equality and non-discrimination law, human rights law, and legal anthropology. She is co-author of *Likestillings- og diskrimineringsrett*, Gyldendal, 2022; co-editor of Women's Human Rights, CEDAW in *International, Regional and National Law*, Cambridge University Press, 2013; and editor of *Human Rights, Sexual Orientation and Gender Identity*, Routledge, 2017.

Anne Laure Humbert, PhD, is Professor of Gender and Statistics and Co-Director of the Centre for Diversity Policy Research and Practice at Oxford Brookes University. Anne has worked extensively on developing methodologies and indicators for measuring gender equality. Recently, she has contributed to the Horizon 2020 funded project UniSAFE, which seeks to measure and address gender-based violence in higher education in Europe. Recent publications include: 'From gender regimes to violence regimes: Re-thinking the position of violence', *Social Politics*, 2022; and *Undoing the Nordic Paradox: Factors affecting rates of disclosed violence against women across the EU*, PLOS ONE, 2021.

Mads Ananda Lodahl is an independent bodyworker, lecturer, and author of both fiction and non-fiction. He has been focusing mainly on queer and trans experiences for the last 20 years in theory, activism, nightlife, therapy, film, and literature. He runs the queer- and trans-centred SPACE clinic for bodywork in Copenhagen and has played a central role in discussions on gender and sexuality in Denmark. Previous publications include: *Soft Boys*, Gyldendal, 2023; *Upassende Opførsel*, Solidaritet, 2018; and *Sauna*, Gyldendal, 2021.

Silje Lundgren is Senior Lecturer at Tema Genus, Linköping University. She is currently working on two research projects about sexual harassment and sexual abuse of power in the Swedish police force, funded by Forte (the Swedish Research Council for Health, Working Life and Welfare) and the Swedish Crime Victim Fund, together with Dr Malin Wieslander (Linköping University). Lundgren is also working on a project funded by the Swedish Research Council on the implementation of policies against sextortion in Tanzania, headed by Principal Investigator Elin Bjarnegård. Silje Lundgren has a PhD in cultural anthropology from Uppsala University (2011).

Maja Lundqvist works as an analyst at the Swedish Secretariat for Gender Research at the University of Gothenburg, Sweden. She holds an MA in gender studies, with a focus on intersectional perspectives. Maja has ten years of experience working in the gender equality research field in Sweden, the Nordic region, and Europe. Her main focus has been the issue of sexual harassment in higher education and workplaces. Previous publications include: 'Sexual harassment in higher education – a systematic review', *European Journal of Higher Education*, 2020; 'Sexual harassment in higher education – a systematic review', *The Swedish Research Council*, 2018; and *Sexual Harassment in the Research and Higher Education Sector: National Policies and Measures in EU Member States and Associated Countries*, ERAC, 2020.

Heta Mulari is a post-doctoral researcher at the Unit of Social Research, Faculty of Social Sciences, Tampere University. Her research interests include youth and girlhood studies, urban studies and feminist ethnography. She is co-editor of *Nordic Girlhoods – New Perspectives and Outlooks*, Palgrave Macmillan, 2017 (with Bodil Formark and Myry Voipio). Her publications also include: 'Emotional encounters and young feminine choreographies in the Helsinki Metro', *Girlhood Studies*, 2020; and '"Everyone here is willing to teach each other": Negotiations over hippie culture and resistance in Helsinki-based flow art community', *Journal of Youth Studies*, 2021.

Angelica Simonsson, PhD in education, is a senior analyst at the Swedish Secretariat for Gender Research, University of Gothenburg. Currently she also works as a postdoctoral researcher in gender studies, Örebro University, studying institutional responses to sexual harassment in higher education in the Horizon 2020 funded project UniSAFE. Her research interests are in the field of gender, sexuality, and education. Her publications include: *Preventive Work against Sexual Harassment in Swedish and Nordic Working Life*, Swedish Secretariat for Gender Research, 2020; and 'Smooth conversations: sexuality as a linguistic resource in a secondary language classroom', *Discourse: Studies in the Cultural Politics of Education*, 2020.

Lea Skewes is Assistant Professor at VIA University College, Aarhus. She is a social psychologist and philosopher who specialises in gender stereotypes and gender discrimination. Her recent work focuses on sexism, gender discrimination, and the backlash against gender equality policies in Danish academia. Skewes has been on the editorial board of *Women, Gender & Research* since 2017. She has also founded the Gendering in Research (GIR) network at Aarhus University. Previous publications include: 'Attitudes to sexism and the #MeToo movement at a university in Denmark', *NORA – Nordic Journal of Feminist and Gender Research*, 2021; and *Attitudes to Sexism and Gender Equality at a Danish University*, *Women, Gender & Research*'s special issue on Gender and Academia, 2019 (both with Joshua Skewes and Michelle Ryan).

Sigbjørn Skåden is a Sámi writer from Láŋtdievvá/Planterhaugen in Northern Norway. He writes in both indigenous Sámi language and Norwegian, and since his debut in 2004 with the epic long poem *Skuovvadeddjiid gonagas* has published one other book of poetry, three novels and a children's book. Skåden has been the Young Artist Of the Year at Riddu Riđđu indigenous festival, the prologue writer for the Arctic Arts Festival, and a profile author for the European poetry platform Versopolis. His book *Våke over dem som sover*, received the Havmann Award for Best North Norwegian Book of the Year, 2014. Skåden has a Master's degree in English literature and a Master's degree on Sámi poetry. His latest book is the novel *Fugl*, Cappelen Damm, 2019.

Sofia Strid is Senior Lecturer in Sociology University of Gothenburg, and Associate Professor of Gender Studies and Research Leader at the Centre for Violence Studies at Örebro University. She is Principal Investigator of Regimes of Violence, Swedish Research Council, and the Scientific Coordinator of UniSAFE, RESISTIRÉ and ACCTING, EUH2020. She has worked extensively on the theory and measurement of violence. Recent publications include: 'Inequalities, isolation, intersectionality', *Women's Studies International Forum*, 2021; 'States of violence', *Journal of European Social Policy*, 2021; and *From Gender Regimes to Violence Regimes: Re-thinking the Position of Violence*, Social Politics, 2022.

Kajsa Widegren, PhD in gender studies, is a senior analyst at the Swedish Secretariat for Gender Research, University of Gothenburg. As an analyst, she works mainly with the working conditions in Swedish higher education, with a special interest in the institutionalisation of interdisciplinary fields. Previous research activities have included publications on feminist cultural studies, girlhood studies, and visual culture. Her publications include: 'The politics of the mask: The Knife as queer-feminists', *Made in Sweden – Studies in Popular Music*, Routledge, 2017; 'Emotionally charged: Parental leave and gender equality, at the surface of the skin', *Challenging the Myth of Gender Equality in Sweden*, Policy Press, 2016; Kärnkraft, jordbävning, krig: Chim↑pom och den relationella estetiken som kärnkraftsmotstånd, *Tidskrift för genusvetenskap*, 2015–16.

Foreword

Ruth Lewis

Northumbria University

Angelica Simonsson, Maja Lundqvist and Kajsa Widegren are ideally placed, in their work at the Swedish Secretariat for Gender Research at University of Gothenburg, to bring together this fascinating collection about sexual harassment. With recent extensive experience of examining aspects of sexual harassment, they have a deep familiarity with the current research and policy landscape and have identified a need to 're-imagine' our approaches to sexual harassment. Such re-imaginaries are required, they contend, in order to move beyond the defining characteristics of much existing sexual harassment research with its focus on prevalence and measurement, and the unproblematic use of juridical terms for conceptualising sexual harassment. In addition, the editors set the parameters and scope of the collection by making a strong case, drawing on Mary Douglas's work about dirt, that we should not view sexual harassment as anomalous but as interwoven into the fabric of everyday practices; rather than being atypical, sexual harassment is a social and cultural phenomenon that is part of the continuum of violence, life and society. In the midst of widespread drives towards 'gender-neutrality' which deny the significance of enduring structures and systems on the material realities of life, this perspective is welcome indeed.

The editors' success in developing new directions is enhanced by one of the book's most compelling features; the union of scholarship (which includes empirical and theoretical insights) written by academics whose primary focus has not been sexual harassment, with essays and 'vignettes' by fiction writers, practitioners, and activists. The contributions generated by this approach – which reflects a long-standing Nordic tradition of facilitating dialogue between researchers, politicians, policy makers, practitioners, and nongovernmental organisations – have provided a fresh perspective that breaks out of the boundaries that so often develop around disciplines, sub-disciplines, professional groups and working practices, not to mention national boundaries.

While the book overall recognises that sexual harassment is a gendered phenomenon and is perpetrated primarily by men against women, the narrative contributions, in particular, present non-traditional accounts of sexual harassment that break away from the common narrow view of it as being perpetrated by men in the workplace. These compelling contributions are careful, thoughtful, empathetic accounts of personal experiences which stayed with me long after I read them, reminding me of the complexities of sexual harassment, power, and gender and the intersecting systems of oppression that are implicated.

A further strength of the book is the care taken by the contributors to provide detailed contextualisation of sexual harassment. The socio-economic, political histories of the Nordic region and of individual Nordic countries are brought into sharp focus and provide fascinating insights, as well as challenging the widespread belief that Nordic social democracy has achieved something close to gender equality. More recent political developments, such as #MeToo, also provide the context in which contemporary considerations of sexual harassment occur but, while recognising its significance, the editors and contributors are careful not to overstate the impact of #MeToo.

The contributions include intersectional perspectives on: sexual harassment in the context of workplace exploitation of 'depleted' female bodies; sextortion as an important conceptualisation of sexual violence and corruption; sexual harassment against young women and its impacts on their engagement with urban spaces; the conditions in academia that are conducive to sexual harassment; judicial approaches to sexual harassment, including restorative justice, carceral feminism, equality and anti-discrimination frameworks; how generations of oppression against the Sámi people may be implicated in contemporary perpetration of sexual violence; and the failure of Nordic welfare states and gender equality models to reduce men's violence against women and girls. In addition, the vignettes invite the reader to contemplate: the challenges for men in 'calling out' abuse; a young trans man's experience of sexual harassment; homophobia and the male gaze; the value of writing in recovery from sexual violence; and a woman's experience of sexualised graffiti directed at her. And yet, each of these contributions is about more than this summary suggests. Each one also engages with the wider contexts in which sexual harassment occurs, with causation, with the diverse, ripple-like effects of sexual harassment, with the limits on women's freedom, and with questions about prevention. Together and individually, they will help the reader think about the complexities of sexual harassment in ways that do not rely on established but contested concepts and approaches and instead encourage readers to engage in re-imagining sexual harassment both in the Nordic region and beyond.

I commend the editors for fulfilling their ambitious aims; they have produced a collection that provides a refreshing provocation which will help generate new directions for scholarship and policy as well as new dialogue between those of us working to end sexual violence in all its guises.

Introduction: Re-imagining sexual harassment

Maja Lundqvist, Angelica Simonsson and Kajsa Widegren

#MeToo happened. But we don't really want to start there, because #MeToo happened in 2017 while sexual harassment has been around for way longer than that.

However, as a direct consequence of #MeToo we found ourselves engaged in an extensive demand for knowledge on sexual harassment. Since 2017, we have reviewed the majority of the research in this field from the Nordic region, and a great deal of the existing international literature, as well as examining policy making at the Nordic and European levels (Simonsson, 2021; Svensson, 2021; Bondestam and Lundqvist, 2018, 2020). These research reviews show how juridical definitions dominate the research field. While a juridical definition is important in legislative contexts, it also presents a risk: it limits our understanding of sexual harassment (Bondestam and Lundqvist, 2020).

There are so many stories about sexual harassment out there. Not only in the way that #MeToo showed, through thousands and thousands of individual accounts of the experience and consequences of being exposed to sexual violence that share both similarities and differences, but also many different stories about what sexual harassment is and what it does in the world. As feminist theorist Donna Haraway suggests, we need to be aware of the demarcations and continuities that we create with our stories (Haraway, 1992). The stories about sexual harassment that we have come across and the stories that we create have made this clear (Franks, 2019).

The juridical approach has influenced both policy and how we understand the phenomenon in some limited ways as something countable – something that lends itself well to a specific definition and understanding, and consequently as something that can be eradicated by means of legislation, policies, and education. We felt frustrated by this and felt a need for new ways to discuss and approach sexual harassment. And we wanted to do this as a part of a long-standing tradition in the Nordic countries: by facilitating dialogues between researchers, politicians, policy makers, practitioners, and nongovernmental organisations (NGOs). The infrastructure for these dialogues already exists, but we wanted to see the topic of the conversation changed: we wanted to see the way that we talk about sexual harassment supplemented by new strands of thought. Quite simply, we think it is time to take these dialogues further.

When one critically engages with research on and policy development to counter sexual harassment, the phenomenon appears on the one hand to be inherently naturalised, as something that is a given in a heteronormative and heterosexist society, something that is integrated into everyday decisions about where to work, where to live, and how and when to move through public spaces (Gunnarsson, 2018; Mellgren, Andersson and Ivert, 2018). Concepts such as 'a culture of silence' attempt to capture this normalisation and how it affects organisations and individuals. Normalisation is yet another way to understand gendered vulnerabilities and the heterosexualisation of relations between men and women (Butler, 2004, 2006).

On the other hand, sexual harassment is understood as an anomaly, a deviation from the normal and the common order (Gottzén and Jonsson, 2012). When presented as anomalous, sexual harassment can be described as not fitting a given set or series of acts, as something that threatens the perceived social structure of society. Sexual harassment as an anomaly, and its relationship to supposedly functioning systems, echoes in a particular way in contexts that put a great deal of trust in the transparency of social structures in well-organised and regulated societies, such as the societies of the Nordic region. The anomalous is often seen as disgusting, disruptive and dangerous. It is treated as something that violates a system of values and therefore something must be done about it.

'Uncleanness or dirt is that which must not be included if a pattern is to be maintained' (Douglas, 1984, p 50). Inspired by the well-known anthropologist Mary Douglas's work, we argue that anomalies are interesting since they say something about the context, the pattern, the supposed 'normal' that the anomaly deviates from: a normal workplace or public space and normal social relationships that have no room for oppression, inequalities and harassment. This is a normality where the idea of someone using sexual acts to harass someone else is an abnormality. The way that sexual harassment emerges in research and policy making relies on the notion of rational and transparent management. It relies heavily on quantitative surveys and the phenomenon of sexual harassment as something that is neatly defined and managed by the enforcement of transparent routines for reporting it, investigations at organisational level, and that is ultimately settled in a court of law.

Douglas' apt formulation: 'Dirt is a matter out of place' comes to mind (Douglas, 1984). Hair on the head is not dirt, hair in your food is. But the hair on your breakfast sandwich is not dirt if you found the sandwich under the table. If you found and picked up a sandwich under the table, from the kitchen floor, the hair on the sandwich is not an anomaly, the hair is not dirt – the whole sandwich is. For sexual harassment to be seen as dirt, the world must be pure, and we know that it is not. In an unequal world, sexual harassment is not an anomaly, it is not dirt. The world is dirt.

The understanding of sexual harassment that comes into view through this way of telling the story does something not only to its supposed normality, but also to the possible ways of thinking, talking, and dealing with it. For us, other ways to produce knowledge will have to start by problematising the very concept of sexual harassment and the specific contexts in which it has been produced as a scholarly, juridical and policy concept. What would happen if, instead of looking at sexual harassment as an anomaly, we were to explore and examine it as a social and cultural phenomenon, as something that – no matter how destructive – is a part of our world? Of course, this is not to say that it is natural, a given or a should-be. Rather, looking at sexual harassment as a social and cultural phenomenon is a way of trying to do the work of taking responsibility for the knowledge we have about how intersecting power relations work and of asking questions about how this relates to issues of sexual violence and harassment.

Theorising re-imagination

Sexual harassment as a field of knowledge production is in need of new imaginaries to think and act with. We have therefore taken the concept of 'imaginaries' as our point of departure. The sandwich on the floor under the breakfast table is a striking image that goes beyond mere illustration. It is an intrinsic part of the conceptualised intellectual work that Douglas takes us through. As a term, imaginary is related to images and notions of, as well as the capacity to imagine beyond, the current situation. The psychoanalytical interest in imaginations stems from Jacques Lacan's analysis of the ego's development through the mirror image of the self: a figure at once more superior and lacking, that is developed through the mirror's imaginaries (Lacan, 2020). In the theoretical tradition of cultural studies, Graham Dawson has contributed the concept of cultural imagination – a way to try to capture broader patterns that form strong conceptualisations, reproduced in actual imaginaries, narratives, and other meaning-making processes as well as in identity formations (Dawson, 1994). In the social sciences, imaginaries have broadened their scope to include the individual micro level, the organisational meso level and the collective macro level of continual, collective, and contested processes. At the collective level, social imagination takes place in the public sphere and through social interactions. Individuals, organisations and movements are involved in these processes, internalising prototypical understandings, challenging and (re)inventing them. 'Social imagination is the essential social-cognitive process that generates, validates, or challenges understandings' (Hart-Brinson, 2016, p 3).

This step – from using imaginaries to deconstruct cultural and social meaning-making processes to using them as a part of an epistemological project where imaginaries are also seen as an intrinsic part of knowledge production – owes much to the feminist philosopher Michèle Le Doeuff. In her collection of essays, *The Philosophical Imaginary* (Le Doeuff, 2002), she argues that the use of metaphors in Western philosophy can be seen as the productive handling of contradictions and tensions. When we use the concept of 'social imaginaries', it relates to the power of describing and creating the world with all its contradictions and tensions, and thus it relates to theoretical and conceptual development as well as the development of research designs that move beyond the current understanding. This 'creation of the world' is fundamental to the possibility of political change, since imaginations might be limited and restricted to the status quo due to dominant structures and systems, and a lack of imaginations relates to a lack of options (Phipps, 2021). However, this does not mean that we leave the critical, deconstructing perspective behind. When Angela Davis calls for conceptual development in the field of studying violence, it is also a call for caution: 'I would like to suggest that we need to forge ways of thinking and talking about these modes of violence – verbal, physical, psychological forms of violence – that do not unintentionally affirm their permanence' (Chandra and Erlingsdóttir, 2020, p 28). The practice of re-imagination takes this warning seriously, in particular because imaginaries of women, women's bodies and sexuality already flood our culture and are often laden with the same seductive force that images themselves are often assumed to have (Nead, 1992).

We need to re-imagine sexual harassment to help us think beyond restrictive concepts and understandings of vulnerabilities. The objective of this anthology is therefore to investigate the field of sexual harassment research from other perspectives, primarily the field of Nordic gender, sexuality, and intersectionality studies, but also from outside of academia. Our intent is to explore other social imaginaries in order to contribute to a more nuanced body of knowledge and to see sexual harassment theorised and expressed in relation to numerous contexts, giving space for particularities rather than abstract definitions. In this book, we explore the ways in which sexual harassment is interwoven into the fabric of practices in everyday life in spaces that we share. How it intersects with conditions in the labour market, in legislation and the practice of law, and in the organisation of the welfare state. We need imaginaries that help us think through the diversity of violence and power relations and challenge dichotomies between regulated work and unpaid care work, between the public and the private, and to think about justice beyond the juridical. We believe that these imaginaries, questions and perspectives are of great importance far beyond the specific geographical region of the Nordic countries.

Nordic modernity, gender equality and historical amnesia

The Nordic region is the context for this edited volume, as well as its empirical starting point. By 'Nordic' we do not mean coming from or even working in the Nordic countries, but 'working with' the structures that take place in and form the imaginaries of the Nordic region. The anthology of course does not have the ambition to cover all aspects of the Nordic region or the countries within it, but calling something a context means that the region has some specificities, and the countries in it some communalities, at the level of societal structures as well as at the level of cultural and social imaginaries. We will broadly describe some aspects of the Nordic region context − historical, economic and political − that are important for framing the chapters of this book, as well as discussing the critical use of the concept of Nordic exceptionalism and the imaginaries that it relies on (Jensen and Loftsdóttir, 2012; Sawyer and Habel, 2014). This forms a cartography of the Nordic region, in Rosi Braidotti's account acknowledging the co-creation of the specific location, the powers that have structured this location, and the possible new ways to imagine it (Braidotti, 2011).

The Nordic countries are not all alike, not historically and not currently. Between the Icelandic North Atlantic, almost deserted coastlines and the pulse of the traffic and nightlife in central Stockholm, there are more differences than similarities. But these differences between urban and rural settings are similar in many regions. In the following, we will focus on some significant areas of resemblance within the Nordic region, especially at a policy level, which have had important structural effects. At the turn of the last century, the social movements for worker's rights, education, religious freedom, sobriety, human dignity and democracy fostered the growth of actual organisations, such as the region's strong social democratic parties, as well as democratic structures across the Nordic countries (Boje, 2008; Brandal, 2013). The politics that brought these movements together used public protests and strikes as their tools, but they were often considered a violent force that threatened to overthrow traditional values and political hierarchies. When the Nordic states allowed universal suffrage, it should be seen in the context of the many revolutionary tendencies throughout Europe in the 1900s, in particular the Russian revolution (Jakobsen and Kurunmäki, 2016). National liberalisations can be described as means to deflect the revolutionary influences coming from the uprising in Russia. The development of democracy in the Nordic countries is thus tightly intertwined with narratives of the benevolent, reasonable government that wants to keep the national order in place. The cultural theorist Slavoj Žižek distinguishes between different forms of violence (Žižek, 2008). What he calls subjective violence are visible acts of violence, while symbolic and systemic violence are inherent to maintaining the status quo. These latter are forms of violence that are intertwined with power structures and are violent because they are communicated as keeping the peace and order. Žižek calls these forms of violence symbolic and systemic as they are integrated into a system and also need symbolic expressions to perpetuate their meanings. With this perspective, the state narrative of the benevolent nation, 'giving' people democratic rights can be interpreted as symbolic violence in Žižek's account.

Parallel to these political developments, societal support for growth based on an expanding industrial sector is also a vital part of the historical narrative of the region (Brandal, 2013). The five Nordic countries – Iceland, Norway, Denmark, Sweden, and Finland – went through fairly similar processes of modernisation and industrialisation throughout the 19th and 20th centuries. Differences in geography and politics have meant that the five countries went in different industrial directions, but their reliance on raw materials such as wood, iron, fish and other food products, and later oil and gas, have been consistent through the region and have meant that all the Nordic countries rely on exports. Being able to refine their raw materials and their development of technology means the Nordic countries have also relied on an expansion of their education sectors, creating educational and social mobility as well as a differentiated labour market – but with industrial production firmly at the centre.

So far, this is a rather unproblematic account of the economic and social development that forms the basis of imaginations of Nordic rational modernisation. That is true, but it is also storytelling of a particular kind. It is vitally important to carefully navigate the specificities of the Nordic context without reproducing what scholars have called Nordic exceptionalism – a deeply integrated collective self-understanding of one's own countries as exceptions from the impacts of and contributions to colonialism and historical and contemporary racist and sexist structures (Keskinen, Stoltz and Mulinari, 2020). The processes of recognising and exposing colonial history and breaking down the cultural amnesia that have dominated the Nordic countries in the 21st century concerning the direct and indirect profits from slave trading and colonial exploitation are ongoing. Denmark and Sweden had colonies in the East Indies, at different times Denmark and Norway have both colonised Iceland, Greenland, and the Faroe Islands. This denial of historical involvement in colonial violence and exploitation is deeply intertwined with the notion of the Nordic countries as modern, enlightened, rational and democratic (Keskinen et al, 2009). Sápmi – the land of the Nordic indigenous Sámi people that is spread across the northern parts of today's Norway, Sweden, Finland and Russia – has not been recognised by these nations as colonised land. All these four nations have failed to acknowledge their involvement in the theft of land, settlement policies, deportations, and the stigmatisation of the Sámi population. In 2021, it was 100 years since the Swedish government decided to establish the State Institute for Racial Biology (SIRB) at Uppsala University, one of the most prestigious universities in the Nordic region. Similar institutes were also established in Norway, Germany and the US at this time. Extensive programmes for 'eugenic sterilisation' were in place in Sweden as well as in Norway and Denmark (Tydén, 2010). The SIRB – which was renamed the Department of Medical Genetics in 1959 – still holds remains of Sámi people and thousands of photographs that were taken of the Sámi population between 1921 and the 1940s as part of this racist policy.

Nordic exceptionalism takes different forms in different countries depending on the history of each nation, but also that of the whole of the Nordic region. Understanding oneself as an exception is supported by notions of one's own country as excelling in having a transparent state apparatus, democratic systems, 'colour-blindness' and gender equality. This self-image also relies on the notion that the Nordic countries are welfare states and the Nordic variants of the welfare state are closely linked to sexual politics. The industrial work on which the Nordic countries have built their wealth has historically been coded as masculine. The idea of the Nordic family is firmly founded on a nuclear structure with complementary gendered roles, which has led to far-reaching structures in the division of work between women and men, in families as well as in the labour market. The notion of welfare as building on 'robust' economic growth and playing the game of the market economy subordinates women's care work and also relegates women to the tax revenue 'consuming' part of the labour market. After the economic expansion that began in the post-war era, the Nordic countries have gone through fairly similar legal and social reforms to support gender equality and building systems for universal welfare. Women's traditional care work was professionalised and institutionalised outside of the private sphere. However, neoliberal restructuring during the 1980s and beyond has led to numerous systemic cuts that affect women's participation as welfare workers as well as the welfare system itself. The public sectors in all five countries have made significant cutbacks in welfare-related spending in the last thirty years. Education, healthcare and pensions have all been subject to privatisation and in some of the countries – Sweden stands out here – formerly state-owned public services have also been outsourced and now operate on the basis of market logics (Lundahl et al, 2013).

Today the Nordic countries have the world's highest rates of female participation in the regulated labour market. The normalisation of a two-breadwinner family model, as well as strong discourses on women's rights to individual fulfilment, can be seen as systemic violence since it offers a myth about gender equality which is no longer systemically supported by the welfare system. Instead, gender equality has become symbolised as a 'Nordic trait' (Griffin, Martinsson and Giritli Nygren, 2016). These discourses reproduce nationalist ideas about equality as a notion of modernity that differentiates 'us', who are forward-looking and developed, from 'them', who are reactionary and burdened by traditions (Vuori, 2009).

In the Nordic countries, #MeToo shed light on the silencing of women's exposure to sexual violence and harassment at work and it is telling that the calls for action against sexual harassment were often organised within occupational categories. #MeToo not only showed that gender equality has not been achieved, but also that there was considerable awareness of and capacity for conducting feminist analyses and utilising a gender equality discourse. Close connections between women's movements, political gender equality goals and gender research have formed a robust feminist discourse, which is also connected to international interventions within the UN, the EU and international social movements.

From the 1990s and beyond, different gender equality indices have been used to compare gender equality between countries, and these indices usually have one or more of the Nordic countries at the top of their rankings. The notion of gender equality as something measurable is highly criticised, as thinking that it is measurable neutralises power inequalities. But the gender equality 'mantra' (as it is called in Griffin, Martinsson and Giritli Nygren, 2016) has also contributed to a strong identification with gender-equal norms and awareness of inequalities based on gender. The reporting of sexual harassment, sexual violence and gender discrimination is high in the Nordic countries, but so is the level of knowledge, and maybe also the tendency to report. So international comparisons will evidently suffer from methodological difficulties.

As Angela Y. Davis notes in *The Routledge Handbook of the Politics of the #MeToo Movement*, the historical development of the Nordic countries and their welfare models shows that closing economic and social gender gaps is in no way a guarantee that a society will be free from gender-based violence and sexual harassment (Chandra and Erlingsdóttir, 2020). On the other hand, the economic gaps between men and women have ceased closing since the economic crises of the 1990s and 2000s. They have instead increased (Swedish Gender Equality Agency, 2022). Universal welfare is a vital aspect of the imaginations of the Nordic region, but these need to be revisited and re-imagined as well.

In the Nordic countries, research on sexual harassment has never formed a research field as such. Gender studies and related research fields, which are extensive and vibrant in all the Nordic countries, have shown little interest in sexual harassment, despite strong fields of research in gender and working life, as well as research on violence against women and intimate partner violence. Some clues to the reasons for this might be found in the historical development of gender research in the Nordic region. Gender studies is institutionalised to varying degrees in the different Nordic countries, but in all five countries there are gender studies researchers working in different parts of the social sciences, medicine, education, technology, and the humanities. The differences in the development of gender research in each of the countries are due to different research policies, but overall gender research was initially closely tied to practical gender equality work driven by women's movements and often in direct dialogue with established political parties and gender equality goals (Alnebratt, 2009; Dahl, 2020). Intimate partner violence against women has had a much more prominent place in the political discourse, in activism and as an independent research field in these countries than sexual harassment. Sexual harassment has been a question for gender equality managers at an organisational level, rather than seen against the background of broader violence regimes. The Nordic field of research on violence against women and intimate partner violence is a crucial source of knowledge, and a broader context within which we can see sexual harassment as a continuum of violence: physical, verbal, discursive, symbolic, and systemic.

The social and cultural imaginations of the Nordic region are vivid and productive, and in need of critical deconstruction. However, while there is an abundance of imaginaries regarding the Nordic region, there seems to be a deficit of these with regard to understanding and theorising about sexual harassment. Or rather, Nordic imaginaries seem to run the risk of preventing other more extensive imaginations of sexual harassment from taking shape, and thus challenging and reconfiguring the complacent image of the Nordic region, almost as if the region's self-image is acting as a protective shield, keeping the Nordic region clean and tidy, and not a messy co-construct of sexual harassment.

Sexual harassment: previous research

We will use three questions as starting points for a discussion on the existing research field. What is sexual harassment? What is wrong with sexual harassment? And what do we *do* with sexual harassment? Through engaging in these questions, we want to describe how the phenomenon of sexual harassment comes into view when critically engaging in research and policy on sexual harassment. We are not trying to capture the entirety of the field, but rather its main traits. The questions are not asked primarily to be answered, but rather to sketch the contours of the field and its main concerns as well as its blind spots and what is implicitly taken for granted. Overall, it will continue this storytelling, and follow the delimitations that the field has established.

The concept of sexual harassment has been disseminated by transnational movements, and ideas and expertise are spread through direct and indirect ties between researchers, activists and policy makers. However, the US has been at the forefront regarding regulation, policy development and the development of the conceptual understanding of sexual harassment (Zippel, 2006). As we have seen, the Nordic field of research on sexual harassment is limited, but the research that does exist is very much influenced by an understanding of sexual harassment developed in the US. Its dominance can be described as both quantitative – the majority of international research is based on empirical data from the US – and qualitative, as it sets the methodological and epistemological frames for research on sexual harassment also in contexts that are not regulated by US law. Consequently, we find ourselves in a situation where we risk reproducing the US's dominance, a risk that prompts us to insist on our critical position in relation on it. This does not mean that we should disregard individual researchers and their work, but rather we aim to capture the epistemological demarcations that have guided their efforts.

What is sexual harassment?

The term sexual harassment was coined in the US in the 1970s (see for example: Farley, 1978; MacKinnon, 1979). When Catharine MacKinnon published her book *Sexual Harassment of Working Women: A Case of Sex Discrimination*, she described sexual harassment as 'an experience for which there has been no name' (MacKinnon, 1979, p 27). Sexual harassment was of course experienced, theorised about, and resisted even before MacKinnon's book in 1979. Women have talked about it, but their voices have not been heard. Even more so, some women's voices have been seen as less important than others. Women of colour are one group whose theorising and conceptual knowledge about sexual harassment has been ignored (Berenstain, 2020).

In these early days of the formation of the research field, sexual harassment as a term was also subject to exploration and operationalised in different methods and forms of measurements. One way of exploring sexual harassment was through following legal cases and court documents (Franke, 1997; Schultz, 1998; Leeser, 2003). This kind of research was plentiful during the 1980s and 1990s and hints at the close connection between research and the development of juridical frameworks at the time. It has subsequently been criticised for its tendencies to decontextualise when trying to arrive at a universal definition through the juridical system:

> As further developments have been made to this definition – through both judicial and tribunal decision-making and legislative tinkering – it has become increasingly apparent that the nature, context and harm of sexual harassment continues to defy simplistic definition. Each time we attempt to improve and refine our legislative understanding of sexual harassment, we run the risk of trivialising or excluding experiences that do not fit the new model. Clearly, these difficulties do not provide an

excuse to be satisfied with the status quo but they do invite us to take a modest view of what can be achieved through legislation. (Mason and Chapman, 2003, p 223)

A focus on prevalence as the main interest of research, and questionnaires as the preferred method of inquiry, also formed the basis for studies of sexual harassment during this period.

Several methodological challenges were later identified in relation to different methodological approaches. One approach was the direct query survey, where respondents were asked to define sexual harassment, and another concerned behavioural experiences, where the researcher defined what constituted sexual harassment. However, these different methods lead to differences in reporting rates: using the respondents' definitions generated one set of results that differed from those in reports that relied on the researcher's definition (Ilies et al, 2003).

The close connection between sexual harassment and the labour market is another common aspect of the field, mediated by legislation and regulation affecting what is understood to be sexual harassment. In Europe, empirical research shows that millions of women suffer from sexual harassment in their workplaces, and discussions of sexual harassment were initially included in a broader context of violations against workers' dignity (Zippel, 2006; Latcheva, 2017). The workplace is also the context in which the majority of research and policy on sexual harassment has been generated (McDonald, 2012). Anti-discrimination law regulates relationships in the workplace, between employees, and between employees and employers. The idea of a labour market with an employer who is legally responsible for their employees is not a given, but dependency on legal definitions of sexual harassment seems to take such simplified relations for granted. Many people work but are not employed or they work outside of regulated employment arrangements. Many are harassed outside the workplace, and so this juridical framework limits the understanding of society's perceptions of sexual harassment.

What has become clear when examining the development of terms and investments in theory over time in the research field as a whole is how a gradual closing of the gap between legal definitions and the scientific definition of sexual harassment is occurring (Bondestam and Lundqvist, 2020). Legal definitions vary by juridical context, but most legislation in the area contains similar elements, such as descriptions of the conduct as unwanted or unwelcome acts of a sexual nature (McDonald, 2012). These definitions in themselves leave many questions unanswered: how do we understand and measure 'unwelcome'; what kinds of 'acts' are to be included, and what actually is meant by 'of a sexual nature'? To some extent these questions have been dealt with in the research, resulting in validated scales for questionnaires such as the Sexual Experiences Questionnaire (SEQ) which includes a variety of different acts that could be understood as sexual harassment (for example Fitzgerald, Gelfand and Drasgow, 1995). There has been far less exploration of what is unwelcome and of a sexual nature, and both of these criteria also entail normative imaginations about heterosexuality and the general availability of women's bodies (Superson, 1993; Anderson, 2006; Saul, 2014).

Other challenges relate to socio-cultural differences in understandings of sexual harassment and the skewed distribution of samples: in the 1980s basically only women were respondents in studies concerning sexual harassment (Bondestam and Lundqvist, 2020). A review article of study context and participants in research on campus-based assault and dating violence in the US showed that the respondents in most of the reviewed research did not reflect the demographics of US higher education. The respondents in the reviewed studies were substantially younger and White, heterosexual and middle-class to a greater extent than US college students were overall at the time (Voth Schrag, 2017).

A culture of silence was explored as a term that acknowledged the social and cultural aspects of difficulties in talking about experiences of sexual harassment. Underreporting is well established as a phenomenon in the research field, and shame, victimhood and fear of retaliation are described as some of the reasons for this (see for example: Superson, 1993; Cairns, 1997; Bergman et al, 2002; McDonald, Backstrom and Dear, 2008). But silence is not only about who speaks or not, it is just as much a question of listening and acknowledging (see for example Fricker, 2007). To not acknowledge minorities, such as women of colour, as knowing subjects limits our understanding of sexual harassment (see for example: Buchanan and Ormerod, 2002; Welsh et al, 2006; Richardson and Taylor, 2009; Berenstain, 2020). The silencing is not just about the execution of power but is also reproduced by the research field that was originally established to break that very silence.

The strong juridical framework, how work and the workplace are understood, and the situating of sexual harassment mainly within these realms all limit the understanding of what is perceived as sexual harassment. The context of employment and labour markets in the Nordic region features collective agreement systems in different industries, within different welfare systems, in parallel with relatively strong anti-discrimination laws. The question 'what is sexual harassment' has been handled as if it is actually possible to contain and draw lines around a universally consistent concept, or, to draw on Mary Douglas: keep the concept clean and separated from contextual dirt. Hence, perspectives exploring the intersectional dimension of exposure to sexual harassment, listening to other voices and investigating different contextual continuums will be the means by which we aim to provide a range of possible answers to the question: what is sexual harassment?

What is wrong with sexual harassment?

'We have constructed the phenomena around the available legal remedies, rather than around a comprehensive normative account of the wrongs at stake' (Anderson, 2006, p 292).

Importantly, no matter how studies are carried out and whether or not respondents described their experiences as sexual harassment, the negative consequences at an individual level are similar. Negative psychological, work-related and health consequences seem to be common ground in experiences of sexual harassment (Magley et al, 1999; McDonald, 2012; Bondestam and Lundqvist, 2020). This is one obvious wrong: the negative consequences of sexual harassment at both individual and societal levels. However, the question of what is wrong with sexual harassment is not very much elaborated on in the majority of studies of sexual harassment. Rather it seems to be an implicit consensus that sexual harassment is wrong in and of itself. So while there seems to be an abundance of efforts to map the prevalence of sexual harassment, efforts to investigate its broader ramifications are scarcer. One of the consequences of this apparent consensus seems to be that difficult questions about the complex situations and contextual factors involved are not often included in studies of sexual harassment.

In the following section, we will let Elisabeth Anderson's 2006 review, 'Recent thinking about sexual harassment: A review essay', exemplify a discussion of the theories regarding sexual harassment as a wrong. In research discussing how to conceive of the wrong of sexual harassment, one central fault line is whether the core wrong consists in an injury to groups or to individuals. Group-based theories, also called equality theories, view the core interest injured by sexual harassment to be equality among social groups, mainly based on sex/gender. Individual-based theories, also called dignity theories, locate the wrong in the means that harassers use to achieve their objectives, where the harm done is done to an individual's standing as a person (Anderson, 2006).

These theories each capture important aspects of the wrong of sexual harassment but both strands of thought also run up against different types of limitations. The equality theories on the one hand take as their point of departure a heteronormative paradigm, and fail to include a variety of sexually harassing acts, behaviours and situations (Anderson, 2006). These theories risk making the understanding of sexual harassment one-dimensional.

Dignity theory, on the other hand, ignores the material disadvantages inflicted by sexual harassment, individualises and depoliticises the harms of sexual harassment, and fails to grasp the ways in which the indignities of sexual harassment are institutionalised in, for example, the gender segregation of the labour market. In the Nordic countries, the wrong of sexual harassment, as far as it has been dealt with at all, seems to have ended up either in the gender equality field (group-based, equality theories) as part of a political ambition to eradicate gender-based violence, or as a question of working conditions and employer responsibility (dignity theory).

Another theory discussing the wrong of sexual harassment is the autonomy theory, where workers' freedom to express their gender and sexuality at work is of importance. This understanding boils down to a conflict between the exercise of one person's sexual liberty and another person's sexual autonomy (Anderson, 2006). Queer-feminist researchers have pointed out that the mere existence of a queer person could be read as sexual harassment by homophobic and/or heterosexist employees, while others pay attention to how sexual harassment laws might collude with managerial motives to suppress different sexual identities in the workplace (Anderson, 2006). This perspective on sexual autonomy shows how previous research tends to unify the category of women in ways that intersectional approaches have interrogated in other fields of research. The unifying of the category 'woman' not only excludes experiences of different forms of oppression based on race, gender, sexual orientation, class or age, but also tends to base its traits on the White, Western, middle-class, heterosexual woman and reproduce broader social and cultural imaginations of (White, young, beautiful) women as victims.

These theories have contributed to the development of the research field, but they still tend to focus on the juridical aspects, the main disciplinary domicile being in philosophy of law (Berndt Rasmussen and Olsson Yaouzis, 2020). The limitations of all three perspectives are their inability to include intersecting power relations along the lines of gender, race/ethnicity and sexual orientation, but also their inability to contextualise and relate sexual harassment to structural circumstances. Ultimately, the research that has been done primarily defines sexual harassment as an occupational health and safety issue which can be remedied by better policies and more frequent reporting till the employer.

What do you do with sexual harassment?

The urge to eradicate sexual harassment, to make it stop, has affected the structure of the research field. Two focuses permeate much of the research on sexual harassment: the focus on prevalence and the focus on prevention. Over and over again, the research field approaches the question in almost the same way: establishing if, how and how much sexual harassment there is in certain industries, workplaces or occupational groups. A vast number of studies of sexual harassment follow this logic. A questionnaire is sent out with questions about experiences of sexual harassment, the percentages are summarised, and the study concludes with a list of recommendations. The recommendations are seldom based on the actual results, but are generic recommendations like establishing a policy, improving leadership, and creating stronger support systems. Despite the repetitiousness of these studies' main features, they are seldom exactly alike, and therefore it is not possible to use them for comparison or longitudinal meta-studies. According to existing research, prevalence rates vary extensively (Bondestam and Lundqvist, 2020). Individualisation and the juridification of sexual harassment can be seen in both the research and preventative measures (McDonald, Charlesworth and Graham, 2015).

All of these starting points contribute to an understanding of sexual harassment as something first and foremost to *do* something about. These kinds of studies might well be of great importance, but they do not seem to generate any kind of foundation for the development of well-targeted preventive measures. Effective prevention would seem to require something else or something more in terms of empirical or theoretical foci.

The focus on doing gives the impression that we all agree, that we already know enough, that we have already got it figured out, and now all we need to do is to write an adequate policy plan, inform all the employers about the reporting systems and routines, or tighten the legislation. This urge to do something and the measures recommended are what Sara Ahmed calls non-performative actions. With a critical use of Judith Butler's performativity concept, Ahmed notes the lack of action in upholding policy: 'Non-performatives describes the "reiterative and citational practice by which discourse" does not produce "the effects that it names"' (Ahmed, 2012, p 117).

This repetitious call for measures can be described as a need to 'name' sexual harassment as a problem: not in the sense of giving voice to a silenced experience, which was Catharine MacKinnon's main project, but as an ambition that this 'naming' in itself will bring about change. What the concept of non-performatives shows is that to name is not to bring into effect. Rather, naming ends up standing in for the effect; thus naming can be a way of *not* bringing something into effect (Ahmed, 2012). The urge to produce studies and attach recommendations with weak relation to the results of these studies, or to write and amend policy documents that end up in a drawer, become non-performative: a stand-in for the effect. The seemingly never-ending need for recommendations, implementability and checklists does do something with knowledge about sexual harassment; it keeps it tidy and manageable without looking at the contexts that enable sexual violence and harassment.

Together these three questions – what is sexual harassment? what is wrong with sexual harassment? and what do we *do* with sexual harassment? – and how they have been dealt with in research, politics, and policy, affect the building of knowledge about and our understanding of the phenomenon of sexual harassment in certain ways. There are obvious conflicts, contradictions, and areas of disagreement that disrupt and make visible the complexity of sexual harassment as a phenomenon in the world. We are interested in exploring what will happen if these are put in the foreground in order to frame, understand and by extension prevent sexual harassment. Can we re-imagine sexual harassment as something else than as an anomaly in the world?

Re-imaginations in the Nordic region

During the time when the institutionalisation of gender studies was at its most intense during the late 1990s and the first part of the 2000s, two important shifts occurred. The first one is related to the institutionalisation of gender studies. This meant academic autonomy, and a distancing from the organised practice of politics and the demands for 'implementable' research results that are implicit in this relationship. The second shift was theoretical currents, such as poststructuralism, queer studies and intersectionality, that turned the research field's interest away from radical feminism and its stable account of the category 'woman'. Intersectionality showed how feminist research had implicitly modelled 'woman' on White, heterosexual middle-class women. Given that most research on sexual harassment builds on a realist, gender-binary conception of men and women as categories that are ontologically stable (although in stages involving historical and social change) the notion of gender as multifaceted, intersectionally scattered, moulded in the complex interaction of social structures, institutions, practices, and cultural and symbolic representations, did not fit the research tradition of sexual harassment studies. But this is a false dichotomy. We need more accounts of violence, not fewer, including the ones that poststructuralist theories taught us, in order to grasp for instance discursive violence, the violence of silenc(ing) and marginalisation, the violence of organisational powers, of dehumanisation, and of economic and corporeal exploitation. We need to follow the entanglements of multiple power structures and resistance in order to facilitate the necessary re-imaginations needed to more fully make sense of sexual harassment.

For this book, we invited scholars who for the most part would not self-identify as sexual harassment researchers. What they bring to the understanding of sexual harassment are concepts, perspectives, knowledge, and stories that have been developed in the broad field of gender studies research in the Nordic region. We also invited writers of fiction to contribute essays and short stories, contributing voices that are not easily captured within the framework of research methods. We need these voices that can show the brutality of the mundane and the micro-resistance that sometimes occurs out of pure coincidence. We owe it to many feminist researchers who have insisted that 'academic language' can be a form of violence in itself with its claim that objectivity is the result of a distanced position.

Danish writer and activist Mads Ananda Lodahl's four short stories form a red thread through the book. These stories describe both transgressions of and submissions to the norms of sexuality in different social locations. The fictional voice and focalisation can be truly loyal to the specific ambivalences that our multiple positions place us in. All four stories take as their starting point a location, stressing the importance of context when we investigate power relations. Their titles – 'In the gents', 'On the freshers' trip', 'On the promenade' and 'At the AGM' (Chapters 15, 5, 9 and 2 respectively) – underline this aspect.

Lodahl's 'At the AGM' (Chapter 2) opens the book's first part, titled 'Cartography of everyday violence in the Nordic region'. It continues with 'Depleted bodies: Intersectional perspectives on workplace violence' by Paulina de los Reyes (Chapter 3). This chapter aims to advance the conceptualisation of workplace violence beyond individual actions to address the structural conditions that make harassment, threats and abuse part of workplace normality. As context, she uses the neoliberalisation of the Nordic labour market and the stratification of the labour market along intersecting lines of power relations that leave immigrant women's bodies and labour in states of depletion. This important contribution to exposing the continuum of depletions as a way to reconceptualise sexual harassment is followed by a theoretical discussion by Sofia Strid, Anne Laure Humbert and Jeff Hearn (Chapter 4). Their chapter, 'The violently gender-equal Nordic welfare states', elaborates on violence as autotelic – the organising principle as a distinct regime of the Nordic welfare states – and as such continues the development of an account of sexual harassment as integrated into regimes of violence.

Following this, we present two chapters with an ethnographic focus on the intersection of gender and age: 'Negotiating sexual harassment and young urban femininities in Helsinki' by Heta Mulari (Chapter 6) and 'Men run academic track; women jump sexist hurdles' by Lea Skewes (Chapter 7). Both chapters map traditionally masculine sites: the urban space and a university department of physics. Mulari's chapter analyses girls' and non-binary youths' experiences not only of sexual harassment and sexual violence but also of empowerment and solidarity on public transport and in urban spaces. Skewes' chapter focuses on student experiences of gender-stereotypical attitudes and sexual harassment in an educational setting where a specific form of masculinity – coined as a 'Hercules' masculinity – is dominant. Normative assumptions in the department about an inherent relation between physics and masculinities lead to the individualisation of women's difficulties in integrating into the department's environment and when exposed to sexual harassment.

The novelist Sigbjørn Skåden's chapter 'Some ten years ago I started writing a novel' (Chapter 8) is a reflection on the social and cultural mechanisms of racist oppression of the Sámi populations in Norway, with a wide historical scope. Skåden sets out these structures as the backdrop for writing *Våke over dem som sover* (*Watch Over Those Who Sleep*) (Skåden, 2014). He asks what links there can be between different forms of abuse of power. As its starting point the novel takes the revealing of extensive sexual abuse of underage girls in the Sámi village Guovdageaidnu/Kautokeino and the silences that made it possible, as well as the silences in its aftermath.

The second part of the book, titled 'Violence, knowledge and imagining justice', takes on different aspects of what we call the juridification of sexual harassment. Juridification is both the notion that sexual harassment can and should be contained, defined, and solved within the juridical system, but also encompasses a specific effect of the close connections between sexual harassment research and the juridical system in the US. One example of how juridical definitions fail is when a changing social situation creates new vulnerabilities to assaults that – for lack of an adequate juridical concept – cannot be condemned. Such is the situation that is analysed in 'Sextortion: Linking sexual violence and corruption in a Nordic context' written by Silje Lundgren, Åsa Eldén, Dolores Calvo and Elin Bjarnegård (Chapter 10). That chapter analyses and discusses two recent and publicly known legal cases that include elements of quid pro quo as sextortion in Norway and Sweden and advocates the need for a framework of sextortion as an answer to practices of Nordic exceptionalism.

Another strand of feminist thinking addresses alternative ways of perceiving and doing justice, sometimes called transformative justice. Two chapters take on these perspectives, from different standpoints and with different methods. Silas Aliki works as a lawyer and publishes opinion pieces regularly in daily newspapers. Their chapter 'I have always thought a lot about the nature of violence: Carceral feminism – sexual violence in the neoliberal state' (Chapter 11) is a powerful confrontation with discourses of 'law and order' and the withdrawal of the state from the responsibility for securing justice and democratic rights. Sexual violence and women's bodies become the battlefield where the marginalisation of the racialised man takes place. Aliki reminds us that feminisms can be politically relevant beyond the cry for longer prison sentences, if they constitute movements for social and economic rights for all women. They propose transformative justice as an alternative to repression. Hildur Fjóla Antonsdóttir on the other hand has interviewed people who have been sexually assaulted, harassed and raped about their views on alternative justice practices. In 'Beyond restorative justice: Survivors' calls for innovative practices in Iceland' (Chapter 12), Antonsdóttir offers a feminist analysis of restorative justice practices, focusing on empirical accounts from sexual violence survivors in Iceland. This ethnographic account captures the ambivalence of the respondents, as restorative justice ultimately means re-exposure for individuals who have already been (made) vulnerable.

The poet Sumaya Jirde Ali's chapter 'I write to tell myself it wasn't my fault' (Chapter 13) is a sharp encounter with the failure of the juridical system. It gives a personal account of the legal, social, emotional and professional aftermaths of being subjected to sexual violence, and not being heard.

Anne Hellum's 'One step forward and one step back: Sexual harassment in Norwegian equality and non-discrimination law' (Chapter 14) is an historical account of the unfolding of the legal context in the Nordic countries, its different political influences, and its shortcomings and possibilities when it comes to convictions in current sexual harassment cases.

In the concluding chapter (Chapter 16), we draw together knowledge from all the chapters, and place them in dialogue with each other, discussing both their similarities and tensions. We discuss in depth not only the consequences of placing sexual harassment on a continuum of violence but also the normalisation of different forms of violence. The effects and limits of the juridification of sexual harassment as well as the limitations of the Nordic gender equality discourse are also discussed. But we also try to summarise some lessons that we think are important for readers of this book to take with them in further dialogues on sexual violence and harassment in the Nordic region, and beyond.

Fifty years of research, lifetimes of experience, and a global #MeToo movement show that sexual harassment is still a persistent problem in society. Through this book we aim to contribute to research and knowledge-building guided by curiosity, exploration, and re-imagination: trying to take responsibility for the difficult questions of power, inequality, and sexuality in our social environments, and confronting the urge to do something with a firm belief that seeking knowledge is not a matter of presenting quick fixes, but rather an expression of a joint commitment to move the world.

References

Ahmed, S. (2012) *On Being Included: Racism and Diversity in Institutional Life*, Durham: Duke University Press.

Alnebratt, K. (2009) *Meningen med genusforskning så som den framträder i forskningspolitiska texter 1970–2000*, Göteborg: Acta Universitatis Gothoburgensis.

Anderson, E. (2006) 'Recent Thinking about Sexual Harassment: A Review Essay', *Philosophy & Public Affairs*, 34 (3): pp 284–312.

Berenstain, N. (2020) 'White Feminist Gaslighting', *Hypatia*, 35 (4): pp 733–58.

Bergman, M.E., Langhout, R.D., Palmeri, P.A., Cortina, L.M. and Fitzgerald, L.F. (2002) 'The (Un)reasonableness of Reporting: Antecedents and Consequences of Reporting Sexual Harassment', *Journal of Applied Psychology*, 87 (2): pp 230–42.

Berndt Rasmussen, K. and Olsson Yaouzis, N. (2020) 'MeToo, Social Norms, and Sanctions', *The Journal of Political Philosophy*, 28 (3): pp 273–95.

Boje, T.P. (2008) 'Velfærdsstat og Civilsamfund: De Nordiske Lande i Komparativt Perspektiv', *Tidsskrift for samfunnsforskning*, 49 (04): pp 595–609.

Bondestam, F. and Lundqvist, M. (2018) *Sexuella trakasserier i akademin: En internationell forskningsöversikt*, Stockholm: Swedish Research Council.

Bondestam, F. and Lundqvist, M. (2020) 'Sexual Harassment in Higher Education – A Systematic Review', *European Journal of Higher Education*, 10 (4): pp 397–419.

Braidotti, R. (2011) *Nomadic Theory: The Portable Rosi Braidotti*, New York: Columbia University Press.

Brandal, N. (2013) *The Nordic Model of Social Democracy*, Basingstoke: Palgrave Macmillan.

Buchanan, N.T. and Ormerod, A.J. (2002) 'Racialized Sexual Harassment in the Lives of African American Women', *Women & Therapy*, 25 (3–4): pp 107–24.

Butler, J. (2004) *Undoing Gender*, New York, London: Routledge.

Butler, J. (2006) *Gender Trouble: Feminism and the Subversion of Identity*, New York: Routledge.

Cairns, K. (1997) '"Femininity" and Women's Silence in Response to Sexual Harassment and Coercion' in Thomas, A. and Kitzinger, C. (eds) *Sexual Harassment: Contemporary Feminist Perspectives*, Buckingham, Open University Press.

Chandra, G. and Erlingsdóttir, I. (2020) *The Routledge Handbook of the Politics of the #MeToo Movement*, London: Taylor and Francis.

Dahl, U. (2020) 'Nordic Academic Feminism and Whiteness as Epistemic Habit', in *Feminisms in the Nordic Region*, Cham: Springer International Publishing.

Dawson, G. (1994) *Soldier Heroes: British Adventure, Empire, and the Imagining of Masculinities*, London: Routledge.

Douglas, M. (1984) *Purity and Danger: An Analysis of Concepts of Pollution and Taboo*, London: Ark Paperbacks.

Farley, L. (1978) *Sexual Shakedown: The Sexual Harassment of Women on the Job*, New York: McGraw-Hill.

Fitzgerald, L.F., Gelfand, M.J. and Drasgow, F. (1995) 'Measuring Sexual Harassment: Theoretical and Psychometric Advances', *Basic and Applied Social Psychology*, 17 (4): pp 425–45.

Franke, K.M. (1997) 'What's Wrong with Sexual Harassment?' *Stanford Law Review*, 49 (4): pp 691–772.

Franks, M.A. (2019) 'A Thousand and One Stories: Myth and the #MeToo Movement' in Fileborn, B. and Loney-Howes, R. (eds) *#MeToo and the Politics of Social Change* [online], Cham: Springer International Publishing, pp 85–95.

Fricker, M. (2007) *Epistemic Injustice: Power and the Ethics of Knowing*, Oxford: Oxford University Press.

Gottzén, L. and Jonsson, R. (2012) *Andra män: maskulinitet, normskapande och jämställdhet*, Malmö: Gleerups.

Griffin, G., Martinsson, L. and Giritli Nygren, K. (2016) *Challenging the Myth of Gender Equality in Sweden*, Bristol: Policy Press.

Gunnarsson, L. (2018) '"Excuse Me, But Are You Raping Me Now?" Discourse and Experience in (the Grey Areas of) Sexual Violence', *NORA: Nordic Journal of Women's Studies*, 26 (1): pp 4–18.

Haraway, D. (1992) 'Otherworldly Conversations; Terran Topics; Local Terms', *Science as Culture*, 3 (1): pp 64–98.

Hart-Brinson, P. (2016) 'The Social Imagination of Homosexuality and the Rise of Same-sex Marriage in the United States', *Socius: Sociological Research for a Dynamic World*, 2, pp 1–17.

Ilies, R., Hauserman, N., Schwochau, S. and Stibal, J. (2003) 'Reported Incidence Rates of Work-related Sexual Harassment in the United States: Using Meta-analysis to Explain Reported Rate Disparities', *Personnel Psychology*, 56 (3): pp 607–31.

Jakobsen, U. and Kurunmäki, J. (2016) 'The Formation of Parliamentarism in the Nordic Countries from the Napoleonic Wars to the First World War' in Palonen, K., Ihalainen, P. and Ilie, C. (eds) *Parliament and Parliamentarism: A Comparative History of a European Concept*, New York: Berghahn Books.

Jensen, L. and Loftsdóttir, K. (2012) *Whiteness and Postcolonialism in the Nordic Region: Exceptionalism, Migrant Others and National Identities*, Farnham: Ashgate.

Keskinen, S., Stoltz, P. and Mulinari, D. (2020) *Feminisms in the Nordic Region: Neoliberalism, Nationalism and Decolonial Critique*, Cham: Springer International Publishing AG.

Keskinen, S., Tuori, S., Irni, S. and Mulinari, D. (2009) *Complying with Colonialism: Gender, Race and Ethnicity in the Nordic Region*, Abingdon: Taylor & Francis Group.

Lacan, J. (2020) *Ecrits: A Selection*, New York: Routledge.

Latcheva, R. (2017) 'Sexual Harassment in the European Union: A Pervasive but Still Hidden Form of Gender-Based Violence', *Journal of Interpersonal Violence*, 32 (12): pp 1821–52.

Le Doeuff, M. (2002) *The Philosophical Imaginary*, London: Continuum.

Leeser, J. (2003) 'The Causal Role of Sex in Sexual Harassment', *Cornell Law Review*, 88 (6): pp 1750–93.

Lundahl, L., Arreman, I.E., Holm, A.-S. and Lundström, U. (2013) 'Educational Marketization the Swedish Way', *Education Inquiry*, 4 (3): pp 497–517.

MacKinnon, C.A. (1979) *Sexual Harassment of Working Women: A Case of Sex Discrimination*, New Haven, London: Yale University Press.

Magley, V.J., Hulin, C.L., Fitzgerald, L.F. and DeNardo, M. (1999) 'Outcomes of Self-Labeling Sexual Harassment', *Journal of Applied Psychology*, 84 (3): pp 390–402.

Mason, G. and Chapman, A. (2003) 'Defining Sexual Harassment: A History of the Commonwealth Legislation and Its Critiques', *Federal Law Review*, 31 (1): pp 195–224.

McDonald, P. (2012) 'Workplace Sexual Harassment 30 Years on: A Review of the Literature', *International Journal of Management Reviews*, 14 (1): pp 1–17.

McDonald, P., Backstrom, S. and Dear, K. (2008) 'Reporting Sexual Harassment: Claims and Remedies', *Asia Pacific Journal of Human Resources*, 46 (2): pp 173–95.

McDonald, P., Charlesworth, S. and Graham, T. (2015) 'Developing a Framework of Effective Prevention and Response Strategies in Workplace Sexual Harassment', *Asia Pacific Journal of Human Resources*, 53 (1): pp 41–58.

Mellgren, C., Andersson, M. and Ivert, A.-K. (2018) '"It Happens All the Time": Women's Experiences and Normalization of Sexual Harassment in Public Space', *Women & Criminal Justice*, 28 (4): pp 262–81.

Nead, L. (1992) *The Female Nude: Art, Obscenity, and Sexuality*, London, New York: Routledge.

Phipps, A. (2021) *Politics Theory Other - #106 The Trouble with Mainstream Feminism w/ Alison Phipps* [online]. Available from: https://soundcloud.com/poltheoryother/metoo [Accessed 30 August 2022].

Richardson, B.K. and Taylor, J. (2009) 'Sexual Harassment at the Intersection of Race and Gender: A Theoretical Model of the Sexual Harassment Experiences of Women of Color', *Western Journal of Communication*, 73 (3): pp 248–72.

Saul, J. (2014) 'Stop Thinking So Much About "Sexual Harassment"', *Journal of Applied Philosophy*, 31 (3): pp 307–21.

Sawyer, L. and Habel, Y. (2014) 'Refracting African and Black Diaspora through the Nordic Region', *African and Black Diaspora*, 7 (1): pp 1–6.

Schultz, V. (1998) 'Reconceptualizing Sexual Harassment', *The Yale Law Journal*, 107 (6): pp 1683–1805.

Simonsson, A. (2021) *Förebyggande arbete mot sexuella trakasserier i svenskt och nordiskt arbetsliv: en forskningsöversikt* [online], Göteborg: Swedish Secretariat for Gender Research. Available from: http://hdl.handle.net/2077/68472.

Skåden, S. (2014) *Våke over dem som sover*, Oslo: Cappelen Damm.

Superson, A.M. (1993) 'A Feminist Definition of Sexual Harassment', *Journal of Social Philosophy*, 24 (1): pp 46–64.

Svensson, M. (2021) *Sexually Harassed at Work: An Overview of the Research in the Nordic Countries*, Nordic Council of Ministers.

Swedish Gender Equality Agency (2022) *Ekonomisk jämställdhet: en uppföljning av senare års utveckling av det jämställdhetspolitiska delmålet (2022:2)* [online]. Available from: https://jamstalldhetsmyndigheten.se [Accessed 30 August 2022].

Tydén, M. (2010) 'The Scandinavian States: Reformed Eugenics Applied' in *The Oxford Handbook of the History of Eugenics* [online], Oxford Handbooks: Oxford University Press.

Voth Schrag, R.J. (2017) 'Campus Based Sexual Assault and Dating Violence: A Review of Study Contexts and Participants', *Affilia*, 32 (1): pp 67–80.

Vuori, J. (2009) 'Guiding Migrants to the Realm of Gender Equality' in Keskinen, S., Irni, S. and Mulinari, D. (eds) *Complying with Colonialism: Gender, Race and Ethnicity in the Nordic Region*, Abingdon: Taylor & Francis Group.

Welsh, S., Carr, J., MacQuarrie, B. and Huntley, A. (2006) '"I'm Not Thinking of It as Sexual Harassment": Understanding Harassment across Race and Citizenship', *Gender & Society*, 20 (1): pp 87–107.

Zippel, K.S. (2006) *The Politics of Sexual Harassment: A Comparative Study of the United States, the European Union, and Germany*, Cambridge: Cambridge University Press.

Žižek, S. (2008) *Violence: Six Sideways Reflections*, New York: Picador.

PART I

Cartography of everyday violence in the Nordic region

2

AT THE AGM

Mads Ananda Lodahl

Translated by Paul Russell Garrett and Nielsine Nielsen

I work as an area manager for a major clothing retailer that has stores all over Europe, and my job consists mostly of driving around in my car to look after the shops in my district.

Once a year the managers, middle management, coordinators, and consultants from the entire Nordic division come together at a big annual general meeting (AGM). We number around five hundred employees plus partners. Nearly a thousand people all told.

It all takes place at a huge conference centre in Aarhus. I've only lived in Denmark for a few years, and this will be my first AGM. Food and lodging are included, and I've brought my wife along. She's never been to this kind of thing before either.

Coffee and croissants are being served in the foyer when we arrive, and my wife and I notice it's almost exclusively men mingling around the coffee tables. The employees. Their partners, almost exclusively women, take the luggage up to their rooms. We glance at each other. My wife notices my apologetic look, and responds with one acknowledging it's not my fault. Then she goes up to the room with our bags, and I grab a croissant with the other men.

This entire setup isn't exactly my cup of tea, but nonetheless, I make an effort, because I don't want to hear anyone say I'm not making an effort to integrate into Danish society. I don't want to be poorly integrated. But I don't want to be standing around networking while my wife is lugging my bags around and sorting out the room. I didn't think it would be like this in Denmark.

Later that morning, there's a presentation and some team-building for the staff. The wives stay in their rooms or hang out in the café. Lunch is served around noon in the form of a huge buffet. The pastry tartlets are really good, and it's nice to be able to hold my wife's hand under the table.

The AGM starts in the afternoon. The atmosphere is formal, serious, and administrative. We go through the annual accounts. The budget for the coming year. One guy isn't happy with the board of directors and tries to get people all riled up. Mostly people are bored. While we hold our meeting, the wives go out shopping. Most of them come from small towns, so it's a chance for them to do a little window-shopping in Aarhus.

People are often surprised this is actually a thing in Lebanon, but before I came to Denmark, I was really politically active in Beirut. I tried to combat the racism that many of the young Sri Lankan au pairs had to deal with. I fought for women's rights, for human rights in general, and for minorities.

When I met my wife, who is Danish, and moved to Denmark with her, I didn't think I'd have to deal with similar issues here. After all, I'd entered the so-called 'civilised world'. It was a massive surprise to see what it was really like. Little things like the wives carrying the bags and going shopping while the men do business. And bigger things. The whole executive management team, for example, is made up of men.

What people really come for is the party. You just have to make it through the AGM, then there's a five-course meal with traditional Danish food. Fjord mussels served with home-made mayonnaise for starters. For mains, roast beef and potatoes with thyme and flakes of Icelandic salt. The dessert is also typically Danish. Ice cream or some sort of cake. Plenty of wine with the food. More than plenty.

The managing director gives a speech to the entire group. I'd be nervous in his position, but he's a natural. Knowledgeable, funny, and rhetorically savvy. There's entertainment afterwards. Some singer named Lis Sørensen. I've never heard of her, but she's not bad.

Out of the nearly five hundred employees, maybe thirty-five of us come from an ethnic minority background. Three in particular are repeatedly mentioned as examples of being well-integrated into society. People refer to the fact that they eat whatever is served, drink alcohol, and treat women properly.

I'd like for people to speak highly of me – I'm not just at the AGM for fun; I'm also here to cultivate my connections within the company. It's an odd mix of business and pleasure.

Even though my official title is area manager, I don't have any real powers when I drive around my district talking to the store managers, even though on paper, they're below me. After all, the shops generate profit for the entire business, so I'm more reliant on them than they are on me. It's my job to keep them more or less in line and make sure they abide by the directives that have been set by management, and all in all to run their stores professionally and efficiently.

If I don't do my job, there's a risk that individual store managers will start slacking off on their responsibilities or just pull out of the franchise. I have some of the Nordic region's biggest stores in my district, so it's important for the entire business that my stores run well. To achieve that, the most important tool I have at my disposal is simply to stay on good terms with the store managers.

There's a seating plan for the dinner, and I end up at the same table as the managers of the three biggest stores in my district (and our wives, of course). My goal is to forge strong enough relationships that they feel an obligation towards me, and thus towards the company. I already know them. I see them almost every week. But the AGM dinner is a good chance to develop my relationship with them. On a more personal level.

The whole situation makes me uncomfortable. As soon as I'd arrived, drinking my coffee, I made the decision to keep to myself. Not to get drunk. To go to bed early. I don't like the other men and I don't like the atmosphere. All the women seem to be on guard. On the other hand, I don't want to seem arrogant, and like I said, I don't want them to think I'm not well integrated. I end up sticking around for the whole party. I get drunk, too. Not too drunk. But enough that the store managers won't think I'm arrogant or weird.

When the alcohol goes in, the wit goes out. It's a Danish saying, they always joke about it. There's an army of waiters running around the tables pouring wine. People get drunk. There have been lewd comments all day, and there's one woman in particular the men are talking about. She's just been hired as a marketing coordinator; she's young, has big breasts, and is there on her own. People are sitting around – even before they're proper drunk – openly talking about how they're going to find a way to touch her breasts. Laughing like schoolboys.

Later on the waiters disappear and the dancing starts. There's an open bar. Behind the rows of spirits bottles and silver-coloured cocktail shakers there are mirrors. People get really drunk, which surprises me. Some get so drunk that they vomit on the floor. The cleaners hurry over to clean it up. A few people are arguing at their tables.

"Don't spoil the good atmosphere!" someone shouts.

Everyone agrees, and then they make up.

My wife has stayed by my side all night, but around one, she gives me a quick peck on the lips and goes back up to our room by herself. I go to the bar for one final drink, and while I'm waiting to order, a Danish guy comes up and puts his hand on my shoulder.

"Are you from Lebanon?" he asks.

"Yes." I flash a big smile. "How did you know that?"

"I picked up on your accent earlier. I've just been down to visit my daughter in Beirut, so the accent is fresh in my mind. She lives down there."

He introduces himself as Anders and tells me his daughter works for an international NGO. We talk about Beirut, about my family's olive trees, which I have to thank for my education and all that I've become, about the majestic cedars in Bsharri, and the Modca café on Hamra Street.

"I thought only tourists went to Modca", Anders laughs.

"No, locals too. I would go there with my friends almost every day."

He knows a lot of the same streets as I do in Beirut, and I talk about my political activism there. It's nice to find a piece of home in the middle of all this. Somebody who knows what they're talking about.

While I'm talking to Anders, the three store managers from my table come up to the bar. They're really wasted, and now we're standing in a little circle. Me and Anders, and the three store managers, who are trying to involve me in their plan to feel up the new marketing coordinator. Anders laughs uncomfortably.

"Just look at her", one of the store managers says, pointing.

The marketing coordinator is standing alone at the other end of the bar.

"Phwoar, how nice is she!" the store manager says.

"Ouch, she is sizzling", the other store manager says, before telling us a trick he knows. "The rest of you crowd around her so she can't move, then I reach over the bar for a drink, and I accidentally brush my hand against one of her tits."

The others laugh.

"The trick is for everyone to stand close enough that she can't tell who's touching her."

"You should give her a proper squeeze", the first store manager interrupts. "Don't just brush up against her. Like this."

He uses his hand to show how he would grab her breast.

They laugh again.

I don't say anything.

Anders doesn't say anything either.

I think about his daughter in Beirut and about my wife up in the hotel room and how I thought things would be different in Denmark. And of course they are. But not in the ways I imagined.

The three store managers are still hatching a plan that will give them a chance to touch the marketing coordinator's breasts when she heads in our direction. She's not looking at us. Maybe she's on her way to the toilet. At least, that's the direction she's going.

Just as she's about to walk past, two of the men step out in front of her and block her path. Now she's trapped between the three drunken store managers and me and Anders. One of the men goes in for a hug. She laughs uncertainly but doesn't resist.

She looks scared, I think.

She's surrounded by five men, and I'm one of them.

"Fancy a dance?" the man asks her.

"I'm just headed to the loo", she replies.

"Come on!" he says, pressing his face against hers.

"Maybe when I come back."

She looks at him playfully, like she's promising him something, but I can see she's just trying to extricate herself from the situation.

He lets go of her, but then the other store manager grabs her and gives her a hug. We're standing around her in a little cluster. I can't move either, the bar is crowded and it's difficult to see exactly what's happening but for a moment, she makes a face like she's in pain.

"She doesn't like that!"

It just flies out of me.

"What did you say?" the store manager asks and lets go of her.

"It doesn't look like she wants you hugging her. Just look at her. Does she look happy?"

She pulls away and disappears without saying a word.

"Aw, now she's gone", one of the store managers says.

"You've ruined everything", the other one says, shooting me an angry look.

I say she didn't seem to be enjoying it and maybe they're a little too drunk and aggressive.

"Danish girls can speak for themselves", one of them says. "Not like where you're from."

I try to tell them about my country. Add some nuance. Anders tries to chip in, but it's all wasted on the three store managers. More talk about Denmark and about ruining the party. More discussions on how they're going to feel her up when she gets back from the loo.

"I touched her breast", the third store manager says. He's been quiet until now.

"You did what?!" the first manager says.

"While you were hugging her, I just slipped my hand under your arm and squeezed her tit."

He holds a hand up and shows how hard he squeezed her.

"Honk, honk!"

The three of them burst out laughing.

I don't know what to say. I look out at the dance floor. The music is really fast tempo, but people are dancing cheek to cheek. I see a hand grabbing someone's arse. Maybe it's okay, maybe it's not.

When I finally crawl into bed, the sheets are crisp and white, and my wife is soft and warm under the duvet. I love staying at hotels. I love my wife.

In the morning we take a long shower together, and when we go down for breakfast, the atmosphere is as unrestrained as it is awkward. There's scrambled eggs, bacon, fruit, bread, cheese and coffee. Some people are so hungover they have to dash out of the dining area to throw up. Many are ashen-faced. The wives are lugging the bags around. The men are laughing as they boast about how much they drank the night before. Some are whispering and sniggering in the corners. I have to try to put things right with my store managers, and if I'm lucky they won't even remember the entire incident at the bar the previous night.

I can't wait to get home. My wife's parents are looking after our daughter. We pick her up on the way home, and for dinner we eat pizza on the couch while watching an animated film. I can't remember the last time we've done that.

3

Depleted bodies: intersectional perspectives on workplace violence

Paulina de los Reyes

Introduction

Women's high labour market participation in Sweden has often been seen as an indication of a successful gender equality model as well as a sign of a modern working life. Thus, the upsurge of a special labour market for women in the 1970s was related to the launch of welfare measures that were intended to provide effective solutions to gender-specific reproduction dilemmas. Universal rights to childcare, tax benefits, access to part-time jobs, and generous maternity leave have commonly been framed as crucial components of a woman-friendly welfare model which has served to reinforce perceptions of Sweden as (one of) the most gender-equal nations in the world. While the Swedish gender equality model is highlighted as a model to follow internationally, recent developments in the workplace suggest the need to examine its pitfalls and negative consequences for women workers in more detail. Two aspects are particularly salient: on the one hand, the persistence of different forms of harassment, abuse and violence against women in the workplace; and on the other hand, increasing levels of ill-health, sick leave and early retirement among women workers (Arbetsmiljöverket, 2021, Jämställdhetsmyndigheten, 2021).

To the extent that sexualised violence in the workplace persists and poor health among women is rising, identifying the conditions that shape and reinforce gendered exposure to violence in the workplace matters more than ever. Current research results indicate, however, that a gender perspective is not enough to address the different forms of threat and harassment that women face in the workplace (Boréus et al, 2021; Sjöstedt et al, 2021). New models of organising labour, as well as differentiation processes based on class, age or migration background, point to the relevance of paying attention to multiple and intersecting hierarchies of power in the workplace and in society (Thörnquist, 2016; de los Reyes and Malmén, 2021). From this perspective, workplace violence must be approached not only as the occurrence of isolated acts of aggression but also as the expression of structural and intertwined hierarchies of power that shape subordinate and vulnerable positions along lines of gender, class, sexuality and national belonging.

A question that remains to be explored is whether an analysis of workplace hierarchies is sufficient to understand how experiences of violence are affecting women's health and wellbeing. As part-time work, pay differences and unstable work conditions have historically positioned women workers as subordinate labour and also as a group particularly exposed to violence, harassment and abuse, the impact of normalised perceptions of a gendered division of labour between the productive and reproductive spheres must be revisited. Moreover, current organisational practices also often rely on gendered perceptions when it comes to low-status, time-consuming, largely invisible work tasks that need to be done in order to maintain the functioning of workplaces (Selberg, 2012; Kalm, 2019).

Drawing on feminist theoretical perspectives of the power relationships implicit in the differentiation between the spaces of productive and reproductive work, it is therefore relevant to interrogate in what ways normative and essentialist perceptions of this divide act to reinforce workplace violence and the normalisation of labour regimes where the bodily integrity of women risks being exposed to (sexualised) violence, harassment or abuse.

Although gender equality policies have been targeted to ameliorate the conflicts between paid work and family work, the reproductive burden on women persists. Moreover, the existence of gender and other hierarchies of power in workplaces has proved to be functional to management models that are based on the fragmentation and particularisation of the labour force (Bhattacharyya, 2018; Thörnquist, 2016).

Taking into consideration that detrimental working conditions affect women's health and general wellbeing, it is necessary to ask whether it is possible to separate experiences of gendered violence in the workplace from women's everyday lives and reproductive responsibilities. Even though the linkages between these spheres have been neglected in most academic investigations in Sweden, in recent years artistic works and fictional narratives have recreated the experience of growing up with mothers exposed to different forms of gendered and racialised oppression in the workplace (de los Reyes, 2022). For instance, an art exhibition MAMI:AMA:MÖDRAR[1] in Stockholm in 2021 brought together art works by writers, performers and other cultural workers that in different ways illustrate a common experience of 'carrying our mothers' broken bodies on our shoulders', as expressed by writer and art historian Macarena Dusant (2021).

Dusant's words, as well as the art works in the exhibition, expose a violence that transcends the bodies of female workers and the concrete workplaces where it occurs. As shown later in this chapter, the artistic works of these new generations reveal important but often ignored dimensions of workplace violence. Moreover, they demonstrate the systemic nature of the intergenerational transmission of experiences of violence, emphasising the need for a comprehensive approach that focuses not only on women's conditions as workers but also on their capacity to reproduce sustainable living conditions for themselves and their families. Against this background, the impact of workplace violence on women's lives outside the workplace must be explored, especially in contexts where women's exposure to workplace violence also affects their capacities for caring and opportunities for replenishment.

In this chapter, the concept of 'replenishment', as well as its opposite 'depletion', addresses the conditions necessary to reproduce human social, physical and psychological capacities in order to make social life (im) possible. Taking social reproduction theories as the point of departure, the analysis in this chapter highlights the necessity of a comprehensive approach that, beyond individual acts and organisational management practices, also interrogates how workplace violence depletes the capacities of female workers to live sustainable lives. In so doing, the chapter highlights the relevance of addressing workplace violence as a structural problem that transcends traditional boundaries between working life and private life.

The chapter is structured as follows. First, I will briefly introduce the concepts used in a discussion that articulates the operation of workplace hierarchies to create different expressions of violence against women. Focusing on intersectional perspectives as the point of departure and based on earlier working life research in Sweden, this section identifies the interaction between different expressions of violence at the workplace level (micro-aggression, sexual harassment, detrimental work environments) and the structural conditions that permeate women's working life experiences. The concept of 'informal hierarchies' is used here to interrogate the dialectics between formal organisational principles and everyday practices of subordination that open the way for and normalise the occurrence of harassment, aggression and violence. The second section discusses the dividing lines between working life and family life, and the separation of paid work from domestic work. The discussion takes as a point of departure the exhibition MAMI:AMA:MÖDRAR and opens the way for a new understanding of the different dimensions of workplace violence and especially of its effects on women's bodies and reproductive capacity. This emphasises the relevance of a comprehensive approach to experiences of violence, aggression and structural deprivation for understanding the dynamics between violence, reproductive failure and depleted bodies. The chapter concludes with a discussion of the relevance of developing theoretical and conceptual frameworks that allow for transformative strategies to combat violence in the workplace.

Gendered violence in the workplace

Even though official documents in Sweden point to violence against women as an extreme form of gender oppression, gender research focusing on violence at work is relatively new. Until recently, the principal concern of this research has been the domestic sphere or such violence has been conceptualised as a cultural feature of particular groups (Eldén, 2003; Eriksson, 2005). However, since the 1980s, researchers have identified an increase in the frequency of violence at work (Estrada et al, 2010; Wikman, 2012). This trend has been particularly evident in occupations coded as female, such as healthcare and education, but in recent years it has also become evident that abuse, violence and harassment affects women workers in a larger range of occupations than those characterised as 'female' (González, 2014; Thörnqvist, 2016; Bondestam and Lundqvist, 2018). As many researchers emphasise, a key problem in assessing the scope and impact of workplace violence is the lack of a unified definition that includes its multiple expressions and consequences (Chapell and di Martino, 2006; Lundqvist and Bondestam, 2020). In this context, the International Labour Organization (ILO) Convention 190 offers a broad definition that permits comparisons between different workplace settings:

> Violence and harassment in the world of work refers to a range of unacceptable behaviours and practices, or threats thereof, whether a single occurrence or repeated, that aim at, result in, or are likely to result in physical, psychological, sexual or economic harm, and includes gender-based violence and harassment. (ILO Convention 190; International Labour Office, 2019)

The ILO definition encapsulates a range of behaviours that, either by themselves or together, constitute expressions of violence. Consequently, individual, social and work-related factors such as workplace culture, work situations and psychosocial hazards frame the occurrence of workplace violence. According to the ILO, sexual harassment and discrimination are considered to be specific forms of violence affecting female workers and racialised workers in particular (International Labour Office, 2020). In highlighting the consequences of these acts, the International Labour Office also establishes a linkage between particular acts of violence and a circumstance of damage to physical or mental health among those exposed to violence. This connection has been amply investigated in different studies that confirm the risk of being affected by mental illness, burnout or sick leave due to experiences of psychological and physical violence (Hogh et al, 2016; Portoghese et al, 2017; Forte, 2020; Coverso et al, 2021).

The connection between sexualised violence and the workplace has been further highlighted since the wave of protests following #MeToo denunciations raised awareness of sexualised abuses of women. In Sweden, workplace narratives after #MeToo often related to workplace conditions that normalise abuse and discrimination (Johansson et al, 2018; Karlsson and Ström, 2019; de los Reyes and Malmén, 2021). Common experiences for many victims are vulnerability and a lack of control due to insecure employment contracts, insecure organisational arrangements and workplace cultures that enable individual and collective acts of abuse and harassment. An interview study conducted with the female staff of eight Swedish universities (de los Reyes and Malmén, 2021) highlights the relevance of hierarchies of power in the workplace for analysing exposure to sexual abuse. According to the interviewees, sexual abuse is often associated with vulnerability and unequal conditions in the workplace: 'Men who harass and rape women [do not] pick any "random" woman. They pick women who are extra vulnerable in different contexts – young women, women with precarious employment, doctoral students' (senior lecturer quoted in de los Reyes and Malmén, 2021, p 35).

Even though inequality appears to be a key condition of workplace abuse, women can also be exposed to sexual abuse from men in similar positions in workplace hierarchies: 'We [have] also seen a lot, at conferences but also during fieldwork, where young girls have had bad experiences, as well as really bad experiences where they have been sexually exploited by superiors but also by their classmates' (researcher quoted in de los Reyes and Malmén, 2021, p 33).

When the interviewee in the second quote notes that sexual harassment also occurs between people in similar positions (classmates), it is also evident that the operation of a structural gender order is also reflected in women's exposure to sexual violence in the workplace.

Testimonies from other industries confirm the linkages between gender harassment and workplace hierarchies. Accounts of the impact of the #MeToo movement indicate that situations of harassment, violence and abuse are everyday experiences for many female workers in many industries:

I have lost count of how many times I have been called 'little girl' by men. Last month I cried in the warehouse because a man refused to take my help and instead my newly hired colleague was asked for help as he felt that I as a woman could not understand him. I have also called security guards several times due to sexual innuendos from customers. (Retail worker quoted in Karlsson and Ström, 2019, p 40)

When she dared to talk to her boss, she was told that she just had to put up with it. Both the boss and the perpetrator are still with the company and what happened was hushed up. (Forest worker quoted in Johansson et al, 2018, p 422)

These quotes indicate that abusive conduct often occurred in contexts of internalised hierarchies where gendered, ageist, sexualised and racialised categorisations operate openly or covertly. In these situations, potential victims are not only exposed to abusive practices like those described in these quotes. They are also reminded of their condition of subordination through more or less offensive comments on their particular position and bodily attributes. References to the body are particularly violent since they signal a perception that reduces the other to an object of desire or to a subordinated position in hierarchies of gender, race, (dis)ability or sexuality. And even apparently innocent comments operate as othering practices when they are repeated and unilateral. For example, questions regarding choice of partners, food habits, parental obligations, and professional experience appeal to a normality which allows some people to question how other people live their lives. Thus, micro-aggression, which can also result in long-term hurt, has an important hierarchising function since it signals who is considered a 'normal' worker and who is not. As expressed in the quotes, micro-aggression is not casual, it is the expression of (in)formal power unbalances where some subject positions at the workplace are constructed as normal, right and superior while others are constantly positioned as deviant, wrong and inferior.

The operation of informal hierarchies in workplaces enables not only acts of abuse and violence but also creates uncertainty about the rules and principles guiding workplace organisations and relationships. "We have good rules concerning the psychosocial work environment, but the problem is that they are not followed"[2] says a union representative in the retail sector. She identifies managers' lack of training in workplace rules as a reason for this problem. Another motive is simply that these rules are not prioritised when organising the distribution of tasks at workplaces. Demands on productivity gains in combination with managerial arbitrariness creates scope for disregard of the established rules and workers' rights to good working conditions, including protection against abuse, bullying, and acts of violence. An interview study conducted among retail workers after #MeToo illustrates how the priorities of the managers affect the rights of the workers:

> I am so extremely disappointed with the managers who refuse to react when a customer is offensive to the staff. I have never felt supported by my boss in unpleasant situations. For example, when a customer resorted to a personal attack on me, whereupon my boss smoothed it over with '[it's] nothing to get upset about'. (Retail worker quoted in Karlsson and Ström, 2019, p 47)

Accounts of victims of abuse being recommended to take sick leave can be seen as a further expression of particularisation that contributes to ignoring the organisational conditions that enable abuse and other forms of workplace violence. In these cases, concrete instances of violence or abuse are accompanied by a lack of recognition – a fact that can be perceived as revictimisation. A reading of working life narratives reinforces the research results that establish a nexus between violence and ill-health. The risk of damage not only to their mental wellbeing but also to their opportunities to replenish their capacity to work is commensurate with the failure of current gender equality measures to protect women workers from being harassed while being compelled to ignore abusive conduct.

In addition to blatant and covert abuse, narratives emanating from the workplace that convey experiences of being considered 'disposable bodies' highlight a further dimension of workplace violence. "If I have to spend the whole day unpacking clothes, I know that my shoulders are not going to resist another workday".[3] Regulations concerning rotation, ergonomic adaptation and rehabilitation opportunities are beyond the reach of many workers. "We know we can be easily replaced"[4] concludes the informant. Workers in precarious employment are seldom in a position to defend their rights. Insecurity and individualisation make collective demands for better working conditions almost impossible. For these workers, as well as part-time workers and other low paid workers who cannot afford to be sick, the constant use of painkillers during workdays is the only way to manage their depleted bodies.

Even though precariousness makes female workers particularly vulnerable to different forms of (sexualised) violence, it is worth stressing that lack of control, stress, anxiety and uncertainty is a transversal trend that, despite variations, affects women workers in a number of sectors (Johansson et al, 2018; Simonsson, 2020; Forte, 2020; Arbetsmiljöverket, 2021). For instance, management modalities in the public sector show similar tendencies. According to Lauri (2016), the Swedish welfare model has undergone a process of standardisation and rationalisation that has severely damaged the professional ethos of social workers giving rise to stress, suffering and anger. The lack of control and the individualisation of organisational shortcomings appear to be important devices of gendered control and subordination.

[I]t feels like you can't do anything to change it. It's a gigantic system that, it doesn't matter what you think or what you say. And more and more it's being transferred down onto yourself, like when I worked with financial support, then I openly expressed what I saw as the problem, and then I was often ill, at home like with fever and such stress from the workload. Then I was sent to some like company health service to check, it was suggested that there was something wrong with me, that I couldn't handle my work. (Social worker quoted in Lauri, 2016, p 204)

The implementation of management models that prioritise customer adaptation, efficiency goals, and slimmed down work organisations have been accompanied by increased levels of sick leave at the same time that new spaces of violence have become an almost normalised feature in many work organisations. Women are not only exposed to explicit harassment but also to management practices that impact their health and sense of self. These trends challenge traditional accounts of gender equality as an ideal to be realised in the world of work. Also, the narrative of progress that frames transformations in the workplace must be revisited in order to find strategies to cope with sexualised violence in the workplace.

Violence, reproduction failures and depleted bodies

Previous research results point to the need for a comprehensive approach to (sexualised) violence, abuse and harassment in the workplace (Thörnquist, 2016; Bondestam and Lundquist, 2018; de los Reyes and Malmén, 2021). Undoubtedly, the interconnections between gendered and racialised patterns in the labour market, informal hierarchies in the workplace, and micro-aggression at an individual level are crucial to understanding the emergence of spaces of violence that severely damage the wellbeing and health of many female workers. In this context, it is necessary to problematise the logics operating behind current management models in order to deal with normalised practices of workplace violence. However, in order to achieve a comprehensive understanding of the long-term consequences of patterns of gendered violence in the workplace, it is also important to consider their impact on the everyday lives of female workers. Analysing the effects of normalised abusive working conditions in a European context, researcher Amelia Horgan identifies problematic linkages:

> In many lines of work, harassment and being spoken down to are so common as to be practically part of the job description. This is particularly the case in the gendered and racialised service sector. If our physiological and spatial orientation are affected by our working days, what about our sense of self? What effect might daily repetition of the gendered and deferential patterns of speech and movement that service work demands have on our self-esteem on our lives outside work? (Horgan, 2021, p 80)

Horgan points to the vulnerability associated with racialised and gendered categorisations and also to demands that form workers' subjectivities beyond the workplace. In Sweden, figures indicating increased ill-health among young women and the proliferation of sick leave due to mental ill-health suggest that harmful working conditions are a phenomenon that transcends workplace settings and affects women's bodies. Research on gendered violence has problematised the separation between working life and family life when it comes to partner abuse. Thus, in recent years, a growing body of research has highlighted the negative impact of partner violence on women's work (McGregor et al, 2021). According to these results, women exposed to partner violence face not only sexual, emotional and physical harm but also work-related impacts such as barriers to employment, lost wages, and decreased work capacity (McGregor et al, 2021). While productivity losses and employers' administration costs have been the focus of many studies, the consequences of work-related violence on family life, domestic responsibilities and caregiving capacity are issues that have been considerably less explored.

Feminist researchers have pointed to the problematic separation of the domestic sphere from the world of work, not least because of its reinforcement of heteronormative household norms and ideas of a male breadwinner. To the extent that the interdependence between those sectors is not recognised, an important sphere of human activity is being ignored and its contribution to social wellbeing remains invisible. Most analyses depart from the economic impact of domestic work, focusing on the provision of food, care and protection. Feminist approaches to social reproduction, however, take a more comprehensive stance on reproductive work, highlighting its centrality for the transmissions of values, cultural traditions and social stability (Elson, 2012; Fraser, 2016; Bhattacharyya, 2018). According to Marxist feminist scholar Sara Farris (2019), a focus on the material conditions of social reproduction allows us to understand the multiple and complex manners in which class exploitation intertwines with gender and racialised systems of oppression.

Focusing on the histories of violence and legacies of (post)colonial trauma that characterise racial capitalism, sociologist Gargi Bhattacharyya (2018) stresses that the hierarchies established on the basis of categories of (productive) work and (reproductive) non-work rely on a continuous differentiation of bodies along lines of gender, sexuality and race. Thus, beyond its specific contribution to the understanding of intersecting relationships of oppression, subordination and violence, social reproduction theory elaborates on the condition of production of human beings and its consequences on (un)sustainable ways of life. As feminist theorist Silvia Federicci points out: 'Unlike other forms of production, the reproduction of human beings is to a great extent irreducible to mechanization, being the satisfaction of complex needs, in which physical and affective elements are inextricably combined, requiring a high degree of human interaction and a most labour-intensive process' (Federicci, 2012, p 107).

Federicci's analysis of the relationship between work and life-producing processes points to the complexity of the different dimensions involved in social reproduction and opens the way for a discussion of the sustainability of life in current contexts of the capitalist organisation of work. Drawing from empirical work on single mothers in the US, feminist economist Diane

Elson argues that an excess of pressure on the domestic sphere in order to compensate for deficiencies in working life may result in the depletion of the human capabilities of those involved in reproductive work (Elson, 2012). Following Elson's analysis, feminist scholars stress the necessity of scrutinising the consequences of harm produced by work modalities where 'the inputs into social reproduction are less than the outputs generated by it' (Rai et al, 2010, p 2).

Combinations of lack of control, excessive workload and the sense of being compelled to perform meaningless tasks are often pointed to as signs of detrimental working conditions. The social workers interviewed by Lauri (2016) seem to be well aware of the need for replenishment in order to cope with these difficulties: 'We are under a lot of strain, or, it's we have a lot to do, always, and we have very few periods of recuperation in this job and we have a burden of documentation that is absurd' (quoted in Lauri, 2016, p 117).

Harmful working conditions arise and the lack of replenishment affects not only social workers but also other professions and female workers, not least in service work and in the public sector. Sociologist Rebecca Selberg identifies these linkages among nurses working in a major Swedish hospital.

> [I cried] right before my vacation … it was stress. I couldn't manage. I take too much responsibility [I've] seen other nurses cry. More and more they cry. They are overwhelmed because they don't know how to prioritise. You always have to prioritise but sometimes it's impossible because everything is equally important. That's when it comes, the tears. (Nurse quoted in Selberg, 2012, p 231)

Narratives of breakdowns are often constructed around the body and perceived as the non-fulfilment of professional demands. In this way, the impact of harmful conditions at work rather than reproductive failures are conceptualised as individual incapacity and transformed into bodily experiences. During her fieldwork at the hospital, Selberg (2012) noticed that:

> Many shared a fear of not lasting till retirement. 'I'm hoping I win the lottery' one nurse said jokingly, because she felt certain she wouldn't be able to work as a nurse until 55 (yes – a decade before retirement age). Nurses in their early thirties complained of back pain, and considered career paths that could take them out of ward nursing. Many complained of feeling exhausted, emotionally and physically. (Selberg, 2012, p 232)

While the combination of physical and mental workload affects women's bodies, their ability to cope with a lack of replenishment, depleted bodies and health problems differs according to their social class and civil status. According to economic historian Soheyla Yazdanpanah (2008), the main preoccupation for mothers with health problems is what will become of their children and how they can avoid their problems affecting their offspring. When Yazdanpanah highlights the mothers' concern, she also acknowledges the effects of ill-health beyond workplaces and their impact on the next generations.

As already mentioned, the intergenerational transmission of workplace violence has been an issue that has not been researched in Sweden. Testimonies of children that witnessed their mothers coming home after work with signs of having been abused or harassed are few and fragmented.[5] An important contribution that challenges the invisibility of this aspect of violence is the artistic work of a generation of young adults who witness, suffer and follow the depletion of their mothers' bodies. These experiences have often taken the form of literary narratives (see de los Reyes, 2021) but are also present in other artistic forms, such as those presented in the exhibition MAMI:AMA:MÖDRAR. Elaborating on these experiences from the perspective of the children, Macarena Dusant (2021) highlights forms of (workplace) violence that transcend the mothers' bodies.

> We are the children who have witnessed how our mothers' lives have been torn apart by a labour market with low wages and exhausting work; mothers who have been thrown out of the system straight into poverty. Their lives reflect an economic system based on an inequality that has contributed to their downfall. As children, we want to break the silence and isolation that surrounds our mothers' lives. We want to write their stories into history and talk about their strengths and their cares, and their declarations of love that have remained silent. (Dusant, 2021, p 8)

The narratives behind this artistic production reveal unformulated questions on mothers' bodies depleted by hard work turned into their children's insights about an unfair social system. The powerlessness of children, who can only guess that something is happening in their mothers' (working) lives, is thus transformed into anger and frustration in a new generation. An important context to the exhibition, and to the stories of depletion that it conveys, is the transformation of the social security system and tougher requirements for acknowledging work-related ill-health and granting early retirement. An important background to the exhibited artistic works is the mothers' stories of denial, misrecognition and suspicion from the Swedish social insurance agency (Försäkringskassa).

In contrast to current perspectives on gendered violence in the workplace, social reproduction theories take a point of departure in women's everyday lives and in the conditions for replenishment of their human capacities. From this perspective, the voices of adult children of female workers provide important clues to understanding how experiences of detrimental working conditions are transmitted to new generations.

Conclusion

"See me as a human being" (Linnea, retail worker[6]).

Taking social reproduction perspectives as the point of departure, the analysis in this chapter explores the different ways that workplace violence depletes women's capacity to replenish their living conditions and ability to deal with everyday life. A central argument has been to highlight the relevance of a comprehensive approach that problematises how workplace violence depletes female workers' capacity to live sustainable lives beyond individual acts and organisational management practices. To this end, it is necessary to transcend traditional boundaries between working life and private life and explore how female workers' experiences of violence are perceived, transmitted and suffered in their affective and social lives.

In contrast to current narratives of progress that frame gender equality and working conditions as a process of constant improvement, the analysis in this chapter shows how gendered, sexualised and racialised inequalities are being reinforced by new management models that deplete the working capacity of an increasing numbers of female workers. However, as demonstrated in most studies, the impact of violence and of gendered violence is not general and affects women differently. Exposure is also associated with racialisation processes, insecure working conditions and management modalities that individualise organisational shortcomings.

Empirical accounts of violence in workplaces and policy recommendations reveal the importance of organisational contexts for understanding how abuse, bullying and sexual harassment affect the wellbeing and health and safety of employees. However, much remains to be done at this level, in particular regarding the role of leadership in normalisation processes that reinforce discrepancies between gender equality and occupational health and safety regulations and the occurrence of different forms of (gendered) violence in the workplace. The testimonies of women during the #MeToo protests reveal not only the inadequacy of current regulations but also indicate the need for a comprehensive approach to the mechanisms of control at work and their impact on workplace violence. Moreover, the linkages between organisational modalities and structural inequalities must be scrutinised in order to understand in what manner (un)equal bodies are reconstructed in workplaces. This is crucial to de-essentialising the subject positions established along lines of gender, class, race, sexual orientation and bodily variation. As shown in this chapter, experiences of violence are closely linked to practices of objectification and subordination which deny the individual the possibility of a sustainable life. When retail worker Linnea, at the beginning of this section, calls for being recognised as a human being, it is hardly possible to ignore the need for a comprehensive understanding of the multiple and complex dimensions involved in workplace violence.

Notes

[1] This exhibition was shown at Botkyrka Konsthall, 26 August 2021.
[2] Interview with a union representative in the retail sector, 22 November 2021.
[3] Interview with retail worker, 15 November 2021.
[4] Interview with retail worker, 15 November 2021.
[5] Testimonies of these events have been gathered within the research project 'Migrant mothers and racialised children. Dilemmas, struggles and visions'. A forthcoming article "Memories in between. Daughters of the Chilean Diaspora in Sweden" in *Memory Studies*, presents some of the results of this project.
[6] https://handelsnytt.se/2021/10/06/se-mig-som-manniska/.

References

Arbetsmiljöverket (2021) *Arbetsorsakade besvär. Arbetsmiljöstatistisk rapport 2021:3*. Solna: Sveriges officiella Statistisk/Swedish Work Environment Authority.

Bhattacharyya, G. (2018) *Rethinking racial capitalism. Questions of reproduction and survival*. London: Rowman & Littlefield.

Bondestam, F. and Lundqvist, M. (2018) *Sexuella trakasserier i akademin: en internationell forskningsöversikt*. Stockholm: Swedish Research Council.

Boréus, K., Neergaard, A. and Sohl, L. (eds) (2021) *Ojämlika arbetsplatser. Hierarkier, diskriminering och strategier för jämlikhet*. Lund: Nordic Academic Press.

Chappell, D. and Di Martino, V. (2006) *Violence at work*. Geneva: International Labour Office.

Converso, D., Sottimano, I. and Balducci C. (2021) Violence exposure and burnout in healthcare sector: mediating role of work ability. *Med Lav,* Feb 23; 112(1): 58–67.

de los Reyes, P. (2022) Migrant mothers: work, nation and racialisation in Swedish official discourses 1970–2000 *Scandinavian Economic History Review,* 70: 2, 123–41.

de los Reyes, P. and Malmén, S. (2021) *Informella hierarkier, könade praktiker och ojämlikhet i akademin*. Rapport 2021:5. Göteborg: Swedish Gender Equality Agency.

Dusant, M. (2021) Förord. MAMI:AMA:MÖDRAR. Stockholm: Labyrint Press.

Eldén, Å. (2003) *Heder på liv och död. Våldsamma berättelser om rykten, oskuld och heder*. Uppsala: Acta Universitatis Uppsaliensis.

Elson, D. (2012) Social reproduction in the global crisis: rapid recovery or long-lasting depletion? In Uttin, P., Razavi, S. and Buchholz, R.V. (eds) *The global crisis and transformative social change*. London: Palgrave Macmillan.

Eriksson, M. (2005) Den onda och den normala fädersmakten? Fäders våld i svensk offentlig politik. *Tidsskrift for kjønnsforskning*, nr 56–72.

Estrada, F., Nilsson, A., Jerre, K. and Wikman, S. (2010) Violence at work – the emergence of a social problem. *Journal of Scandinavian Studies in Criminology and Crime Prevention*, 11: 1, 46–65.

Farris, S.R. (2019) Social reproduction and racialized surplus populations. In Osborne, P., Alliez E. and Russell, E.-J. (eds) *Capitalism: Concept, idea, image – aspects of Marx's Capital today*. Kingston upon Thames: CRMEP Books, pp 121–34.

Federicci, S. (2012) *Revolution at point zero. Housework, reproduction and feminist struggle*. Brooklyn: Common Notions.

Forte (2020) *Våld i arbetslivet inom hälso - och sjukvård, socialt arbete och utbildningssektorn*. Stockholm: Swedish Research Council for Health, Working Life and Welfare.

Fraser, N. (2016) Contradictions of capital and care. *New Left Review, 100*, 99–117.

González Arriagada, A. (2014) Hot och våld i skolan. Räcker det med jämställdhet? In de los Reyes, P. (ed) *Inte bara jämställdhet. Intersektionella perspektiv på hinder och möjligheter i arbetslivet*, SOU 2014:34. Stockholm: Fritzes.

Hogh, A., Conway, P.M., Clausen, T., Madsen, I.E.H. and Burr, H. (2016) *Unwanted sexual attention at work and long-term sickness absence: a follow-up register-based study*. BMC Public Health 2016; 16: 678.

Horgan, A. (2021) *Lost in work. Escaping capitalism*. London: Pluto Press.

International Labour Office (2019) International Labour Conference. Convention 190. *Convention concerning the elimination of violence and harassment in the world of work*. Geneva: ILO.

International Labour Office (2020) *Safe and healthy working environments free from violence and harassment*. Geneva: ILO.

Jämställdhetsmyndigheten (2021) *Könsdiskriminering, sexuella trakasserier och ohälsa i arbetslivet*. Rapport 2021:6, Göteborg.

Johansson, M., Johansson, K. and Andersson, E. (2018) #Metoo in the Swedish forest sector: testimonies from harassed women on sexualised forms of male control. *Scandinavian Journal of Forest Research*, 33(5):1–7.

Kalm, S. (2019) Om Akademiskt hushållsarbete Och dess fördelning, *Sociologisk Forskning*, 56(1): 5–26.

Karlsson, M. and Ström, G. (2019) *#obekvämarbetstid - en rapport om #metoo-uppropet inom handeln*. Stockholm: Handelsanställdas förbund.

Lauri, M. (2016) *Narratives of governing. Rationalization, responsibility and resistance in social work*. Umeå: Umeå University.

Lundqvist, M. and Bondestam, F. (2020) *Efforts to prevent sexual harassment in academia.* Stockholm: Swedish Council for Higher Education.

McGregor, J., Oliver, C., MacQuarrie, B. and Wathen, C. (2021) Intimate partner violence and work: a scoping review of published research. *TRAUMA, VIOLENCE, & ABUSE* Vol. 22(4): 717–27.

Portoghese, I., Galletta, M., Leiter, M., Cocco, P., D'Aloja, E. and Campagna, M. (2017) Fear of future violence at work and job burnout: A diary study on the role of psychological violence and job control. *Burnout Research* 7 (2017): 36–46.

Rai, S., Hoskyns, C. and Thomas, D. (2010) *Depletion and social reproduction. CSGR Working Paper 274/11.* Centre for the Study of Globalisation and Regionalisation, Department of Politics and International Studies, University of Warwick.

Selberg, R. (2012) *Femininity at work. Gender, labour and changing relations of power in a Swedish hospital.* Lund: Arkiv förlag.

Simonson, A. (2020) *Förebyggande arbete mot sexuella trakasserier i svenskt och nordiskt arbetsliv – en forskningsöversikt.* Gothenburg: Swedish Secretariat for Gender Research.

Sjöstedt, A., Giritli Nygren, K. and Fotaki, M. (eds) (2021) *Working life and gender inequality: Intersectional perspectives and the spatial practices of peripheralization.* New York, NY: Routledge.

Thörnquist, A. (2016) *Lite får man tåla – eller? Strukturella och intersektionella perspektiv på hot och våld mot personal i hemtjänsten,* Arbetsliv i omvandling/ Work Life in Transition 2016:1. Lund: Work, Technology and Social Change (WTS), Lund University.

Wikman, S. (2012) *Våld i arbetslivet.* Stockholm, Stockholms Universitet.

Yazdanpanah, S. (2008) *Att upprätthålla livet. Om lågavlönade ensamstående mödrars försörjning i Sverige.* Stockholm: Acta Universitatis Stockholmiensis.

4

The violently gender-equal Nordic welfare states

Sofia Strid, Anne Laure Humbert and Jeff Hearn

Introduction

Sexual harassment is recognised as a form of violence against women and as discrimination on the grounds of sex, gender and/or sexuality. It includes non-consensual physical contact, such as grabbing, pinching, slapping, or rubbing against another person in a sexual way. It also includes non-physical forms, such as catcalls, sexual comments about a person's body or appearance, demands for sexual favours, stalking or non-consensual exposure of sex organs (UN, 2018). Sexual harassment is a violation of the principle of equal treatment of women, men and further genders.

Sexual harassment is one of the most common forms of violence against women (FRA, 2014), although there is a lack of research and empirical evidence on its prevalence, consequences and how to prevent it (Latcheva, 2017). This evidence matters, as there is a need for research-based preventive instruments to tackle sexual harassment (Simonsson, 2020). The different forms that sexual harassment takes range widely in their degree of severity. All forms, however, create a cultural environment that harms, whether or not it provides an 'entry point' to other forms of violence against women, including embodied acts of sexual or physical violence. If violence against women is understood as autotelic – meaning here that different forms are interrelated and thus correlated – then sexual harassment can be taken to be indicative of a broader climate of violence against women. Thus, in this chapter we focus on empirical measurements of violence and violence against women, with the understanding that it nevertheless is informative about the sexual harassment taking place within the Nordic countries.[1]

The largest prevalence survey on violence against women, including sexual harassment, in the EU – conducted by the European Union Agency of Fundamental Rights (FRA) – ranks the Nordic countries at the top compared to other EU countries when it comes to disclosed[2] levels of physical violence, psychological violence, sexual violence, and sexual harassment (FRA, 2014) (see Figures 4.1 and 4.2).

Figure 4.1: Disclosed levels of physical and/or sexual violence against women since the age of 15 in the EU (FRA, 2014)

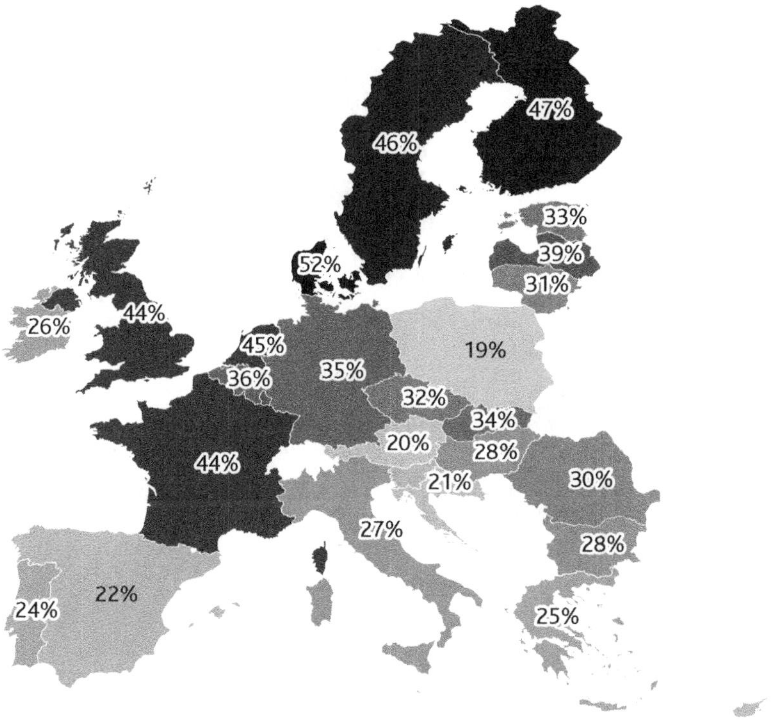

Source: https://fra.europa.eu/en/publications-and-resources/data-and-maps/survey-data-explo
rer-violence-against-women-survey @ GeoNames, Microsoft, OpenStreetMap, TomTom

This is at odds with the Nordic countries being ranked in various composite indices as the most gender-equal, or as 'women-friendly' (Hernes, 1987) welfare states, a phenomenon referred to as the 'Nordic paradox' (see Figure 4.3) in the literature (Gracia and Merlo, 2016).

While gender equality and the Nordic welfare state models are widely debated, mainstream comparative analyses of these welfare models have not adequately covered gender (Orloff, 2009) or violence (Strid et al, 2021). Welfare state regimes research, with a very long history in the social sciences (Titmuss, 1963; Therborn, 1983; Esping-Andersen, 1990) including that on gender welfare regimes (Lewis, 1992; Duncan, 1995, 2002; Sainsbury, 1999), once indicated that some welfare states were more women-friendly than others. Women-friendliness, a contested concept originally used by German-Norwegian political scientist Helga Maria Hernes (1987), views the women-friendly welfare state as an instrument for the empowerment of women as citizens, workers and mothers, as these welfare states propel women's social status closer to that of men – and towards system equilibrium.

Figure 4.2: Disclosed levels of sexual harassment against women since the age of 15 in the EU (FRA, 2014)

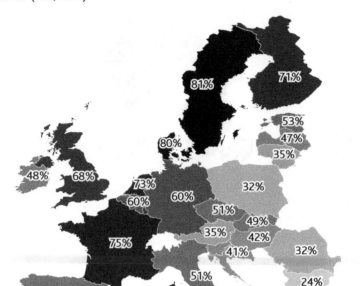

Source: https://fra.europa.eu/en/publications-and-resources/data-and-maps/survey-data-explo rer-violence-against-women-survey @ GeoNames, Microsoft, OpenStreetMap, TomTom

In a welfare state regime analysis, the social democratic welfare states, such as the Nordic welfare states, come out as more women-friendly than those that are conservative/corporatist or liberal.[3]

However, the claim of being a women-friendly welfare state has been heavily criticised. In the welfare state, as elsewhere, the gender system operates through gender segregation and hierarchy, positioning women as both subordinate to and separate from men (Hirdman, 1988).[4] Other critics have suggested a reformulation and contextualisation with gender equality as the key notion, focusing on *which* social policies can be considered to be women-friendly, and for *which* women (Borschorst and Siim, 2002; Sainsbury, 2006). Feminist scholars have also challenged the idea of the women-friendly state by questioning conventional understandings of the welfare state and women's relationship to it (for example: MacKinnon, 1989; Elman, 1996; Weldon, 2002), including for example the relationship between feminist mobilisation and progressive policy on gender-based violence (Htun and Weldon, 2012; see also Strid et al, 2021). More recently, the welfare state

Figure 4.3: Gender Equality Index vs levels of disclosed violence against women since the age of 15, 2012

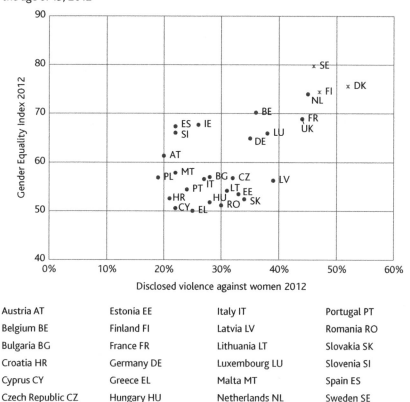

Austria AT	Estonia EE	Italy IT	Portugal PT
Belgium BE	Finland FI	Latvia LV	Romania RO
Bulgaria BG	France FR	Lithuania LT	Slovakia SK
Croatia HR	Germany DE	Luxembourg LU	Slovenia SI
Cyprus CY	Greece EL	Malta MT	Spain ES
Czech Republic CZ	Hungary HU	Netherlands NL	Sweden SE
Denmark DK	Ireland IE	Poland PL	United Kingdom UK

Sources: https://fra.europa.eu/en/publications-and-resources/data-and-maps/survey-data-explorer-violence-against-women-survey and https://eige.europa.eu/gender-equality-index/2015

regime typology and its notion of women-friendliness have been further challenged by intersectional perspectives, and criticised in particular for neglecting diversity, migration, multiculturalism, and 'race' (Sainsbury, 2006; Siim and Borchorst, 2017; Dahlstedt and Neergaard, 2019).

This chapter takes a step further and considers what could be learnt from placing violence centre stage in debates on gender equality and welfare states, and the extent to which the Nordic welfare states are women-friendly. Despite the range of critiques of the women-friendly welfare state, it is notable that the empirical bases on which welfare regimes typologies and their critics build when classifying and theorising about the women-friendly welfare state, with few exceptions, continue to exclude men's violence against women as an indicator of women-friendliness or indeed gender equality. Hence, while there is a long tradition of feminist research on gender equality and the welfare state, research on men's violence against women *and* the welfare state is less prevalent (see, for example Haavind and Magnusson, 2005; Tanhua, 2020). Recently however, these themes, and the tensions between them, have been picked up and explored from a different angle, namely through exploring the so-called 'Nordic paradox' (Gracia and Merlo, 2016). The 'Nordic paradox' literature departs from the observed positive correlation between gender equality and disclosed levels of violence against women in the Nordic countries. A naïve interpretation of this correlation would suggest that the more gender equality there is in a country, the more violence against women there is, which of course needs to be – and has been – further analysed in relation to a range of factors, not least attitudes and understandings of gender-based violence as violence (Humbert et al, 2021).[5] This counterintuitive correlation suggests either that a violence regime is independent of gender equality regimes (Hearn et al, 2020; Strid et al, 2021), and/or that the Nordic welfare states are not as women-friendly as once argued. What is clear is that the 'Nordic paradox' points towards a complex relationship between gender equality and violence against women, which needs to be further explored.

In this chapter, we interrogate why formally gender-equal welfare states such as the Nordic welfare states report comparatively higher levels of violence against women, including sexual harassment, while at the same time are ranked as the most gender-equal and women-friendly welfare states. This primarily conceptual chapter starts by problematising this vision of the Nordic welfare states as gender-equal and 'women-friendly' by showing that this may not hold true if violence against women – including sexual harassment – is taken into account. However, before violence can be incorporated into an assessment of how gender-equal the Nordic countries are, it is necessary to further discuss the concept of violence: what counts as violence, violence as a system (Strid and Meier-Arendt, 2020) and how it relates to (gender) inequalities. The aim is to move towards alternative conceptualisations of welfare states in relation to gender equality, ones which fully integrate the problem of violence against women, including sexual harassment. The chapter discusses what violence is and asks what happens when we focus primarily on violence as a central question for analysing the Nordic welfare state(s). It thus contributes to the debate on gender power relations in the Nordic countries by simultaneously placing violence at the centre of such relations.

Theoretical perspectives with violence centre stage

The complexity of violence against women and gender equality takes us back to the question posed earlier in this chapter: 'Why are formally gender-equal welfare states substantively unequal?' There are multiple approaches to responding to that question. Turning to theory, and to classical feminist (political) theory, different responses, or emphases, are offered. This chapter relies mainly on a radical feminist analysis and focuses on men's violence as a root cause of inequality (Atkinson, 1969; Firestone, 1970). Radical feminists do not view gender equality as sameness – and hence do not see gender equality as equal participation in the same practices or in the same places – and instead locate inequalities in patriarchal gender relations, in institutions, ideologies, discourses and practices of sex/intimacy and, more importantly here, violence against women.

Alternatively, some liberal feminist theories view gender equality in terms of sameness across gender, sex/gender role difference, or rooted in legal inequalities and lack of equal opportunities and equal treatment (Okin, 1991), while some other liberal feminists draw on radical feminism to focus on the examination of the nature of violence (Nussbaum, 1999). Marxist feminists also vary in their analysis, with many viewing gender equality as sameness, and locating inequalities in private ownership, individual property ownership and oppression under capitalist modes of production (Friedan, 1963; Fergusson, 1989), although some also stress questions of sex and reproduction as fundamental (see Hearn, 1991 and O'Brien, 1981, for discussions). Finally, socialist feminists address the interconnectedness of capitalism and patriarchy, and sometimes also imperialism, to explain and transform the oppression of women (Hartmann, 1979; Ferguson, 1989).

Drawing on an analysis of society informed by radical feminist ideas, this chapter places men's violence against women centre stage in the analysis of gender relations. It understands violence as an expression of power and calls for a transformation of society where the institutions and norms that uphold men's material and discursive privileges are both challenged and transformed. Such transformation requires an analysis of patriarchy and the welfare state in which violence and violence against women take centre stage (Atkinson, 1969; Firestone, 1970). Doing so places violence, in its many forms, at the centre of patriarchy and conceptualises violence as its 'organising principle' (Strid and Hearn, 2021). The concept of an organising principle is borrowed from the natural sciences where it is a/the core assumption from which everything else by proximity can derive a classification or a value. Violence is treated and conceptualised as the central reference point that allows all other objects to be located, and used, in a conceptual framework. For example, the idea of the solar system is based on the 'organising principle' that the sun is located at a central point, around which all planets revolve.

Using the thought experiment of an organising principle can help simplify and get a handle on a particularly complicated field, domain, set of social relationships, or phenomena. It allows a shift in understanding, particularly by going beyond heterotelic interpretations of violence, meaning here an understanding of how violence is used as a means to achieve another goal.

An example is the use of violence to maintain control over women or to uphold patriarchal institutions – such as via sexual harassment or economic forms of violence. In this view, violence is complex and understood in line with a radical feminist analysis of violence as an expression of power, but *not reducible* to power; violence is understood as dominance, but it is *not reducible* to dominance. While violence is connected to power and dominance, it is not about power or dominance for their own sake, but transcends these to achieve another goal. While heterotelic understandings of violence are useful, the argument here is that they are not enough and should be combined with autotelic understandings of violence. Violence can be viewed as autotelic when it is a goal in itself, an activity, process and institution that contains its own meaning or purpose (Schinkel, 2004, 2010; Hearn et al, 2020, 2022). Autotelic violence means that violence is not merely a tool, it is also self-perpetuating and an end in itself, as can occur with, for example, organisation(al) violence (Hearn and Parkin, 2001), structural violence (Galtung, 1969), cultural violence (Galtung, 1990), and epistemic violence (Spivak, 1988). The approach concerns the ontology of violence and questions whether violence is always to be explained by something else, for example, as social exclusion, economic marginalisation or individual pathology (Strid and Meier-Arendt, 2020; Hearn et al, 2020, 2022).

In the following discussion, the chapter engages with these themes and tensions. First, it engages with debates on gender equality and (the lack of) violence in welfare state research. It then discusses the concept of violence, what counts as violence, and violence as a system (Strid and Meier-Arendt, 2020). The chapter then relies on an analysis of violence regimes, and uses a recently constructed composite measure of different forms of interpersonal violence including homicide, femicide, physical violence, and sexual violence and harassment, to show that violence against women in the Nordic welfare states operates relatively independently from other measures and indicators of gender equality (Strid et al, 2021). These results are then discussed in relation to systems of violence and oppression, gender equality and feminist theory. Finally, the chapter proposes violence as a means of understanding gender relations in the 'violently gender-equal' Nordic countries.[6]

Welfare regimes

The often-referred-to work of Esping-Andersen (1990), *Three Worlds of Welfare Capitalism*, led to an entire industry of research analysing or fitting welfare states in Europe and beyond into ideal-type categories (Liebfried, 1991; Goodin et al, 1999) and feminist critique thereof (Sainsbury, 1991, 1999; Lewis, 1992; Orloff, 1993). Esping-Andersen was predominantly occupied with class and commodification (rather than gender and violence). His well-known distinction between liberal, conservative, and social democratic regime types moved away from expenditure as the sole criterion for welfare efforts, and instead replaced it with the notion of the impact of the decommodification of labour, social stratification and the public–private mix of social provisions. The liberal US, conservative Germany and social democratic Sweden typified the ideal models/types of each welfare state category. Esping-Andersen was in 'good company' when he omitted gender in his original analysis; most post-war writing on welfare states makes little, if any, mention of women or gender (for example: Titmuss, 1963; Goodin et al, 1999). The feminist critique of Esping-Andersen stresses the importance of gender as both an outcome and an explanation of outcome: that is, gender and gender relations as both independent and dependent variables in social policy and welfare regime research. In particular, these critiques focus on notions of the family, unpaid work and care (Lewis, 1992; O'Connor et al, 1999; Sainsbury, 1999) and on women's dependency on the welfare state, drawing on earlier feminist work on private and public patriarchies (Siim, 1987). These feminist critiques have further developed the welfare state regime typology by gendering it. They concluded that a wider range of issues needed to be included in the theorisation and comparison of forms of gender regime, violence being one of them (Walby, 2009, 2013). Yet, the gender regime framework took neither violence nor women's and men's relationship to violence into account, not even ten years later (for example, Sörensen and Bergqvist, 2002). Any conclusions about how some welfare state regimes are 'more women-friendly' than others therefore need to be revisited.

Gender-based violence is an extensive global problem with significant impacts on individuals, families and societies. It is defined by the EU (EC, 2021), the Council of Europe (2011), the UN (1993) as a cause and a consequence of gender inequality. It has pandemic proportions: one in three women has been subjected to some form of physical or sexual violence in her lifetime (FRA, 2014). More than one in two women in the EU, on average, have experienced sexual harassment since the age of 15 (FRA, 2014) (see Figure 4.2). For Denmark, Finland and Sweden – three Nordic welfare states often labelled the most gender-equal countries in the world (World Economic Forum, 2001, 2022; EIGE, 2021, 2019) – the disclosed prevalence of physical and sexual violence against women is even higher: between 52, 47 and 46 per cent respectively (FRA, 2014; see also Lundgren et al, 2002 and Westerstrand et al, 2022 for Sweden) (see Figure 4.1). To some, the FRA data point towards a paradox, namely the coexistence of high levels of gender equality and high levels of violence against women (Gracia and Merlo, 2016). The growing debates about the 'Nordic paradox' examine the interpretation of these data including: the extent to which questions about violence, definitions of violence and violent experiences have the same meanings in different national and linguistic contexts (Martín-Fernández et al, 2020); the extent to which violence, or rather different kinds of violence, are accepted and normalised (Gracia and Merlo, 2016); and the extent to which responses of exposure to violence are affected by social shame (Enander, 2009; Weiss, 2010) and gender equality. Others have explained the apparent paradox with contextual and situational factors (Humbert et al, 2021) and pointed to the relative independence of gendered violence from other gender equality indicators (Strid et al, 2021). Nonetheless, violence seems key to understanding gender inequality and gender relations, and the relationship between violence and gender equality remains an interesting topic to explore.

This also raises questions about how to understand violence against women, and violence more generally in relation to societal context, and poses the very question of 'what is violence?' in an even more fundamental way (Lawrence and Karim, 2007; Ray, 2018). There are multiple contestations of what violence is, including physical violence, assault, sexual violence, coercive control, homicide, and genocide, as well as less directly physical violence, such as cultural, symbolic, epistemic and systemic violence (Bourdieu, 1998; Žižek, 2008). Violence includes, but is not limited to, state violence, economic violence, terrorism, gender-based violence, violence against women, anti-lesbian, gay and transgender violence, intimate partner violence, gang violence, hate crime, cyberviolence, and stalking. The societal contextualising of violence and violence against women problematises any simple definition of violence and its boundaries (Walby et al, 2017; Walby and Towers, 2017; Bjørnholt and Hjemdal, 2018).

Violence is still often framed and defined in terms of physical violence, even to the extent that sometimes (physical) sexual violence is separated from physical violence and not even discussed as part of physical violence, as we have argued elsewhere (Humbert et al, 2021). Feminist activists and scholars have long argued that domestic violence, gender-based violence and intimate partner violence also include non-physical forms of violence (such as economic, psychological and emotional violence) (Kelly, 1998; Hearn, 2013). Accordingly, violence and violence against women need to be understood in relation to societal conditions, broadly based structures of inequality, governance and welfare state regimes, as well as social movements. For example, inequalities and entrenched oppressions may mean that the act or use of violence, especially physical violence, is not necessary to maintain oppressive or unequal social relations, as long as the potential for and threat of violence are available (Hearn, 2013), such as in cases of symbolic violence (Bourdieu, 1998) and structural violence (Galtung, 1969). In these circumstances, the very act of physical violence is not necessary to control and dominate – that is, the setting is so unequal that direct or physical violence as a means of more inequality is not needed. Paradoxically, 'violence, or at least direct, interpersonal and physical violence, may not be used as necessary in some very violating contexts' (Humbert et al, 2021, p 3). The question then is, as framed by Hearn and colleagues (2022, p 2), 'is violence a set of material bodily actions and effects? A range of discursive constructions? Is violence more structural in character, as, for example, through institutions or structural inequalities? Or all of these – all intersectionally gendered?'

Violence and violence regimes

There is a very long tradition of feminist research on violence (Brownmiller, 1975; Kelly, 1988; Hearn, 1998; Hester et al, 2008), although recently it seems to have fallen out of fashion.[7] There is also a very long tradition of feminist research on violence and the state (MacKinnon, 1989; Elman, 1996; Hearn, 1998), challenging our understandings of the welfare state and women's relationship to it. One of the more explicit approaches is MacKinnon's (1989), who argues that the state itself is patriarchal through male dominance and violence. Nonetheless, violence is not as yet fully addressed by mainstream social theory, with the role of violence as a source of social stratification within and between welfare states underexplored (Strid et al, 2021). The importance of violence, from welfare regime research to contemporary research, is often either underestimated or rendered invisible, not least in mainstream social sciences and social theory, but also in contemporary gender studies (Hearn, 2013; Walby, 2013). The consequences, when considering welfare responses to gendered violence are, first, that one might miss greater differences between the same welfare regimes and gender regimes than commonly assumed (Pringle, 2005; Lister, 2009), and second, that welfare regimes deemed women-friendly may not turn out to be women-friendly at all.

While there have been movements, both gendered and non-gendered, towards a more cohesive analysis of the regulation and deployment of violence, which hint at the potential of the further integration of theories of violence (Enloe, 2000; Scheper-Hughes and Bourgois, 2004; Gregory, 2004; Roberts, 2008), the separation of the study of different forms and levels of violence in different disciplines has led to fragmented theory and explanations (Lundgren in Norrby, 2012; Walby, 2013; Hearn et al, 2020). However, some research has indicated extensive similarities across forms of violence and extensive differences between countries in the organisation of violence. Research has further indicated that its many forms – interpersonal (such as crime, gender-based violence), interstate (war), state–citizen (such as the use of the death penalty) and group–state (such as terrorism) – may be connected so that an increase in one form is likely to lead to an increase in other forms, and a decrease in one is linked to a decrease in others (Walby, 2009). These links, the interconnectedness of different forms of violence, may constitute different and distinguishable systems of violence, or 'violence regimes' (Hearn et al, 2020).

Violence regime is a relatively new concept developed to set up a theoretical framework by which states/societies can be compared and contrasted according to how violent they are and how much violence they produce at micro, meso and macro levels (Hearn et al, 2020; Strid et al, 2017, 2021).[8] Violence regime includes the relationship between violence and the institutions and policy set up/implemented to counter violence. Violence as a regime, where violence is approached holistically, addresses the fragmentation of the study of violence.

An approach to violence that considers the co-variance and interrelationships between different forms of violence and shows how many forms of violence are interrelated or interconnected can be used to derive different systems of violence. This has been measured empirically through the creation of a Violence Regimes Index (Strid et al, 2021), where the relationship between deadly violence (homicides, and so on) and damaging violence has been examined (see Figure 4.4). The interconnectedness of different forms of

Figure 4.4: Violence Regimes Index: relationship between the scores for 'deadly violence' and 'damaging violence'

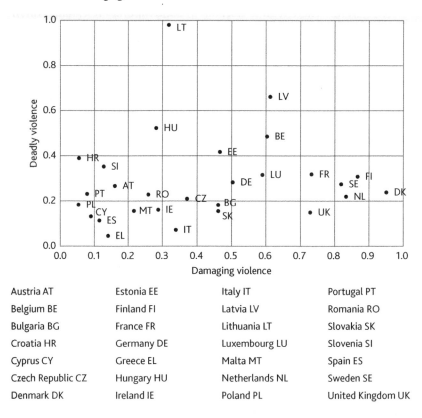

Austria AT	Estonia EE	Italy IT	Portugal PT
Belgium BE	Finland FI	Latvia LV	Romania RO
Bulgaria BG	France FR	Lithuania LT	Slovakia SK
Croatia HR	Germany DE	Luxembourg LU	Slovenia SI
Cyprus CY	Greece EL	Malta MT	Spain ES
Czech Republic CZ	Hungary HU	Netherlands NL	Sweden SE
Denmark DK	Ireland IE	Poland PL	United Kingdom UK

Note: Scores are normalised on a range from 0 to 1, with higher scores associated with higher levels of violence

Source: Strid et al., 2021

(autotelic) violence can then be used to derive different systems of violence using violence regimes. This use of regime is analogous to Esping-Andersen's, who used the term regime to draw attention to 'the complex ways in which welfare states ... can both reshape and reproduce inequalities' (Hudson, 2018, p 48). As others have shown (Walby, 2009), different forms of violence on interpersonal, intra-state and interstate levels correlate, so that increases on one form of violence co-vary with increases in other forms of violence, thus constituting a domain or regime of violence.

As argued elsewhere (Hearn et al, 2020, 2022; Humbert et al, 2021; Strid et al, 2021), this approach to violence regimes requires outlining what is to be meant by violence, and the problem of what violence is, or could be, pervades these discussions. In alignment with previous and ongoing collaborative work,[9] we see violence as a form of inequality, beyond the mere physical and measurable (or indeed 'countable', see Myhill and Kelly, 2019). This approach concerns the ontology of violence, and calls into question whether violence should always be explained by something else, for example, as social exclusion, economic marginalisation or individual pathology – or, as argued here, an inequality, as power and as privilege.

Conclusion

The Nordic countries consistently rank high on different gender equality indices. But they also show higher levels of violence against women and sexual harassment compared to other EU countries. Does this suggest that the Nordic countries – formally regarded as gender-equal welfare states or women-friendly welfare states – have not been capable of reducing or preventing violence against women and sexual harassment? More importantly for this chapter, violence against women is not analysed as central to the welfare state, gender equality or gender relations. If violence were placed centre stage in theoretical and empirical analyses of gender relations, the levels of gender equality in the Nordic countries would drop.

The significance of violence in the mainstream social sciences, social theory and contemporary gender studies is growing, but there is still an underestimation of its importance in the analysis of gender relations. Sexual harassment, with higher levels disclosed in the Nordic 'women-friendly' welfare states compared to other EU countries, is no exception. This failure to incorporate violence has led to analyses that are less relevant and nuanced than they could be, and to policy interventions that could be better evidenced and substantiated.

The positioning of violence as a central organising principle, and the analysis of violence regimes, is an attempt to bring violence back into the analysis, to place it at the centre of the analysis, and to identify the pivot of unequal gender relations. Furthermore, it calls into question welfare state regime research, including gendered regimes, which has concluded that some welfare state regimes are 'more women-friendly than others'. The analysis in this chapter, which has built on collaborative and previous work, challenges this idea and shows how the empirical bases for such conclusions have not fully, or sometimes not at all, considered violence. Finally, the exclusion of violence means that welfare state regime research has overlooked one of the most substantial and deep-rooted causes and consequences of gender inequality.

Contrary to the body of work challenged here, this chapter argues that violence regimes operate somewhat independently from gender equality regimes and welfare regimes, hence pointing to the autotelic nature of violence. The implications of taking violence into account in the regime concept for Nordic countries and developing, both theoretically and empirically, violence regimes, is that it helps us understand that the 'Nordic paradox' is, in fact, not so much of a paradox.

Notes

[1] This chapter builds on previous results, partly published and partly unpublished, from collaborative work within the Swedish Research Council (VR) funded project *Regimes of Violence* (grant number 2017–01914), including Associate Professor Sofia Strid (Gothenburg and Örebro Universities, Sweden), Professor Anne Laure Humbert (Oxford Brookes University, UK), Senior Professor Jeff Hearn (Örebro University, Sweden), and Associate Professor Dag Balkmar (Örebro University, Sweden).

[2] This chapter refers to the disclosed prevalence of violence against women to recognise that survey-based data underestimate actual prevalence as they can only measure the incidents disclosed by respondents.

[3] The term 'regime' carries different meanings. It has been used to capture and denote: (1) 'principles, norms, rules, and decision-making procedures around which actor expectations converge on a given issue-area' (Krasner, 1982, p 185), explicitly including informal institutions; (2) modes of rule or management; (3) forms of government, or the government in power; (4) a period of rule; and/or (5) a regulated system. The notion adopted here draws on all five and is a flexible concept, incorporating macro, meso and micro levels. Hence, our notion of regime can accommodate both more systemic approaches (Walby, 2009), as well as more institutional ones (Connell, 1987).

[4] Both Helga Maria Hernes and Yvonne Hirdman have had a significant influence on scholarly and policy debates in this space, particularly in Norway and Sweden.

[5] The coexistence of high levels of gender equality and violence against women has been explained in many ways, from rejecting the evidence due to methodological issues with the FRA survey (Walby and Olive, 2014), to violence as a backlash reaction to gender equality. However, this relationship, the apparent paradox, can also be explained away, and 'undone'. By using a range of methodological, demographic and societal factors to contextualise the disclosed levels of violence in the FRA study (2014), the multilevel analytic approach deployed by Humbert and colleagues (2021) considers how macro and micro levels contribute to the prevalence of violence, which makes the 'Nordic paradox' disappear. The results

suggest that the 'Nordic paradox' cannot be understood independently from a wider pattern of violence in society, and should be seen as connected and co-constituted in specific formations, domains or *regimes* of violence.

[6] This formulation is owed to Dr Jenny Westerstrand, President of ROKS, the National Organisation for Women's Shelters and Young Women's Shelters in Sweden.

[7] As an example, of the last four Swedish national gender studies conferences, none have addressed the modalities of violence. At *g14: National Gender Studies Conference* Umeå, Sweden in 2014, there was only one panel organised on the topic of men's violence. Two years later, at g16 in Linköping in 2016, despite 'sexualised violence' being a conference keyword, only one panel addressed violence ('The intersections of violence') (see http://liu.diva-por tal.org/smash/get/diva2:1064192/FULLTEXT01.pdf). Three years later, at g19 in Gothenburg in 2019, there was one panel on gender-based violence. Finally, at the g22 in Karlstad in 2022, the only panel addressing violence addresses not its modalities, but its discourses ('Discourses of #MeToo') (see https://www.kau.se/en/centre-gender-studies/date/national-gender-studies-conference-g22/open-panels).

[8] As acknowledged in our previous work, the concept of *violence regimes* is not entirely new. It draws on Weber's understanding of the modern state, where Kössler (2003) uses regimes of violence to discuss the state's monopoly on the legitimate use of violence after 9/11. It also uses Schinkel's (2013) subsequent introduction of the idea that a regime of violence describes the relationship between various forms of violence and that, in their different forms, they constitute a way of governing conduct via the medium of violence. This conceptualisation of *violence regimes* is useful and moves the theorisation of violence forward, but it is different from the way *violence regimes* is developed here, namely as a framework for comparative state analysis and as a form in which states themselves are constituted; as the theorising (and ultimately empirical operationalisation) of autotelic violence; and as a system of interrelated forms, aspects and manifestations of violence, including institutions, policy and violence production (Hearn et al, 2022).

[9] For example, in the project 'Regimes of Violence: Theorising and Explaining Variations in the Production of Violence in Welfare State Regimes' funded by Swedish Research Council (grant number 2017–01914), and the EU H2020 project UniSAFE, funded under grant agreement 101006261.

References

Atkinson, T.G. (1969) *Radical Feminism*, New York: The Feminists.

Bjørnholt, M. and Hjemdal, O.K. (2018) 'Measuring violence, mainstreaming gender: Does adding harm make a difference?', *Journal of Gender-Based Violence*, 2(3): 465–79.

Borschorst, A. and Siim, B. (2002) 'The women–friendly welfare states revisited', *NORA: Nordic Journal of Women's Studies*, 10(2): 90–8.

Bourdieu, P. (1998) *La Domination Masculine*, Paris: Seuil.

Brownmiller, S. (1975) *Against Our Will. Men, Women, and Rape*, New York: Simon & Schuster.

Connell, R. (1987) *Gender and Power*, Cambridge: Polity.

Council of Europe (2011) *Convention on Preventing and Combating Violence against Women and Domestic Violence* (Council of Europe Treaty Series No 210), Istanbul: Council of Europe.

Dahlstedt, M. and Neergaard, A. (2019) 'Crisis of solidarity? Changing welfare and migration regimes in Sweden', *Critical Sociology*, 45(1): 121–35.

Duncan, S. (1995) 'Theorizing European gender systems', *Journal of European Social Policy*, 5(4): 263–84.

Duncan, S. (2002) 'Policy discourses on reconciling work and life in the EU', *Social Policy and Society*, 1(4): 305–14.

EC (European Commission) (2021) 'Gender-based violence by definition', Website [retrieved 2 May 2021]: https://ec.europa.eu/info/policies/just ice-and-fundamental-rights/gender-equality/gender-based-violence/ what-gender-based-violence_en#relatedlinks.

EIGE (2019) *Gender Equality Index 2019*, Luxembourg: Publications Office of the EU.

EIGE (2021) *Gender Equality Index 2021*, Luxembourg: Publications Office of the EU.

Elman, A. (1996) *Sexual Subordination and State Intervention: Comparing Sweden and the United States*, Providence, RI: Berghahn.

Enander, V. (2009) '"A fool to keep staying": Battered women labeling themselves stupid as an expression of gendered shame', *Violence Against Women*, 16(1): 5–31.

Enloe, C. (2000) *Maneuvers*, Berkeley: University of California Press.

Esping-Andersen, G. (1990) *The Three Worlds of Welfare Capitalism*, Cambridge: Polity Press.

Ferguson, A. (1989) *Blood at the Root*, London: Pandora.

Firestone, S. (1970) *The Dialectic of Sex*, London: Jonathan Cape.

FRA (EU Agency for Fundamental Rights) (2014) *Violence Against Women: An EU Wide Survey – Main Results Report*, Luxembourg: Publications Office of the EU.

Friedan, B. (1963) *The Feminine Mystique*, New York: W.W.: Norton.

Galtung, J. (1969) 'Violence, peace, and peace research', *Journal of Peace Research*, 6(3): 167–91.

Galtung, J. (1990) 'Cultural violence', *Journal of Peace Research*, 27(3): 291–305.

Goodin, R.E., Headey, B., Muffels, R. and Dirven, H.-J. (1999) *The Real Worlds of Welfare Capitalism*, Cambridge: Cambridge University Press.

Gracia, E. and Merlo, J. (2016) 'Intimate partner violence against women and the Nordic paradox', *Social Science & Medicine*, 157: 27–30.

Gregory, D. (2004) *The Colonial Present: Afghanistan, Palestine, Iraq*, Oxford: Blackwell.

Haavind, H. and Magnusson, E. (2005) 'The Nordic countries. Welfare paradises for women and children?' *Feminism & Psychology*, 15(2): 227–35.

Hartmann, H. (1979) 'The unhappy marriage of Marxism and feminism: Towards a more progressive union', *Capital and Class*, 8(2): 1–33.

Hearn, J. (1991) 'Gender: biology, nature and capitalism', in T. Carver (ed), *The Cambridge Companion to Marx* (pp 222–45), New York: Cambridge University Press.

Hearn, J. (1998) *The Violences of Men*, London: Sage.

Hearn, J. (2013) 'The sociological significance of domestic violence: Tensions, paradoxes and implications', *Current Sociology*, 61(2): 152–70.

Hearn, J. and Parkin, W. (2001) *Gender, Sexuality and Violence in Organizations: The Unspoken Forces of Organization Violations*, London: Sage.

Hearn, J., Strid, S., Humbert, A.L., Balkmar, D. and Delaunay, M. (2020) 'From gender regimes to violence regimes: Re-thinking the position of violence', *Social Politics: International Studies in Gender, State & Society*, 29(2), 2022: 682–705.

Hearn, J., Strid., S., Humbert, A.L. and Balkmar, D. (2022) 'Violence regimes: A useful concept for social politics, social analysis, and social theory', *Theory and Society*, 51(4): 565–94.

Hernes, H.M. (1987) *Welfare State and Women Power. Essays in State Feminism.* Oslo: Norwegian University Press.

Hester, M., Westmarland, N., Pearce, L. and Williamson, E. (2008) *Early Evaluation of the Domestic Violence, Crime and Victims Act 2004*, Ministry of Justice Research Series, 14/08.

Hirdman, Y. (1988) 'Genussystemet – reflexioner kring kvinnors sociala underordning', *Tidskrift för genusvetenskap*, 3: 49–63.

Htun, M. and Weldon, L. (2012) 'The civic origins of progressive policy change: Combating violence against women in global perspective, 1975–2005', *American Political Science Review*, 106(3): 548–69.

Hudson, J. (2018) 'Social justice and social welfare', in G. Craig (ed), *Handbook on Social Justice* (pp 46–65), Cheltenham: Edward Elgar Publishing.

Humbert, A.L., Strid, S., Hearn, J. and Balkmar, D. (2021) 'Undoing the "Nordic Paradox": Factors affecting rates of disclosed violence against women across the EU', *PLOS ONE*, 16(5).

Kelly, L. (1988) *Surviving Sexual Violence*, Cambridge: Polity Press.

Kelly, L. (1998) 'How women define their experiences of violence', in K. Yllö and M. Bograd (eds), *Feminist Perspectives on Wife Abuse* (pp 114–32), Thousand Oaks: Sage.

Kössler, R. (2003) 'The modern nation state and regimes of violence: Reflections on the current situation', *Ritsumeikan Annual Review of International Studies*, 2: 15–36.

Krasner, S.D. (1982) 'Structural causes and regime consequences: Regimes as intervening variables', *International Organization*, 36(2): 185–205.

Latcheva, R. (2017) 'Sexual harassment in the European Union: A pervasive but still hidden form of gender-based violence', *Journal of Interpersonal Violence*, 32(12): 1821–52.

Lawrence, B.B. and Karim, A. (2007) *On Violence: A Reader*, Durham: Duke University Press.

Lewis, J. (1992) 'Gender and the development of welfare regimes', *Journal of European Social Policy*, 2(3): 159–73.

Liebfried, S. (1991) 'Towards a European welfare state? On the integration potentials of poverty regimes in the EC', *Working Paper*, Bremen University Centre for Social Policy.

Lister, R. (2009) 'A Nordic nirvana? Gender, citizenship, and social justice in the Nordic welfare states', *Social Politics: International Studies in Gender, State & Society*, 16(2): 242–78.

Lundgren, E., Heimer, G., Westerstrand, J. and Kalliokoski, A.-M. (2002) *Captured Queen: Men's Violence against Women in 'Equal' Sweden*, Stockholm: Fritzes Offentliga Publikationer.

MacKinnon, C.A. (1989) *Toward a Feminist Theory of the State*, Cambridge: Harvard University Press.

Martín-Fernández, M., Gracia, E. and Lila, M. (2020) 'Ensuring the comparability of cross-national survey data on intimate partner violence against women: A cross-sectional, population-based study in the European Union', *BMJ Open*, 10(3).

Myhill, A. and Kelly, L. (2019) 'Counting with understanding? What is at stake in debates on researching domestic violence', *Criminology & Criminal Justice*, 21(3): 280–96.

Norrby, A. (2012) 'Forskningsfältet som sköts i sank, intervju med Eva Lundgren, Gun Heimer och Jenny Westerstrand', Swedish Secretariat for Gender Research.

Nussbaum, M.C. (1999) *Sex and Social Justice*, New York: Oxford University Press.

O'Brien, M. (1981) *The Politics of Reproduction*, London: Routledge & Kegan Paul.

O'Connor, J., Orloff, A. and Shaver, S. (1999) *States, Markets, Families*, Cambridge: Cambridge University Press.

Okin, S.M. (1991) *Justice, Gender, and the Family*, New York: Basic.

Orloff, A. (1993) 'Gender and the social rights of citizenship state policies and gender relations in comparative research', *American Sociological Review*, 58(3): 303–28.

Orloff, A.S. (2009) 'Gendering the comparative analysis of welfare states: An unfinished agenda', *Sociological Theory*, 27(3): 317–43.

Pringle, K. (2005) 'Neglected issues in Swedish child protection policy and practice: Age, ethnicity and gender', in M. Eriksson, M. Hester, S. Keskinen and K. Pringle (eds), *Tackling Men's Violence in Families: Nordic Issues and Dilemmas* (pp 155–70), Bristol: Policy Press.

Ray, L. (2011/2018) *Violence and Society*, London: Sage.

Roberts, D. (2008) *Human Insecurity: Global Structures of Violence*, London: Zed Books.

Sainsbury, D. (1991) 'Analysing welfare state variations', *Scandinavian Political Studies*, 14(1): 1–30.

Sainsbury, D. (ed) (1999) *Gender and Welfare State Regimes*, Oxford: Oxford University Press.

Sainsbury, D. (2006) '"Immigrants" social rights in comparative perspective: Welfare regimes, forms in immigration and immigration policy regimes', *Journal of European Social Policy*, 16(3): 229–44.

Scheper-Hughes, N. and Bourgois, P. (eds) (2004) *Violence in Peace and War*, Malden: Blackwell.

Schinkel, W. (2004) 'The will to violence', *Theoretical Criminology*, 8(1): 5–31.

Schinkel, W. (2010) *Aspects of Violence: A Critical Theory*, Basingstoke: Palgrave Macmillan.

Schinkel, W. (2013) 'Regimes of violence and the *Trias Violentiae*', *The European Journal of Social Theory*, 16(3): 310–25.

Siim, B. (1987) 'The Scandinavian welfare states', *Acta Sociologica*, 30(3/4): 255–70.

Siim, B. and Borchorst, A. (2017) 'Gendering European welfare states and citizenship: Revisioning inequalities', in P. Kennett and N. Lendvai-Bainton (eds), *Handbook of European Social Policy* (pp 99–127), Cheltenham: Edward Elgar Publishing.

Simonsson, A. (2020) *Förebyggande arbete mot sexuella trakasserier i svenskt och nordiskt arbetsliv* 2020:1, Göteborg: Nationella sekretariatet för genusforskning.

Sörensen, K. and Bergqvist, C. (2002) *Gender and the Social Democratic Welfare Regime*, Arbetslivsinstitutet.

Spivak, G.C. (1988) 'Can the subaltern speak?', in C. Nelson and L. Grossberg (eds), *Marxism and the Interpretation of Culture* (pp 271–313), Urbana-Champaign: University of Illinois Press.

Strid, S., Balkmar, D., Hearn, J. and Humbert, A.L. (2017) Regimes of violence: Theorising and explaining variations in the production of violence in welfare state regimes. Research Project funded by the Swedish Research Council, Grant 2017–01914.

Strid, S. and Meier-Arendt, D. (2020) 'Våld som system: Våld, maskulinitet och förändring', *Socialmedicinsk Tidskrift*, 97(2), 235–47.

Strid, S. and Hearn, J. (2021) 'Violence and patriarchy', in Kurtz, L. (ed), *Encyclopedia of Violence, Peace, and Conflict*, Academic Press.

Strid, S., Humbert, A.L., Hearn, J. and Balkmar, D. (2021) 'States of violence: Exploring welfare state regimes as violence regimes by developing a violence regimes index', *Journal of European Social Policy*, 31(3): 321–36.

Tanhua, I. (2020) *Gender Equality and Nordic Welfare Societies*, Norden 2020. https://stm.fi/documents/1271139/8492720/Report+Gender+equality+and+Nordic+welfare+societies.pdf/60fcbf91-669b-4d10-9b16-01a51657eb58/Report+Gender+equality+and+Nordic+welfare+societies.pdf?t=1527854184000

Therborn, G. (1983) 'Why some classes are more successful than others', *New Left Review*, 138: 37–55.

Titmuss, R.M. (1963) *Essays on the Welfare State*, London: Allen and Unwin.

UN (1993) *Declaration on the Elimination of Violence against Women*, New York: United Nations.

UN (2018) *Towards an End to Sexual Harassment: The Urgency and Nature of Change in the Era of #MeeToo*, New York: Office of the Executive Coordinator and Spokesperson on Addressing Sexual Harassment and Discrimination at UN Women.

Walby, S. (2009) *Globalisation and Inequalities*, London: Sage.

Walby, S. (2013) 'Violence and society', *Current Sociology*, 61(2): 95–111.

Walby, S. and Olive, P. (2014) *Estimating the Cost of Gender-based Violence in the EU*, Luxembourg: Publications Office of the European Union.

Walby S. and Towers, J. (2017) 'Measuring violence to end violence: Mainstreaming gender', *Journal of Gender-Based Violence*, 1(1): 11–31.

Walby, S., Towers, J., Francis, B. and Strid, S. (2017) *The Concept and Measurement of Violence against Women and Men*, Bristol: Policy Press.

Weiss, K.G. (2010) 'Too ashamed to report', *Feminist Criminology*, 5(3): 286–310.

Weldon, S. L. (2002) *Protest, Policy and the Problem of Violence Against Women: A Cross-National Comparison*, Pittsburgh: University of Pittsburgh Press.

Westerstrand, J., Strid, S., Carsbring, A. and Ekbrand, H. (2022) *Kvinnors trygghet. Ett jämställt samhälle fyllt av våld*, Stockholm: Roks.

World Economic Forum (2021) *Global Gender Gap Report 2021*, Geneva: WEF.

World Economic Forum (2022) *Global Gender Gap Report 2022*, Geneva: WEF.

Žižek, S. (2008) *Violence*, London: Profile.

5

ON THE FRESHERS' TRIP

Mads Ananda Lodahl

Translated by Nielsine Nielsen and Paul Russell Garrett

The toilets on the freshers' trip – that's where it happens. I'm sure other things happen in those toilets, but I just want to write about my own experience. We're at a scout hall somewhere outside of the capital, I don't know exactly where. I've just moved to Copenhagen, so I don't know anything about the geography of Zealand. All I know is that we meet up at the University of Copenhagen Amager Campus and drive out to the countryside, and the trip involves neither boats nor bridges.

On Friday morning, when we meet at the bus and set off on the freshers' trip, the mood is bordering on manic. Some of the other male students are already drunk. They're drinking from hip flasks and slapping each other on the back, even though no one knows each other yet. We're only a few weeks into the start of term. We haven't even set up study groups.

I'm not going to write loads about the trip and the programme and the other students. It's pretty straightforward. There are around fifty students in total. Nearly all of us go on the freshers' trip, because most of us have just moved to Copenhagen from other parts of Denmark, and people are hoping to make new friends. No wonder everyone is a bit on edge.

The tutors are meant to be there to help, but they're drinking more than we are, and they're scaring us with their stories and sarcastic remarks. Sexual innuendo is shooting back and forth on the bus. It's hard to compete with that kind of atmosphere: you can either let yourself get swept up in it or be left behind. Having a normal conversation isn't really possible in a situation like that.

On the bus, one of the women from my class asks what I think about the fact that almost eighty per cent of our class is female, and I say I think it's great.

"The more the merrier", I tell her.

She grins.

"More to choose from."

Just saying it makes me uncomfortable, but I'm trying to fit in, and the words roll off my tongue of their own volition. We all have something at stake here. We all have something to lose, and the next few years of my

67

life will be spent with these people. I don't know any of them. None of them know me or my past. I'm just trying to make a good impression, even though I'm embarrassing myself. Trying to play my cards right, although it feels like I'm stumbling in the dark.

When we reach the scout hall, the tutors organise sleeping arrangements. There's a common room for the tutors, where the food and alcohol are kept. Some of us pass out on the grass outside the scout hall. Others start making dinner for everyone.

I'll be sleeping in a mixed dorm with 20 other students. Aside from the dormitories there's a large dining hall, which also serves as a lounge, a commercial kitchen, and a long corridor leading to the toilets and communal showers. The whole place is shades of brown and beige: the tiles, the dowdy wallpaper, and the ceiling beams. There are spiderwebs in every corner and heavy candy-striped curtains on every window.

We're served goulash with potatoes for dinner. Afterwards there's a quiz led by two of the tutors. Lyrics from '80s pop songs have been run through Google Translate four times, and now we have to guess the songs. If you guess wrong, you have to drink. If you guess right, you get to drink. I cheat and just hold the bottle to my lips. I notice others doing the same.

I stay more or less sober, and I stay close to those who are doing likewise. One of them is Vibeke, who is flirting with me. At least, that is my immediate impression, but it's hard to get a read on her. She's been like this since the beginning, but it's like she takes it to another level on the trip. She laughs at my jokes, asks a lot of questions about me, and listens attentively. Maintains eye contact for a long time.

"Are you seeing anyone?" she asks.

"No."

"Good", she says with a laugh.

There's another icebreaker outside the scout hall, and right after there's a treasure hunt in the woods. It's dark, and you're not allowed to use the light on your phone. I get separated from Vibeke, and I don't really want to continue, but I do anyway.

Later into the night, there's a bonfire outside. There's loud music playing in the dining hall, even though only a few people are in there talking. I go and sit by the bonfire, partly because I'm hoping to spot Vibeke if I'm being honest. Someone is playing 'Wonderwall' on the guitar, and people are singing along. I'm looking into the flames when Vibeke suddenly sits down next to me.

We chat for a long while. She asks a lot of questions. Too many questions. At some point we stop talking, we just stare into the fire, and I try holding her hand, but she pulls it back and laughs at me. She gets up and joins some of the others, but she keeps looking back at me. It looks like she's talking about me.

I see her bum a smoke from someone, then she sits down on a large rock in the car park and starts smoking. Our eyes meet, but when I get up to go to her, she walks away. I wander around for a bit. Glance at my phone. Decide to go to bed.

You're all by yourself in the toilets. It's a small room with cool, brown tiles and square ceiling lights. I look in the mirror while I brush my teeth.

My dad says I've always had a way with the ladies. Thinking about it makes me laugh. I always feel a little uncomfortable when he says it, but he means well. That's just his somewhat awkward way of saying he loves and respects me. And that he thinks I belong in some sort of community of men.

I can hear music and voices coming from the dining hall. Tomorrow is a new day. Maybe I can go for a walk while the others are sleeping off their hangovers. With Vibeke, if she's awake.

After having a pee, I take another look at myself in the mirror. Smooth out my hair. Try to assess my appearance. It's not bad. I'm happy with it. I think about going to university and setting off on a new chapter in my life.

When I open up the door to the corridor, Vibeke is standing right there. Right in front of the door. I can see she's still sober. I want to ask her if she'd be up for a walk in the morning, but she speaks before I can bring it up.

"What's up, little man?" she asks.

I don't know how to answer. She's right, I am small. She is taller and broader than me, and that's fine. I think she's attractive, but right now she's scaring me.

I say I'm off to bed.

"With me?" she asks.

I laugh nervously.

Then she puts both hands on my chest and forces me back into the toilet. She follows, and once we're both inside, she shuts the door and locks it. Then she puts both hands on my chest again and squeezes.

"What have you done with them?" she asks.

I feel a knot forming in my stomach.

"What do you mean?"

"Oh I think you know."

"Umm …"

"Is it true you're really a girl?"

I ask her again what she means.

"I heard you're transsexual."

"Where did you hear that?"

Her gaze is hard and focused. I can't look her in the eyes.

"Around. People talk. So is it true?"

I try to get past her, but the toilet is too small, and she's blocking the exit.

"Let me see what you've got down there", she says, reaching between my legs.

"No, stop."

"I said, let me see!"

We struggle. She could easily molest me, but instead she laughs, steps back and leans against the door so it's impossible for me to leave.

"Okay, I'll stop", she says.

"Thank you", I mumble, and I'm close to crying. It's infuriating. This type of thing hasn't happened to me since before I started passing as a man. It catches me completely off guard and brings back memories of a time I thought I'd left behind.

"Can I please leave now?" I ask her.

"This is what we'll do. If you answer my question – honestly – then I'll let you go."

I beg her to let me leave.

"Just answer me, then I'll let you go."

I hesitate.

"Yes … it's true."

"What is?"

"That I'm trans."

"That you're really a girl", she corrects me.

I lower my eyes.

"Say it!"

I don't say anything.

"Guess I'll have to see for myself."

She reaches for the top button of my trousers, and when I grab her wrist to stop her, it's clear to me how much stronger she is.

"I'm really a girl", I say. "Can I go now?"

Without a word, she steps aside and lets me pass. She holds out her hand like she's a member of staff showing me the way, all the while smiling like she's won an argument.

I don't go back to the dorm. I'm scared she'll come find me if I'm alone, so I go sit with the others and have a strong rum and coke. I am not a girl. I only said that to get away. To keep things from escalating. I know who I am, but it's a vulnerable position to be in when you're starting university in a new city. I don't tell anyone what happened. I try to laugh when other people laugh. To drink when they drink.

It's been three years since the freshers' trip and I've just finished my BA. Vibeke and I are starting the same Master's programme in the autumn, but as far as I know, she hasn't told anyone what happened in the toilet. I haven't told anyone either, until now, because then I would also have to tell people I'm trans, and I'm just one of those trans people who think it's a personal matter. Something I share with people I'm close to.

What's been tormenting me most is that I said I was a girl. It felt like the ultimate defeat, her getting that out of me. Obviously, there's nothing wrong with being a girl, but I think people can understand why it was hard for me to say those words, and ... . Right, I just need to ... .

It's just, it's like, now I'm in a position where I have to defend myself as I'm writing this ... like I feel the need to explain to someone, to convince them that I'm fine with being trans, but I am. My dad is fine with it. I have a girlfriend now, and she's fine with it. Most of my friends know, and they're all fine with it. Some of my classmates know, too, because I told them. They're also fine with it. The point is, I should be the one to decide who knows and when, and under what circumstances, but as I'm describing what happened in the toilet, it feels like I did something wrong. Because, yeah, I could have been proud and open and out of the closet and all that. Waved a flag around. Told the whole world I was trans. Then none of this would have happened.

6

Negotiating sexual harassment and young urban femininities in Helsinki

Heta Mulari

Introduction

'A group of guys got in [the tram] and they sat down there opposite me and started calling out to me and saying really gross things to me. That's not okay, of course, but then when one of them decided to touch me … That's what really crossed my line. […] The fact that nobody intervened, although I noticed there were lots of people around me … That made me feel very lonely. It makes everything even worse because people allow this to happen.'

This excerpt is from a short black-and-white video clip, published on YouTube[1], where a young woman sits in a tram, looks straight at the camera and talks about her distressing experiences of getting harassed on public transport in Helsinki. The video is part of a campaign launched by HSL and HKL (the public transport companies in the Helsinki area) and the Finnish League for Human Rights in 2017. Through videos, articles, posters and stickers, displayed in trams, buses and trains, the campaign aimed to increase knowledge about harassment and racism on public transport as well as providing concrete guidelines for passengers on how to intervene and help out in these situations.

In the past five years, gendering as well as sexual insults and harassment in the public space have been frequently discussed themes in both traditional media and on Finnish social media. In the aftermath of the feminist #MeToo movement, experiences of harassment have become more visible and recognised. Importantly, the key subjects in these societal, mediated debates have been young women: both as targets of sexual harassment and as those who have voiced criticism and shown resistance (see also Dahl, 2014; Aaltonen, 2017; Honkatukia et al, 2022). Furthermore, the percentages of young people who have experienced sexual insults and harassment have risen in recent years. According to the annual School Health Promotion Study (2021) conducted by the Finnish Institute for Health and Welfare, 50 per cent of Finnish girls in secondary school or high school (approximately between the ages of 14 and 18) have experienced sexual harassment in the current school year. Nearly 20 per cent of girls have experienced sexual harassment in a public space and 41 per cent have experienced sexual harassment online. Experiences of sexual insults and harassment are more common among young people who are disabled, belong to sexuality, gender or ethnic minorities (School Health Promotion Study, 2021; on sexual harassment and intersectionality, see also Honkatukia et al, 2022).

As a youth and girlhood studies scholar, I am interested in looking behind these numbers at young people's experiences, narratives and emotions regarding sexual insults and harassment. In this chapter, I will discuss how 16–17-year-old girls and non-binary young people describe and negotiate sexual insults and harassment as well as gendered and age-related power relationships in the city. The young woman's story narrated on the video echoes what I have heard from many young people while I was doing ethnographic fieldwork and interviews with my colleagues in Helsinki in 2016–17. While our original research questions in the project did not explicitly cover sexual harassment, especially girls and non-binary young people foregrounded this theme spontaneously in almost every interview. Gendering and harassment were things that almost everyone recognised as part of urban life. For many, growing up as an urban dweller meant compulsory learning and internalising of gendered, age-related and racialised urban hierarchies as well as unofficial, silent and embodied rules on how to act in the public space (see Georgiou, 2013; Ahmed, 2016; Honkatukia and Svynarenko, 2018; Tolonen et al, 2021; Honkatukia et al, 2022).

In this chapter, I will first discuss how girls and non-binary young people talked about occupying their own place in the city. This chapter draws on material from a research project that explored young people's experiences on public transport in Helsinki, especially the Helsinki metro, which is why the analysis mainly focuses on public transport as an urban space. Second, I will discuss sexual harassment as shared knowledge, something that nearly all participants recognised as an unfortunate part of the urban experience. Third, my focus will be on how the participants talked about how different young femininities are intertwined with gendering and sexual harassment. And finally, I will foreground different embodied and digital strategies the young people used to cope with difficult situations.

Urban encounters, young femininities and gender equality

In terms of theory, this chapter links to previous Nordic research on girls' and women's experiences of gendered and sexual harassment (for example, Koskela, 1997, 1999; Saarikoski, 2001; Aaltonen, 2006, 2017; Tolonen et al, 2021; Honkatukia et al, 2022) as well as theorisations on intergenerational inequalities and control in the public space (Walkowitz, 1992; Georgiou,

2013; Honkatukia and Svynarenko, 2018; Mulari, 2020). Regarding theorising about complex power relationships in the urban space, I have been inspired by feminist philosopher Sara Ahmed's theorisations of (urban) encounters and how, in each encounter, previous encounters between other people or material spaces are always present. These encounters are embodied and affective, evoking emotions such as happiness, fear, sadness, compassion, belonging or anger in us, and concretely moving us in the urban space. Thus, when we encounter people in different urban spaces, interpretations of safeness, danger, familiarity, and strangeness are evoked in each encounter, often subconsciously, as part of our internalised urban experiences (Ahmed, 2000, 2016).

Also, this chapter is informed by feminist theorisations of young femininities, emotions and power (Skeggs, 1997; Ahmed, 2000, 2004, 2016; Ambjörnsson, 2004; Saarikoski, 2009; Österholm, 2013; Dahl, 2014; Mulari, 2015; Mulari, 2020). I understand femininities as simultaneously material, social and discursive, constantly expressed and challenged in lived, embodied experiences. Doing young femininities is always social and connected to different material spaces. Thus, making a young feminine self is a process, actualised through encounters with other people and material spaces (Massey, 2005; Pyyry, 2015; Rentschler and Mitchell, 2016; Sixtensson, 2018). For example, as Sara Ahmed puts it, 'Becoming a girl is here about how you experience your body in relation to space' (Ahmed, 2016, p 25). Different femininities are also continuously regulated in power-related public discourses, exemplified in social norms that define how to dress and behave as a young feminine person in the public space (Driscoll, 2002; Gill and Scharff, 2011; Dahl, 2014; Mulari, 2015; Ahmed, 2016).

Importantly, in the Nordic context, the Nordic gender equality discourse (with its local variations in each Nordic country) is an important example of a power-related set of public discourses which define acceptable and denied norms for young femininity. As many girlhood studies scholars have argued, in many ways young femininity has become an essential figuration for gender equality, and the image of a strong, independent Nordic girl is seen as the ideal representative for the gender egalitarian project. Middle-class, White girlhood in particular has been at the centre of the societal gender-egalitarian figuration of strength and individualistic independence (Eduards, 2007; Honkasalo, 2011; Mulari, 2015; Aaltonen 2017; Formark et al, 2017). Furthermore, understandings of gender-egalitarian girlhood are constantly being redone and reinterpreted in different power-related institutions, such as the school. In many ways, girls in particular have to juggle contradictory messages and expectations: they are simultaneously told that they live in one of the most gender-equal countries in the world and they are expected to be independent and confident, but still they are warned about dangers in the public space and how to become 'street-smart' to avoid getting harassed or insulted.

While many experiences we heard about in the interviews echoed frustration, anger, fear and unease, it is also important to foreground the emotions of belonging, joy and happiness in the public space. Thus, for young people, the city is a multidimensional and constantly changing web of different encounters and emotions, not only those characterised by unwanted experiences. Here, I find it fruitful to foreground Ulrika Dahl's (2014, pp 185–9) figuration of the 'flaneuse', a feminine counterpart of the urban flaneur. Free to move around in the city, the flaneuse challenges urban dichotomies and the male gaze and occupies the urban space in the feminine body.

Data and methods

This chapter draws on semi-structured pair and group interviews that my colleagues and I did as part of the research project Digital Youth in the Media City in 2016–17.[2] The project focused on how digital and material spaces are intertwined with young people's everyday urban lives in Helsinki. Our focus was mainly on public transport, especially the Helsinki metro as an urban arena for travelling, hanging out and socialising. The interviews were collected as part of art workshops organised by the City of Helsinki Youth Department during the summers of 2016 and 2017. In these workshops, groups of young people were recruited as summer workers at youth clubs situated in different parts of Helsinki, near different metro stations. The groups worked for a month to make artworks for the metro stations, supervised by professional artists.

All in all, the groups were dominated by middle-class, White girls. Nearly 80 per cent of all participants identified as girls. A couple of young people identified as gender-fluid or non-binary. Around 10 per cent of all participants belonged to an ethnic minority. Regarding social class, the groups during summer 2016 were quite heterogeneous, but during summer 2017 the participants were predominantly from a middle-class background. All participants who agreed to participate in 2017 were currently studying at high school, many in high schools with a focus on creative arts such as music, visual arts or theatre. The interview themes ranged from metro experiences to different urban spaces that the participants used in their everyday lives; from social media to their understandings of locality, urban social interactions and different neighbourhoods in Helsinki.

Occupying their own spaces

As Myria Georgiou argues, urban space can be understood as a complex network of power relationships, where different groups of people struggle for the right to occupy the space and to become visible and audible (Georgiou, 2013; see also Walkowitz, 1992). Our societal power structures are remade, learned and challenged in different social encounters in the city (Ahmed, 2000, 2004, 2016; Massey, 2005, Honkatukia and Svynarenko, 2018) and different places are lived and experienced socially. As a young girl or a non-binary young person, encountering different urban spaces – as well as other people occupying the same spaces – means complex (and often internalised and unnoticed) negotiations over power and control of each space, as well as a range of different emotions ranging from joy and belonging to fear and anger.

Before moving forward to discussing sexual insults and harassment, it is necessary to take a look at how the informants made sense of moving around and spending time in different urban spaces in Helsinki. The participants often found encounters with strange adults ambiguous, which affected their sense of belonging/not belonging in different urban spaces. While their experiences included pleasant encounters with adults, such as pleasant chatting on the metro, many mentioned a desire to distance themselves from the adult gaze and adult attention. As Päivi Honkatukia and Arseniy Svynarenko have argued in their article about social and intergenerational control in the public space, many young people recognised the internalised pressure against simply hanging out in the urban space. They claimed that adults often accuse young people of loitering in the urban space, which, for them, made it difficult to hang out in peace (Honkatukia and Svynarenko, 2018). Thus, for the participants, spaces such as cafés as well as peaceful corners at shopping malls and in parks provided urban arenas where they could safely distance themselves from adults' comments and social control and create their own social bubbles in the city.

However, while the participants enjoyed spending time in cafés, some of them recalled adults criticising them for talking too loudly: "They stare at you if you speak even a bit louder and then they start complaining" (Pinja, 17), which is why many of them chose to stay outside instead. Most of our informants recognised the lack of free spaces for young people in Helsinki – especially as many of them felt that youth clubs were either for younger kids or had been occupied by certain subculture groups. Furthermore, they felt that spending time in a space specifically made for young people, just based on their age, didn't feel natural. Thus, the participants often spent their time in free places such as public libraries, shopping malls or, in the summertime, parks. For example, Emma (16) preferred to spend time in peaceful parks where "there aren't so many controlling authorities around", referring to security guards and other authorities as well as the general adult gaze. Furthermore, Pinja explained that she preferred to spend her free time in parks because "if you want to go to a café you have to pay for it". Thus, claiming a space in a neoliberal city is always also a question of social class.

Shopping malls in particular were mentioned quite often as spaces that allowed young people to spend free time without them having to pay anything. However, as the following interview quote from Sofia (16) demonstrates, shopping malls often become a battleground for the right to the space. Sofia explains how a particular shopping mall had planned new places to hang out for young people, but adults and older people had occupied these spaces.

'When they renovated [a shopping mall in an eastern Helsinki suburb], they advertised a lot that there would be lots of sofas and other places to hang out for young people downstairs. But now that I've been there, all the sofas have been occupied by adults, and, like, some grannies who are tired of walking. The space has become a resting area for them, and young people can't fit in anymore.'

Many of our informants spent quite a lot of time weekly on public transport, either on a bus, metro, local train or tram while travelling to school, for hobbies or to meet friends. As Honkatukia and Svynarenko conclude, previous research suggests that public transport is an ambiguous space for young people and experiences of uncomfortable or threatening experiences are rather common (Honkatukia and Svynarenko, 2018; see also Tuominen et al., 2014; Ojanen, 2018). However, it has to be said that in our interviews, most narratives about public transport were neutral, some even positive. Some young people even considered public transport as a convenient space to hang out with friends or by themselves. One example is Emma, who described her sense of joy as a young urban traveller:

'I have always loved public transport. I don't like local trains that much, but I like all the others. Somehow it's so nice to sit in the metro when it's not crowded. ... I usually listen to music and look around me, like that. I look at the city and people and so on.'

Here, Emma's description resembles Dahl's (2014) theorisations of the flaneuse, a feminine urban dweller, a counterpart to the male flaneur. In many interviews, we could hear a joy in moving around freely in the city, travelling through different neighbourhoods, looking at different people, listening to music, reading a book. These experiences exemplified feelings of belonging in the urban space and, perhaps, a new-found freedom to move around the city independently. Many of the participants had rather recently started high school further away from their home, which meant longer periods of daily commuting in the city, new places to hang out, and new people to meet.

As seen in these examples, young people constantly make meaning of the urban space through interaction with their peers, other people and the material spaces. Occupying a space was often talked about in a collective sense: when spending time with friends in cafés, libraries, shopping malls, parks or even on public transport, the participants transformed the space into their own where they could feel joy and belonging. These spaces, such as peaceful parks, beaches or empty corners in shopping malls, were often liminal, as girlhood studies scholar Ann-Charlotte Palmgren has put it: situated away from the adult gaze and control (Palmgren, 2016). This is exemplified by Naava (16), who told us that their "favourite place is under a bridge which is in danger of collapse".

However, alongside pleasant moments of moving around and hanging out in the urban space, the young people also talked about more ambiguous encounters, especially with adults. The participants often situated these unwanted encounters in everyday spaces such as on public transport, at metro or train stations, in shopping malls or streets. Next, I discuss sexual insults and harassment as examples of uncomfortable and threatening encounters.

'Perhaps it's just part of this society': sharing knowledge

Many of my early experiences of feeling wronged, as a girl, involved unwanted male attention.

Ahmed, 2016, p 22

As Honkatukia and Svynarenko (2018) (see also Tolonen et al, 2021) state, young people's ambiguous encounters with adults in public spaces include sexual harassment and other forms of derogatory remarks and insults, such as comments on appearance, clothes, make-up, and behaviour, such as not standing up and giving your seat to an older person. These forms of adult control demonstrate how public transport, as an urban space in general, is always a space which is intersected by gendered, racialised and age-related hierarchies (Georgiou, 2013; Räthzel, 2000). Also, our informants recalled seeing and hearing racist insults and some also had personal experiences of being insulted. For example, Lisa (17) told us about her experiences of being shouted at in the city: "We as a collective group look like we are from somewhere else, and, well, we are. We have heard all kinds of comments, such as f**king immigrants and go back to where you came from."

When we asked our informants about their unwanted encounters in the city, they often started talking spontaneously about sexual harassment. The majority of the girls and non-binary young people had either witnessed harassment, heard experiences from their friends, and/or had experienced different forms of harassment themselves (see also Honkatukia et al, 2022). The acts they named harassment ranged from unwanted looks and sexist gestures to catcalling, from direct chatting, such as a person persistently asking for their phone number, to being followed and physically touched. Sexual insults or harassment in the public space were a problem everyone recognised, and most of the informants thought it rather common in Helsinki:

Interviewer:	Is it common, then?
Rakel (16):	Yep, it's super common.
Lisa (17):	Too common. Way too common.
Rakel:	So many of my friends … At school, at health education class, we started talking about how many have been harassed … It is, like, how you define it yourself, a nasty stare can be enough for you.

In this interview excerpt, Rakel points to the fluid understanding of sexual harassment: sometimes, a nasty stare is enough. This fluidity was present in the interviews as well. While not all participants named being talked to or comments about their appearance harassment, they still shared an understanding that these encounters were not pleasant.

All participants talked about girls and young women as typical targets of sexual harassment. As Lisa explained it for example: "I've never seen or heard anyone go and sit next to guys and harass them". Furthermore, they shared an understanding of the perpetrator as being typically an adult, a middle-aged male, who was looking for contact with underage girls. In comparison, in a study by Honkatukia et al (2022) of young people and sexual harassment in Finland, young women described the perpetrators as boys of a similar age (see more Aaltonen, 2006; 2017) or adult men, but found the unwanted attention by adult men especially distressing. Sometimes, but not always, the perpetrator was drunk or under the influence of some other substance. For example, Linda (17) described a common, disturbing situation as follows:

'These situations are very common and I, like, try to make it clear that, no, I'm listening to music now and I'm going home. I'm only 17 and, like … And suddenly he says that he's 20 years old, like, although he really doesn't look like it and [tails off] … They don't ever do anything else besides chat, but I'd like some peace especially if I'm going home really late. It's very disturbing then.'

For many informants, these situations seemed to be an inevitable part of being a young woman, commuting or hanging out alone in the city. Some mentioned that they had encountered these kinds of situations already at the ages of 12 or 13, which coincided with the age they had started using public transport independently. Thus, experiences of sexual insults or harassment went hand in hand with learning about independent commuting and hanging out in the urban space. In the following excerpt, Elisa (16) links being called out to or whistled at to being a young woman walking alone in the city:

Elisa:	Well … People whistle or call out to me because I'm a young woman walking alone somewhere so …
Interviewer:	Sexist remarks, like?
Elisa:	Yep. But, well … I don't get scared because I know it's normal, sometimes these things happen.

Furthermore, Elisa states that being called out to doesn't scare her because it is so "normal", something that just happens as part of the urban experience. Also, Tina (16) commented that these situations happen "all the time": "For example, what happened to me precisely this week was … In the metro here in this neighbourhood someone said to me something like 'Hey baby, I like the way you look'." Furthermore, Riina (16) pondered that the problem isn't linked to public transport only: "Perhaps it's just part of this society … It's about the whole world." Many girls talked about these kinds of comments in almost a laconic tone: this is what happens quite often, and you just have to learn how to deal with it as you grow up as a young woman in Finland. As Ahmed (2016, p 24) puts it: 'Maybe you adopt a certain kind of fatalism: these things happen; what happens will happen; whatever will be, will be.'

This doesn't, however, mean that the girls would have been fine with being called out to or whistled at, or complimented on their appearance. Many said that they were annoyed or frustrated by it. Furthermore, tolerating harassment to some extent is indicative of adopting a coping mechanism in an unequal society (which praises itself for its gender equality). Sociologist Sanna Aaltonen has written about downplaying sexual harassment as a strategy that girls adopt in Finnish society, which emphasises gender equality and the image of a strong, Nordic woman. A strong girl is not scared but deals with difficult situations confidently and doesn't let them affect her: 'downplaying experiences of harassment allows women to escape the position of helpless victim' (Aaltonen, 2017). Thus, the figuration of a strong, Nordic girl and the understanding of a gender-equal society become ambiguous in the context of experienced harassment. It seemed that many participants adopted an understanding of harassment as being an inevitable part of society and, to cope with this, they reflected themselves in the image of a strong, street-smart girl, who is independent and strong enough to place herself above these unfortunate situations. Of course, this is problematic, since it leaves these girls coping with harassment on their own.

Furthermore, the participants also described situations that evoked strong, shared feelings of fear or anger (see Dahl, 2014). As Ahmed states, spaces and people become 'sticky' with certain emotions. Travelling alone on public transport in the evening or at night was often linked to uncomfortable feelings of fear and being constantly on guard (Ahmed, 2004). Many informants recognised the situation of encountering a group of loud, drunk people on a late evening metro train as a shared experience that evoked distress, even fear in them, made them look or walk away, and affected their sense of belonging in the metro space. Furthermore, they talked about fearful situations of travelling alone on public transport, in the evening or at night, and encountering a scary stranger in an empty bus or metro train. For example, Lisa explained:

'This has happened to me a couple of times on an empty bus ... Someone comes and sits down next to you; you don't feel very safe there. There's no one but you and this other person here on the bus and they decide to sit next to you. Then you feel a bit, like, I'm gonna get off at the next stop rather than stay here and take the risk. My friends have told me horror stories. They have been alone on the bus and then someone suddenly says to them: "Hey you, little girl ...".'

Ahmed writes about embodied memories that accumulate from these kinds of experiences and affect the ways in which people situate themselves in public spaces. In the horror stories and experiences of dangerous strangers, a stranger in a public space becomes equated with fear and anxiety: 'Stranger danger is an effective as well as affective script: some bodies become dangerous, some endangered' (Ahmed, 2016, p 24), and the young feminine body becomes smaller, anxious, trying to disappear from the situation.

The participants characterised public transport as spaces where interaction with strangers was kept to a minimum. The participants pondered on the social norms of keeping to oneself or talking to your own group and not communicating with – not even looking at – other people. Often, they found these norms quite pleasant and talked about being absorbed in listening to music, scrolling through social media or reading a book while travelling on public transport. However, this 'norm of silence' (Honkatukia and Svynarenko, 2018; Mulari, 2020) became problematic in cases of sexual insults or harassment. The participants shared an understanding that they could not rely on getting any help from other passengers if someone started insulting or harassing them. Here, again, the social norm of not intervening can be mirrored in gender equality discourses: as a 'strong, independent girl' it is difficult to ask for help. You are trusted to manage on your own. Furthermore, sexual harassment is often silenced in the gender-equal society and swept under the carpet: this is something that a gender-equal society simply does not allow to happen (although it does happen). When we asked how other passengers react in alarming situations, many participants replied: "Well, they don't intervene" (Tina); "They don't do anything" (Ronja, 16); "They kind of said nothing to this person" (Ruska, 16). Ilana

(17) recalled a scary incident that had happened to her at the age of 12 or 13 where no one intervened or helped her out:

Ilana:	I was around 12 or 13 I think, so it would have been good if someone would have said something, because ... Well.
Interviewer:	Was the situation scary or ...?
Ilana:	Well, yep, it was because he was an older man and he smelled a bit of alcohol and I was scared because I didn't know what he would do and then he, like, touched my shoulder and I was, like, help me, what's going on here and ... You can't escape in those situations, so it's important that there should be more social interaction, a sense of community there.

Ilana asks for more social responsibility in the public space and an attitude change towards a situation where sexual insults and harassment would not be tolerated anymore. For many, this situation seemed to be quite far in the future. For example, Aino (17) pondered: "I feel that it would need a bigger attitude change for something to change. That everyone would actively step up and say they don't approve of it and wouldn't let these things happen." Here, it is important to note that our interviews took place before the #MeToo movement, which has successfully foregrounded open resistance and speaking out against sexism and sexual harassment. As Honkatukia et al (2022) argue, in their more recent interviews young women discussed #MeToo as a welcome movement which has lowered the threshold for speaking openly about experiences of sexism and harassment.

Young women and edgy teens: navigating different femininities

When I was a teenager in the late 1990s, I used to travel to the neighbouring town with my friends on the weekends. The town was considerably bigger and more exciting than our own small hometown. We used to hang out in the streets, hamburger restaurants, shopping malls and, in the summertime, parks of course. Once I remember walking down the main street in the dark with my best friend. I must have been around 14 years old. Suddenly a car stopped next to us, there were young guys in the car, and one of them looked directly at us, imitating giving a blow job. I stopped and looked straight at the guy, then at my friend, confused: "What does he want us to drink?" My friend gave me long look, raised her eyebrows, sighed and pulled me along as we walked faster away from the car. She didn't say anything, but I suddenly realised what the situation had been about. An overwhelming feeling of shame filled me: shame at not understanding what the guy had meant, shame at not turning around and walking away faster, shame for being in the body of a teenage girl. And the fear of the car possibly following us.

Sara Ahmed writes about these kinds of childhood and teenage experiences and about how gendering, sexism or harassment are internalised in our bodies as lived memories and emotions that not only affect our ways of occupying public spaces but also change our ways of inhabiting our bodies. From a young age, girls learn how to regulate their bodies in relation to the space and how different ways of expressing young femininity are simultaneously admired but also controlled, even condemned in our society (Ahmed, 2016). As historian Carol Dyhouse argues, concerns and moral panic, especially regarding sexuality, have characterised the construction of our understanding of modern girlhood. Girlhood has been defined at the intersections of (consumerist) admiration, freedom and strength on the one hand and, on the other, the threat of victimisation (Dyhouse, 2013; see also Saarikoski, 2001; Aapola, Gonick and Harris, 2005; Renold and Ringrose, 2013). Furthermore, in our Western culture, it has historically been easier to imagine male flaneurs, admired urban dwellers who walk around alone freely, to observe and feel with the city (Dahl, 2014).

The possibilities for being able to walk around independently and feel a sense of belonging in the city intersect in many ways with understandings about different femininities. For many participants, being young and feminine in the urban space was a sensitive topic to talk about. For example, they listed certain appearance-related signs they linked to being young and feminine and which therefore carried a symbolic meaning of risk and the threat of becoming harassed (see Saarikoski, 2001; Ojanen, 2011). Skirts, dresses, shorts and make-up were among the signs they linked to performing a young, feminine self. For example, as Rakel put it: "Super many young women have experiences of people coming up to them and saying things to them if they're wearing a skirt or something". Riina continued: "I wear fishnet stockings super often and then all the old men start wanking off". Furthermore, Lisa said, in an annoyed tone: "If someone wears a lot of make-up and not that many clothes, that makes it okay to harass them or catcall them or shout nasty things." Furthermore, she explained her unease and worry about her friends, who she felt dressed in a more feminine way than she did:

'I have lots of friends who … They are, like, traditionally very feminine, they use a lot of make-up, and they like to look like young women, like, this is the time of our lives. So, I always worry about them because they get a lot of negative attention so … What could happen to them on the bus or the metro at night?'

In this quote, the heartfelt phrase "this is the time of our lives" reveals the unfair situation girls and young women have to deal with. If you want to use make-up and wear a dress or a skirt, to "look like young women", you have to be on constant guard for possible negative attention, even harassment. Lisa pondered on femininity from several viewpoints and how she is seen and treated very differently depending on her clothing style. Lisa defined her usual appearance and style as "not very feminine" and herself as "a really edgy teen", which, in most cases, protected her from getting insulted or harassed. However, if she occasionally decided to dress in a more feminine way, she had to be prepared for unwanted encounters:

'I would like for once to look like, if I'm going out with my friends somewhere and we look like we have put an effort into how we look. So, it seems to be an invitation for people to come and harass us and, like, say awful things to us and ... They just assume that it is an invitation from us to them, like: "Here we are, look at us, touch us".'

Ruska, who identified as non-binary and gender-fluid, shared similar thoughts about how they were constantly gendered in the public space and how they attracted people's attention when wearing clothes such as short skirts. For Ruska, experiences of how people approached them differently depending on their clothing and make-up style were rather common. Furthermore, Lisa continued that her gender-neutral and 'edgy' style gave her more courage to move confidently in public spaces, and even confront perpetrators if she witnessed sexual insults:

'For me it's a bit easier because I'm quite tall and so ... According to my dad I look like a dyke, so I do have the courage to go and intervene, like, what the actual [tails off] ... I don't feel like I'm very feminine or typically tiny or weak or anything like that.'

Both Ruska's and Lisa's experiences exemplify how embodying different kinds of femininities affects how they felt in public spaces and which kinds of encounters they experienced. Unfortunately, wearing clothes they named 'traditionally feminine', such as dresses or skirts, meant taking the risk of getting unwanted attention. Furthermore, as seen in Lisa's quote, she equated young and feminine with being smaller and weaker, and she distanced herself from this position by calling herself "a really edgy teenager". From Lisa, we also heard experiences of intervening if she witnessed sexual insults or harassment in a public space. She linked her courage to not being typically feminine, but, instead, quite tall and more masculine.

As Ahmed has argued, the process of 'girling' teaches girls from a very young age to be cautious in public spaces, to be on guard, to be wary and modify your appearance, make yourself smaller and less visible. Furthermore, girling operates in the process whereby young femininity is equated with having less mobility and freedom in public spaces (Ahmed, 2016). Thus, for some participants, normative young femininity was something they distanced themselves from, in order to feel more confident and safer. Furthermore, Lisa's experiences can be mirrored in the idea of 'tough femininity', which Honkatukia et al, have located in their interviews. An example of performing tough femininity – and a small act of resistance – could be a conscious facial expression that differed from 'normative, sociable and friendly femininity' (Honkatukia et al, 2022).

Embodied and digital responses and solidarities

'It is quite sick that you have to teach girls how to prevent someone from raping them. Or touching them. You'll have to wear clothes that aren't easy to take off, talk on your phone so you'll look like you are in contact with a real person, don't move around by yourself, don't walk past any car doors at a close distance because someone might pull you in, don't stay in the car for a long time but leave right away. It's sick, because although this is a very safe country and so on … I'd rather live here than somewhere else. But still, we are taught about how not to get raped, or not to get harassed.'

In this long quote, Lisa insightfully draws a conclusion about the internalised, embodied and affective rules she feels that society teaches girls. Here, she refers to health education classes at school, but, as is echoed in many of the interviews, many of these rules are learnt and internalised as part of unspoken social rules on how to act in public spaces. Ahmed's understanding of 'girling' comes close to this: 'to become girl as becoming wary of being in public space' (Ahmed, 2016, p 26). Also, earlier research on sexual harassment and young women suggests that girls and young women adopt different safety routines to 'monitor their interactions and risky situations and places' (Honkatukia et al, 2022). These strategies and routines can be understood as safety work through which girls and young women situate themselves in public spaces.

Furthermore, Lisa's quote echoes teaching about stranger danger: as girls occupying public spaces, one needs to be cautious of strangers. Furthermore, the socially widely repeated understanding of Finland as a safe and gender-equal country clashes with girls' everyday experiences. This foregrounds the problem of the often overwhelming discourse of gender equality: in a country celebrating gender equality, are you allowed to talk about experiences of sexual harassment or are they just swept under the carpet? As a strong, Nordic girl, are you allowed to get sad or scared (Aaltonen, 2017)? And why is it that the girls still seem to be those who need to control their behaviour and appearance, and learn to be cautious in order not to get sexually harassed?

As Honkatukia et al (2022) have argued, public debate on sexual harassment often excludes and pays no attention to young people's complex, intersectional agency and knowledge. This is also why I have wanted to underscore young people's agency in difficult situations: they develop coping mechanisms and strategies, both consciously and subconsciously. The most widely used strategies to escape from unwanted encounters or sexual harassment when travelling or hanging out alone in the city were embodied and spatial: staying still or moving in the space. For example, Minna (16) explained that she tries to avoid certain metro and train stations and walks away as quickly as possible. Furthermore, many were talking about how they chose their seat in the metro car or on the bus: close to the window, far away from others or next to a safe-looking person, who was often defined as female. Thus, participants were used to monitoring their material surroundings as well as the people around them, both consciously and subconsciously. For example, Lisa explained: "If someone who makes you anxious comes and sits next to you, you can always leave and sit next to someone else". Lotta (17) continued: "I'm always, like, OK there's a woman, I'll go and sit next to her".

Furthermore, the participants talked a lot about being immersed in their own digital bubble, where they could spend time simultaneously in a private and social space through listening to music, scrolling through social media or communicating with friends using apps such as Snapchat or WhatsApp. This digital bubble allowed them privacy in a social setting. For example, Minna told us about immersing herself in scrolling through Twitter so that she could protect herself from any unwanted attention.[3] Furthermore, some told us about reading a book or writing in a diary. Riina used poetry books quite creatively on public transport: on the one hand, to create privacy and, on the other hand, to make contact with people with similar interests. "I bring a fancy poetry book with me and then I take it out of my bag flamboyantly. I hope that someone will come and talk to me, like 'Oh, you're reading that book, too!'."

The participants didn't talk that much about openly talking back when experiencing or witnessing sexism or sexual harassment. This is understandable, given their shared understanding about the norm of silence on public transport and in other urban spaces: if you decide to resist and talk back, you can't rely on getting support from other people. Elisa gave us one example of talking back to men who had called out to her on the street:

'A couple of times I've gone to talk to them after they had called out to me, like "Hey girl, come over here". Then I've said to them, like, "Hi, how are you?" and "Well, do you have something to say to me?". They've been super confused and said: "Well, I don't know ...". Then I've been, like "Well then, have a nice day!".'

Another example of direct confrontation was Ruska's experience of becoming harassed on the metro. They explained this situation in a very annoyed and frustrated tone, simultaneously slapping their hand on the table.

'Especially if you're wearing a skirt, in the summertime or something, so the guys come and sit next to me and once, for example, someone just put their hand on my leg and started moving it and then, like, I just hit him on the hand and walked away.'

In this interview, Ruska and their friend Nakki (16) talked very openly about sexism and sexual harassment, sharing their experiences and frustration. While listening to them and many other participants talk about sexual insults and harassment, one key way of coping seemed to be peer solidarity, both in real life and online. Ruska and Nakki's knowledge about open resistance, confrontation and talking back stemmed from many digital feminist platforms on Tumblr and Instagram that they followed frequently (see Morrison, 2016) Furthermore, peer solidarity stemmed from a shared understanding of the perpetrator being almost always an adult male and thus urban sexual harassment as being intergenerational. Rakel pondered on the age of the perpetrator as follows: "Guys my age have never come to harass me". Lisa continued:

'I feel there's a certain solidarity in my age group. ... Although there are idiots, of course, still I feel that our generation is a lot more, like ... liberal and everyone's a lot more accepting. People our age don't come and say to you "Hahaha, f★★king gay, f★★king dyke", they don't touch you or harass you.'

Furthermore, solidarity was seen in how the participants talked about taking care for each other, calling each other to make sure they were safely back home, or talking on the phone if someone was in a worrying situation. Importantly, the urban space often transformed quite drastically when the participants talked about spending time together with their friends. For example, a metro car might transform into a youth cultural arena with loud music, chatting and dance (see Lähteenmaa, 1992). For example, Aino explained: "Metro cars have those poles, and once we went to dance there". Pinja told us about creating a peer bubble in the metro car: "The metro is a very nice place; you can sit there with your friends in your own seat set and chat there in peace. Also, the metro is quite loud, so my loud voice doesn't disturb anyone there."

Conclusion

Calling out, whistles, comments on appearance, persistent chatting, physical touching. These were the most common acts of sexism or sexual harassment that girls and non-binary young people told us about in the interviews. For many, these situations were an unfortunate part of everyday urban life. While listening to their narratives and experiences, the urban space as a gendering network of different power relationships where the struggle for belonging is constantly present was painfully reaffirmed.

Furthermore, the young people's experiences echoed cultural figurations and understandings about, not only young femininity but also adult masculinity. The campaign and the video I referred to in the beginning of this chapter repeat the narrative of the urban space being dangerous to girls and young women travelling alone. While I don't question the participants' narratives about solely adult male harassers and young feminine targets, I do also feel that this narrative is rooted very deeply in our Western cultural understandings about adult males dominating public, urban spaces and (middle-class) women occupying the private sphere, as those in need of male protection. In the narrative of stranger danger and fear, young femininity becomes equated with smallness and weakness and the urban space becomes 'sticky' with feelings such as anxiety and fear (Ahmed, 2004; Dahl, 2014, pp 160–3). In the participants' narratives, this dichotomous understanding of the urban space was constructed and imagined in various contexts ranging from health education classes to media debates and peer culture.

Also, young femininity should always be understood as intersectional, constantly being negotiated in relation to attributes such as ethnicity, ableness, sexuality, age and social class. Our research was dominated by middle-class White girls who have also been the key target of most lively cultural debates on girls' sexual agency and vulnerability in public spaces (Aaltonen, 2017). Many participants struck a balance between putting up with some sexual insults without making a big deal out of them, without expressing anxiety or anger, as if to maintain their position as a strong individual: your behaviour can't affect me.

Our participants also talked about small flaneuse moments of travelling alone in the city, looking at people, listening to music, becoming immersed in one's own thoughts and the rhythm of the city. And, even more eagerly, they talked about sharing pleasant moments of belonging and joy with their friends: of creating pockets of youth culture in the city. Perhaps we would need even more visibility for these kinds of figurations, not only those that tell girls to be cautious and wary?

Notes
[1]   The video *Päätepysäkki syrjinnälle* can be found here: https://www.youtube.com/watch?v=eaii-tg3OkI
[2]   The project was funded by the Kone Foundation and conducted by the University of Helsinki, Tampere University, the Finnish Youth Research Society and the Higher School of Economics, St Petersburg, Russia. The interviews were done by researchers Olli Haanpää, Päivi Honkatukia, Heta Mulari and Arseniy

Svynarenko. These articles are referred to and analysed further in the analysis sections of this article. In total we did 31 interviews with 57 young people. Participation was voluntary and around 10 young people in total declined to participate. The interviews were analysed by using thematic close reading and qualitative content analysis.

3 In these interviews, we didn't explicitly talk about sexual harassment in digital spaces and social media. See more on young people's experiences on online harassment in Finland, in Honkatukia et al, 2022.

References

Aaltonen, S. (2006) *Tytöt, pojat ja sukupuolinen häirintä*. Helsinki: Helsinki University Press.

Aaltonen, S. (2017) Grin and Bear It! Downplaying Sexual Harassment as Part of Nordic Girlhood, in Formark, B., Mulari, H. and Voipio, M. (eds) *Nordic Girlhoods: New Perspectives and Outlooks*. New York: Palgrave Macmillan, pp 83–102.

Aapola, S., Gonick, M. and Harris, A. (2005) *Young Femininity: Girlhood, Power and Social Change*. New York: Palgrave Macmillan.

Ahmed, S. (2000) *Strange Encounters: Embodied Others in Post-coloniality*. London: Routledge.

Ahmed, S. (2004) *The Cultural Politics of Emotion*. Edinburgh: Edinburgh University Press.

Ahmed, S. (2016) *Living a Feminist Life*. Durham: Duke University Press.

Ambjörnsson, F. (2004) *I en klass för sig: Genus, klass och sexualitet bland gymnasietjejer*. Stockholm: Ordfront förlag.

Dahl, U. (2014) *Skamgrepp: Femme-inistiska essäer*. Stockholm: Leopard Förlag.

Driscoll. C. (2002) *Girls: Feminine Adolescence in Popular Culture and Cultural Theory*. New York: Columbia University Press.

Dyhouse, C. (2013) *Girl Trouble: Panic and Progress in the History of Young Women*. London & New York: Zed Books.

Eduards, M. (2007) *Kroppspolitik: Om Moder Svea och andra kvinnor*. Stockholm: Atlas.

Formark, B., Mulari, H. and Voipio, M. (2017) Introduction, in Formark, B., Mulari, H. and Voipio, M. (eds) *Nordic Girlhoods: New Perspectives and Outlooks*. New York: Palgrave Macmillan, pp 1–22.

Georgiou, M. (2013) *Media and the City: Cosmopolitanism and Difference*. Cambridge: Polity Press.

Gill, R. and Scharff, C. (2011) Introduction, in Gill, R. and Scharff, C. (eds) *New Femininities: Postfeminism, Neoliberalism and Subjectivity*. New York: Palgrave Macmillan, pp 1–20.

Honkasalo, V. (2011) *Tyttöjen kesken: Monikulttuurisuus ja sukupuolten tasa-arvo nuorisotyössä*. Helsinki: Nuorisotutkimusverkosto & Nuorisotutkimusseura.

Honkatukia, P. and Svynarenko, A. (2018) Intergenerational Encounters on the Metro: Young People's Perspectives on Social Control in the Media City, *Emotion, Space and Society*.

Honkatukia, P., Peltola, M., Aho, T. and Saukkonen, R. (2022) Between Agency and Uncertainty: Young Women and Men Constructing Citizenship through Stories of Sexual Harassment, *Journal of Social Issues* https://doi.org/10.1111/josi.12512

Koskela, H. (1997) Bold Walk and Breakings: Women's Spatial Confidence Versus Fear of Violence, *Gender, Place and Culture*, 4(3): pp 301–19.

Koskela, H. (1999) 'Gendered Exclusions': Women's Fear of Violence and Changing Relations to Space, *Geografiska Annaler. Series B, Human Geography*, 81 (2): pp 111–24.

Lähteenmaa, J. (1992) Tytöt jännitystä etsimässä: sukkulointia ja irrottelua, in Näre, S. and Lähteenmaa, J. (eds) *Letit liehumaan: tyttökulttuuri murroksessa.* Helsinki: Suomalaisen Kirjallisuuden Seura: pp 155–71.

Massey, D. (2005) *For Space.* London: Sage.

Morrison, C. (2016) Creating and Regulating Identity in Online Spaces: Girlhood, Social Networking and Avatars, in Mitchell, C. and Rentschler, C. (eds) *Girlhood and the Politics of Place.* New York: Berghahn, pp 244–60.

Mulari, H. (2015) *New Feminisms, Gender Equality and Neoliberalism in Swedish Girl Films, 1995–2005.* Doctoral thesis, University of Turku.

Mulari, H. (2020) Emotional encounters and young feminine choreographies in the Helsinki metro, *Girlhood Studies*, 13(1), pp 50–66.

Ojanen, K. (2011) *Tyttöjen toinen koti: Etnografinen tutkimus tyttökulttuurista ratsastustalleilla.* Helsinki: Suomalaisen Kirjallisuuden Seura.

Ojanen, K. (2018) Erojen yhdentekevyydestä jokapäiväiseen rasismiin: Monikulttuurisia kohtaamisia Helsingin lähiöissä. *Alue ja ympäristö*, 47(1): pp 17–30.

Österholm, M. M. (2013) *Ett flicklaboratorium i valda bitar: Skeva flickor i svenskspråkig prosa från 1980 till 2005.* Stockholm: Rosenlarv förlag.

Palmgren, A.-C. (2016) Teini-ikäisten tyttöjen liminaaliset tilat Turussa, Turun kaupunki, Kaupunkitutkimusohjelma: Tutkimuskatsauksia 3/2016.

Pyyry, N. (2015) *Hanging Out with Young People, Urban Spaces and Ideas: Openings to Dwelling, Participation and Thinking.* Helsinki: University of Helsinki.

Räthzel, N. (2000) Living Differences: Ethnicity and Fearless Girls in Public Spaces. *Social Identities*, 6(2): pp 119–42, https://doi.org/10.1080/135046 30050032035.

Renold, E. and Ringrose, J. (2013) Feminisms Refiguring 'Sexualization', Sexuality and 'The Girl', *Feminist Theory*, 14(3): pp 247–54.

Rentschler, C. and Mitchell, C. (2016) Introduction: The Significance of Place in Girlhood Studies, in Mitchell, C. and Rentschler, C. (eds) *Girlhood and the Politics of Place*. New York: Berghahn, pp 1–18.

Saarikoski, H. (2001) *Mistä on huonot tytöt tehty?* Helsinki: Tammi.

Saarikoski, H. (2009) *Nuoren naisellisuuden koreografioita: Spice Girlsin fanit tyttöyden tekijöinä*. Helsinki: Suomalaisen Kirjallisuuden Seura.

School Health Promotion Study (2021) Helsinki: The Finnish Institute for Health and Welfare [online]. Available at: https://thl.fi/fi/web/lapset-nuo ret-ja-perheet/hyvinvointi-ja-terveys/vakivallan-ehkaisy/seksuaalivakivalta [Accessed 5 February 2022].

Skeggs, B. (1997) *Formations of Class and Gender: Becoming Respectable*. London: Sage.

Sixtensson, J. (2018) *Härifrån till framtiden: Om gränslinjer, aktörskap och motstånd i tjejers vardagsliv*. Malmö: Malmö University.

Tolonen, T., Aapola-Kari, K., Lahtinen, J. and Wrede-Jäntti, M. (2021) Miten kaupungista tulee oma? Kaupunkipääoma ja nuorten eriytyneet suhteet kaupunkitilaan, in Vehkalahti, K., Aapola-Kari S. and Armila P. (eds) *Sata nuorta, sata polkua aikuisuuteen: Laadullinen seurantatutkimus Nuoret ajassa*. Helsinki: Nuorisotutkimusverkosto/Nuorisotutkimusseura, pp 57–80.

Tuominen, M., Joronen, T. and Laihinen, E. (2014) *"… sanoi että näytän aivan ****** ja alkoi solvaamaan"*. Helsinki: Helsinki City Urban Facts.

Walkowitz, J. (1992) *City of Dreadful Delight: Narratives of Sexual Danger in Late-Victorian London*. Chicago: University of Chicago Press.

7

Men run academic track; women jump sexist hurdles

Lea Skewes

The personal is institutional [original emphasis]. When we talk about sexism, we are often referring to something that is personal, but also in the world, reproduced by institutions; sexism is habit, orientation, series, structure, assembly, sexism is material. ... Making a feminist case thus requires [that] we can show how sexism is a set of attitudes that are institutionalized, a pattern that is established through use, such that it can be reproduced almost independently of individual will.

Ahmed, 2015, p 10

Introduction

Ahmed's quote captures the idea that, by exploring individuals' experiences of sexism, we can shed light on the institutionalised sexist habits that are currently in place. That is, we can bring to light which habits or norms have become institutionalised and therefore have often receded from view (Ahmed, 2012, p 21). Ahmed also emphasises that by naming the problem – sexism – we are also calling out these attitudes and behaviours as 'wrong' and 'unjustified' (Ahmed, 2015, p 9). Calling something sexist means calling for change. In this chapter, I aim to show how individual students' narratives can help us unveil institutionalised sexism which typically recedes from view in everyday work and study life. I aim to show that, while the men in an actual university department are able to run academic track, women have to jump sexist and sexual harassment hurdles. However, before we get that far, we need to place the study within the Danish context in which it was conducted.

It is well-documented that women are overrepresented in humanities degrees, while men are overrepresented in science, technology, engineering and mathematics (STEM) degrees. This gender asymmetry is especially pronounced in rich Western countries such as the Nordic countries. Therefore, more and more initiatives have been launched in recent years to reduce the underrepresentation of women in STEM.

However, the Nordic countries have handled gender equality challenges quite differently (Nielsen, 2017; Borchorst and Dahlerup, 2020). Denmark has become the black sheep on gender equality measures compared to the other Nordic countries. While Iceland, Finland, Norway and Sweden can lay claim to being among the top five on the World Economic Forum's *Global Gender Gap Index*,[1] Denmark has plummeted to number 29 (Gender Gap Index, 2021). This great difference in gender equality *results* is partially driven by the different *approaches* in each of these countries. Not surprisingly, this country-level difference in approaches has had an effect in educational settings.

Nielsen (2017) shows that Denmark's approach to gender equality in academia is vastly different to Sweden's and Norway's approaches. In contrast to both Sweden and Norway, Denmark has prioritised what is labelled a 'fixing the women' approach − as opposed to more structural approaches aimed at changing the organisation's norms and values. This 'fixing the women' approach is described as follows:

> Traditionally, women's underrepresentation in academia has been explained as a problem related to the women, rather than the organisation. This interpretation is built on a liberal vision reducing career advancement to individualistic matters such as ambition, motivation, and merit. Inequalities are attributed here to women's deficiencies in work experience and insufficient requisite training. (Nielsen, 2017, p 299)

In line with this 'fixing the women' approach, the goal in Denmark has typically been to strive to change women's motivation to take on STEM subjects, rather than improving the study and work conditions for the women who have already made this choice. Unfortunately, this approach marks women as 'deficient' academics, and implies that there is no need for structural and normative changes.

Possibly due to this ineffective 'fixing the women' approach to gender equality in academia in Denmark, gender norms and values that build on sexism and sexual harassment are still a major challenge. We have previously documented that Danish university employees in general − and employees in male-dominated faculties in particular − have sexist attitudes (Skewes et al, 2019) and tend to delegitimise speaking out against sexual harassment via the #MeToo movement (Skewes et al, 2021). We have also shown, in a sample of 300 Danish academics (primarily women), that almost 60 per cent reported experiences of *sexist hostility* in their workplace. Furthermore, more than 40 per cent reported *sexual hostility*, and 13 per cent had been exposed to *unwanted sexual attention*[2] (Einersen et al, 2021). This indicates that academic institutions in Denmark − and in particular STEM environments

– are a high-risk context for women. The interviews I conducted for this study also captured extensive challenges with sexist/sexual hostility and unwanted sexual attention.

In the Danish-based studies about sexism mentioned earlier, we used a combination of the Modern Sexism Scale (Swim et al, 1995) and open questions about attitudes to gender equality policies and to the #MeToo movement to capture patterns of sexist attitudes in academia in Denmark (Skewes et al, 2019, 2021). We complemented this with a Sexual Experiences Questionnaire (SEQ) (Fitzgerald et al, 1995) to capture concrete experiences with sexual harassment (in the form of sexist/sexual hostility, unwanted sexual attention, and sexual coercion) in the academic environment in Denmark (Einersen et al, 2021). We now strive to capture how these sexist attitudes held by individual academics, along with the victims' reports of concrete experiences with sexism and sexual harassment, paint a picture of institutionalised sexism. Inspired by Ahmed (2015), I interpret the personal as institutional. That is, I embrace Ahmed's (2015) argument that painting one group (in this case, women) as a poor fit for academia, or even as 'deficient' as academics, reflects a set of sexist attitudes which have become institutionalised through repeated expression in universities. This institutionalised sexism means that many men experience academia as a 'comfortable fit' – because the institution has been made 'fit' *for* and *by* them – while many women in contrast experience a 'discomfort' (Ahmed, 2017) or a 'lack of fit' (Heilman, 2001) with their academic environment.

These Danish context findings about sexism and sexual harassment are supported by other studies showing that belonging to a minority in an academic degree or a workplace puts you at risk of sexist/sexual hostility and unwanted sexual attention (Fitzgerald et al, 1995). This research shows that sexist/sexual hostility and sexual harassment are much more likely to occur if a workplace or study environment has power differentials between men and women, where men are overrepresented or hold positions of higher status than women (Illies et al, 2003; McCabe and Hardman, 2005; Willness et al, 2007; Easteal and Judd, 2008; O'Connor et al, 2021). It is precisely this asymmetrical power constellation that we typically see in STEM degrees, as well as the physics department from which we collected concrete data.

A cross-cultural study of physicists in Denmark, Finland, Estonia, Poland and Italy allows us to zoom further in to explore what we might expect of the academic environment of a Danish physics degree. In their analysis of 208 interviews with physicists working in academia, Hasse and Trentemøller (2008) identified three types of archetypical or 'ideal' physicists. They found that the most common in Denmark is the type they labelled the 'Hercules' type.[3] This type is described as a masculine nerd figure who is very single-mindedly focused on physics (Hasse and Trentemøller, 2008, pp 100–26). He is very hardworking and competitive and focuses very intensely on his academic career at the expense of social relationships. Social relationships only matter if they are advantageous to him in the physics world (Hasse and Trentemøller, 2008, pp 101–5). Unfortunately, the 'Hercules' type's perception of women and how one ought to relate to them is quite sexist:

> As Hercules believes that everything in the physics world is his to be won [and] everything is up for grabs, including other people, women are neither 'protected' by formal hierarchies or macho culture (where men feel obliged to protect 'their' women). On the contrary, they might be perceived as sexual entities – and up for grabs. (Hasse and Trentemøller, 2008, p 125)

Therefore, it is relevant to explore what it is like to be a woman in physics. Do we find similarities to Hasse and Trentemøller's (2008) 'Hercules' type in our data? And if so, what kinds of challenges or hurdles does this seem to entail for the female students?

Methods and materials

It is important to note that I was invited by a Danish physics department to explore why they might be experiencing high drop-out rates among their female students. The department wished to get a better understanding of what hurdles might be getting in the way of women completing the physics degree they had already embarked on. The department's invitation was posed as a gender-binary project. That is, I was asked to explore the gender difference between female and male students. Hence, the data collection, the reporting and the analysis reproduced a gender binary. I recognise that not all people identify as either female or male.[4]

Participants

I strove to recruit every woman in one particular year of the physics Bachelor's degree, but a few declined the invitation to participate in the study. I successfully recruited 10 female students and 12 male students from the same year. All the participants were Danish, and all but one were White. To ensure the anonymity of the participants, I am deliberately vague about when the data was collected. Furthermore, I have changed all the participants' names to make it difficult to identify any individual.

Coding

After transcription, the interviews were coded bottom-up. I found it important to allow for themes to unfold which I had not asked about or invited. I explored the interviews to see which themes arose. An example of this theme coding was 'defining STEM as male or masculine', which was then followed up by a code of 'positioning oneself as masculine'.[5] used these codes to determine which themes came up for most students and then strove to paint a picture of how all these themes shaped the culture of the degree for both genders.

Funding

Payments to the student assistants who transcribed the interviews were funded by the Independent Research Fund Denmark – Project Number: 8108-00034B.

Results and analysis

In the following, I strive to capture the students' experiences and interpretations of their study environment in their own words. The students were asked about: (a) their motivation for choosing physics; (b) their learning and instruction preferences; (c) their sense of belonging; and (d) their gendered experiences in the degree. In the following, I do not touch upon the theme of preferred learning and instruction styles because we found no gender differences. Instead, I focus on the coded themes which came up for most students, as well as the ones which refer indirectly or directly to gender-discriminatory practices such as sexist/sexual hostility and sexual harassment in the form of unwanted sexual attention. We cover the themes of: (a) motivation for embarking on a STEM degree (in this case, physics); (b) associating the degree with male gender stereotypes or behaviours; (c) attitudes to and experiences of gender representation; (d) negative evaluations of female lecturers; and (e) unwanted sexual attention.

Motivation for embarking on a STEM degree

The majority of students we spoke to had only considered studying STEM subjects. All the women were passionate about physics and most of them had been so from when they were very young:

'Since I was 10 or 11 years old, I have been interested in physics and astronomy.' (Gabriella)

'For me it would probably never have been anything else than science and technology because I have been interested in that since I was a child.' (Dora)

Ten out of the 12 men shared the same passion for their degree:

'Most of my life I have been interested in how things work and in high school I found out that both maths and physics were exciting.' (Christian)

If there is any gender difference in the passion for STEM it is that some of the men seemed to have developed their passion slightly later than the women. Most of the women were committed to studying STEM prior to high school.

Where the two genders do differ is in the reasons given for *why* they developed their interest in the first place. Here, the men almost exclusively referred to their own internal passion for the field that, at least in their narratives, seems to have arisen without any external influence. This interpretation maps well onto the 'Hercules' type's belief that his ability in physics is 'inborn' (Hasse and Trentemøller, 2008, p 107). In contrast, five out of the ten women point out that their fathers invited them into the STEM world, with only three out of the 12 men even mentioning their fathers in relation to their choice of degree:

'My father and I used to go outside looking at stars very often. I think it was because he thought it was fun that we could do it together and then he would tell me about different stuff.' (Dora)

'I think I have always wanted to know how things work, but also my father is an engineer so I had seen part of that world.' (Hannah)

'My dad is a mathematician, or he works with programming, so I think much of my inspiration for maths comes from him. When I needed help with maths and physics, he was the one I went to because he knows more about it than my mum.' (Barbara)

Of the three men who *do* mention some degree of inspiration from their fathers, two of them have flat narratives. One of them (Liam) simply mentions that his father is a physicist as well, without commenting on how this might have affected his choice of degree, while Hugo describes it as follows:

'I think that my father who is an engineer might have had something to do with it [my choice of degree], but I have just always thought maths was cool.' (Hugo)

Only one male participant has a fully relational narrative:

'My father was always interested in physics ... and through him I tried to do some experiments at home.' (Kasper)

In interpreting these responses, one might want to keep Margolis and Fisher's (2002) classic longitudinal study of computer science students in mind; this suggests that, even though the male students often have an individualistic narrative of how they developed their passion for their discipline, they have in fact very often been supported and inspired by parents or other family members. Thus, it may be that this gender difference in narrative could be driven by cultural norms inviting women to think of and speak about themselves in relational narratives, while men are invited to apply individualistic narratives. Whether these gender differences in narrative are driven by gender stereotypes or not, these responses identify that forming a relational bond around STEM activities has been key for developing their passion for STEM for these women. Their fathers invited them to participate in their passion – independent of gender and gender stereotypes – thereby showing them that they could belong in this field, too.

Defining STEM as male

Hasse and Trentemøller's (2008) cross-cultural research shows that the most common 'ideal type' for a physicist in Denmark is what they labelled the 'Hercules' type, which they define as a dominant and individualistic male. The Hercules type is a 'nerd who shuns human society' (Hasse and Trentemøller, 2008, p 101). How does this match up with our findings?

Many of our students comment on physics as a male-typed degree defined by male 'geek' culture:

'I think many people's prejudice about physics is that it's a bunch of boys that sit and do I don't know what – but basically a bunch of geeks, right?' (Hannah)

'We are all a bunch of geeks – there is not so much diversity. It's not a secret there are many boys compared to girls … . This creates a kind of uniformity. … If you need diversity you have to go to medicine or something.' (Hugo)

'I'm very geeky – and so are the others. I'm a boy – and so are the others. So, in that way I fit in.' (Kasper)

'You sense that it is very boyish sometimes because it gets inappropriate and goofy – there is just a different dynamic when the boys outnumber [girls].' (Hugo)

'Maybe having this many men in the degree has created a bit of a "boy culture" where we do "boy things".' (Christian)

Which types of 'boy things' the students offer as examples of this 'boy culture' vary, but drinking beer, playing computer games, Dungeons & Dragons, trading card games and watching Star Wars movies all recur across multiple interviews. While the students seem to align with Hasse and Trentemøller's (2008) findings that physics is understood as male and nerdy, our physics students seem to be quite socially oriented. However, it is noteworthy that the types of social activities they engage in are highly (male) gendered. This difference in social orientation between the two research samples might arise because Hasse and Trentemøller's (2008) study is based on interviews with physics employees, while ours is based on interviews with physics students at first-cycle level. One would imagine that being successful in physics at first-cycle level requires significantly less effort and dedication, compared to being successful as a researcher.

However, even if the socially hostile side of the 'ideal type' physics employee is not replicated in our study of students, we did replicate the finding that the 'ideal' physicist is understood as male. One student even goes so far as to pathologise the gendering of the degree in a way which aligns well with Baron-Cohen's (2003) theorising of autism as the extreme version of what he labels the 'male brain'. Benjamin says:

'I didn't start to feel normal until I started studying physics, because I was used to being *the* geek. But compared to the geeks here I'm rather normal. I don't have a psychiatric diagnosis – there are quite a lot of autistic people, as in clinically diagnosed autistic, or Asperger people [here]. So, we have this joke: "Benjamin you might not be officially an autistic person, but I think you have more or less turned into one by now".' (Benjamin)

Frederik offers an explanation for why women might not want to take on physics, which also aligns well with a gender-essentialist interpretation:

'I feel that it's because men are more interested in things such as physics and that sort of stuff. Just like there are more men laying bricks – I don't think women want to do that, and [just like] there are more female nurses in Denmark. I think it's because of [a gendered] interest.' (Frederik)

Frederik's interpretation is definitely a common attitude in academia in Denmark. However, it is not unproblematic in a study or work environment because Skewes et al (2018) show that such gender essentialist attitudes are positively correlated with acceptance of gender discriminatory behaviour.

The women, on the other hand, interpret the cause of the gender discrepancy differently:

'I think the only reason that I think about this as a male dominated subject is because I have been told that it was when I was choosing [disciplines]. ... One encounters this [attitude] already at primary school – that girls do arts and men do maths.' (Barbara)

'Maybe when people think it is a discipline dominated by men, they feel less like choosing it.' (Dora)

One male student moves beyond just describing what the study environment is like and adds an expectation that the female students need to adapt to, or cope with, the male-typed culture if they wish to stay:

'There are significantly more of us [men] – probably around 90 per cent men. So, you need to be able to handle locker room talk because there is a lot of catfighting [among the boys][6] or whatever you want to call it.' (Daniel)

Asked how or where the boys 'catfighting' unfolds, he continues:

'The humour and the topics [of conversation]. I think it is hard for girls to fit in ... they have to tolerate it ... to us it just makes us feel at home.' (Daniel)

Daniel expresses an expectation that the female students must adapt to the male-dominated study culture (not vice versa). This aligns well with the 'fixing the women' approach documented in academia in Denmark. Daniel does not consider that the male students might need to adapt to the female students' needs, even though he does seem to be aware that the culture which makes the men feel comfortable or even 'at home' might be exactly what makes the women feel uncomfortable. That is, Daniel's interpretation of the consequences of the gendering of his degree aligns well with Ahmed's (2017) analysis of academia as being a 'comfortable fit' for some (men), while being an 'uncomfortable fit' for others (women). However, there is one important difference; while Daniel sees no need to change or challenge this male privilege of comfort, Ahmed uses this awareness of a discrepancy between comfort levels to call for organisational change in academia.

Positioning oneself as one of the boys

How do the female students cope with studying in a male-typed degree among a majority of male students? Many of them strive to overcome the conflict between their gender and their study environment by positioning themselves as more male than the typical female. Some of the men are also aware of this adaptation strategy:

'I sometimes fear that they [the women] feel like they have to be a man to be part of the group ... or maybe it's just a kind of physics geek culture that you might mistake for a male culture ...?' (Christian)

Speaking of a female student who fits in well, Hugo says:

'It's not because she is a tomboy in that way, but there is a geeky part – a science-geeky part – that I might associate with something male.' (Hugo)

Thus, Hugo makes clear that assimilating into the male-typed culture is the way in which the female students can fit in. Seven of the ten female students do explicitly comment on how they model themselves on a kind of male-typed identity – thereby positioning themselves as a good fit for the degree even though their gender marks them as not belonging:

'I have always fitted in better with boys than girls, so I don't have a problem with it [the overrepresentation of men].' (Dora)

'For me it's not a problem that there aren't many women ... I have got loads of male friends in physics, and I think I generally fit in well in a male environment.' (Emma)

'When I was younger and shyer, I did have a lot of good girl friends, but none of them were into programming and physics. So, in that way it's great to come to a place like this where everyone is just geeky.' (Julia)

Some of the female students express their belonging to the male-typed study culture in the form of a deselection of more female-typed cultures or relationships. That is, they show how they fit into their current male-typed culture by distancing themselves from a female-typed culture:

'All that catfighting[7] and all that gossip, that was never something I was very interested in. I always had to pretend I was interested when I was sitting with groups of girls.' (Hannah)

'I don't mind that there aren't many girls doing this degree – because I got enough of the catfighting when I was studying to become x [a female-typed occupation].' (Isabella)

Both Hannah and Isabella are explicitly disavowing female stereotypical characteristics to show how they do fit into their male-typed degree. Other studies of physics degrees have found similar mechanisms of disavowing one's female gender or femininity in order to fit in (Hasse and Trentemøller, 2008). This mechanism of turning away from one's female gender to increase a perceived fit with one's degree has also been documented in experimental settings (Pronin et al, 2004). It captures an awareness that one's female gender is perceived as standing in the way of one's qualifications in male-typed disciplines. However, this identity strategy to compensate for the perceived female 'lack' is only necessary because of the male normative backdrop.

Gender representation

Gender representation[8] is one of the topics the female and male students disagree on the most. Five male students mention that it matters to some degree, but it seems to be in terms of an added bonus to a study environment which is already quite well suited to them. Overall, the male students are quite comfortable with the way things are and many of them have reflected only minimally or not at all on gender in relation to their study environment. Asked how it is to be a male in his degree, Liam answers:

'It's fine, I guess. I don't think about it at all.' (Liam)

Issac adds:

'It's rather easy. I have never been discriminated against or had any problems.' (Issac)

This lack of awareness or indifference to gender is a typical example of 'privilege blindness'. Pratto and Stewart (2012) sums up privilege blindness and its effects as follows: 'Powerful groups are culturally and mentally normalized, which disguises their privilege as "normal" while highlighting inferiority and stereotypes about other groups' (p 28). In other words, when one belongs to the privileged (male) group, one is less likely to consider gender a salient group category or see any need for change.

Out of the five men who do care about gender representation, four of them say that it would be nice to have a few more female students, primarily for social or sexual reasons:

'I have thought that it might be nice to have some more girls in the degree – because it makes for a different dynamic. But I have never reflected on being a man in the degree.' (Kasper)

'One of my friends made the joke that the only real consequence [of the lack of female representation] was that he had to attend other Friday bars to try and find a girlfriend.' (Benjamin)

One person is even openly hostile about being asked for any gender representational considerations:

'If you see a problem with there not being many [women] – and I know there are some people who think there should be a lot of female students – then they should just go to one of the health sciences where there are lots [of women] … If you have a problem then you should have chosen a different degree, that is, if you think it's a big problem. I don't think it is [a problem] at all.' (Gordon)

Gordon encourages us to either not recognise the problem of representation at all, or to classify it as a problem which only has a solution at the individual level. That is, women who are unhappy in the degree have to leave. This aligns well with the 'fixing the women' approach – in that the solution to the clash between a university culture and the female students wellbeing is placing the blame on the women, rather than the culture. From Gordon's position, all organisational or structural interventions are rejected. If you do not feel you belong – that *proves* you do not belong.

In sharp contrast to the male students' perspectives, *all but one* female student thinks there is a serious representational problem in the degree. This aligns well with the normalisation of men as the norm: 'One consequence of normalizing dominant groups is that group membership will be more salient for members of the subordinated groups than for the members of the dominant group' (Pratto and Stewart, 2012, p 31). However, this only makes it more important that we draw attention to what the minority is exposed to.

According to the women, the representational problems start at a very basic level. They are so used to male-dominated language that they are thrown when a more progressive language choice is made. Barbara describes the reflections she had about a lecture that simply offered an example of a person using a female pronoun:

'I was puzzled for a bit. I was like, why is he writing "her", but then I was like "why am I getting confused about this?" It irritated me a bit. But I thought that it was a great low-key way of dealing with it. He couldn't change the fact that he was a man or that there aren't many female researchers, compared to males. But it was a fine way of emphasising that "Of course women can also be involved in this even though there aren't as many". It shouldn't be unnatural, but in my head, it was: Oh my God he is saying "she!".' (Barbara)

Sadly, this quote shows that even the women doing physics internalise an expectation that their study environment is made *by* and *for* men. But at the same time, the example offers hope for change, because even the smallest adjustments to indicate that women also belong get noticed. This student feels seen and included, simply because the lecture includes a fictional example with a woman – a very simple strategy which could easily be adopted in any context: talking about (fictional) characters of all genders in lectures.

Some of the female students were angry about the lack of representation:

'I'm so sick of being underrepresented in general. I feel like when you are studying physics it is just boys. There are boys everywhere, there are male lecturers everywhere and [male] instructors everywhere, and I feel sometimes I just need someone who understands me in a different way. Not that it requires that instructors understand me as a human being, but I would prefer to have a relationship with my instructor that is good enough that I feel comfortable asking for help.' (Alberte)

Despite setting the bar extremely low – not needing the instructor to understand her as a human being but just being willing to take her questions in a comfortable atmosphere – she clearly does not feel that her needs are being met. She feels her degree is constantly reminding her that she does not belong – that this is a degree where only men can be comfortable and seen as human beings.

Some of the women focus on the lack of female representation among researchers and lecturers and explain why it matters to them:

'Yes, it is a bit strange not to see your own gender represented at the higher end of the scale … I think I have had two female lecturers and you can get a bit "Okay, this does not bode well in the other end", right?' (Charlotte)

Barbara adds:

'You feel because you are less represented than others, not necessarily that you are worth less or looked down upon because of your gender, but rather "Okay, I'm a rare sight". … I thought it was great to see there were some female lecturers here because I didn't know they existed at all before I had one … One could at least make sure we had one female lecturer per semester because then you could be like "Well, then I actually belong here".' (Barbara)

Charlotte shows that the lack of female staff members has a demotivating effect on her future career plans in physics. Charlotte interprets the lack of representation as an indication that she herself does not belong in the department as a future staff member. Barbara feels a more immediate need to see female staff around to maintain a sense that she belongs as a student. She needs someone to confirm that she belongs – which of course indirectly suggests that she is having doubts, or that she feels her belonging is questioned by others.

Alberte also adds that it might have a positive effect on the male students' attitudes to female students if they were exposed to female staff more regularly:

'I think it might help [my fellow male students'] attitudes to female physics students if there were more female instructors or more female lecturers.' (Alberte)

This suggests that she is used to male students casting doubt about whether she belongs. She needs the females represented on the staff to prove to these male students that women do in fact belong in the degree and are capable physicists. This captures how the present lack of representation can end up being used as a norm or a prescription for how things ought to be. The male norm recedes from view, while the females 'deviating' from this norm are cast as the problem.

Negative evaluations of female lecturers

As the theme mentioned earlier shows, the few male students that do care about gender representation primarily focus on gender representation among the students (for social purposes), whereas the female students focus more on gender representation among the physics department's employees (as a form of countervailing or a protective shield against the male-dominated environment and the gender-stereotypical attitudes which are entangled in this asymmetrical gender representation). Therefore, it is important to explore how the few female employees were treated.[9]

What stands out most about the male students' comments about the female lecturers is that they do not notice them. Two of the students have forgotten all or some of the female lecturers they have had. For instance, Jacob has to be reminded of one of them:

'Oh, that's true. I had just forgotten her. But that's true and it's not that long ago [that she taught us].' (Jacob)

This, of course, supports the findings mentioned earlier that female representation among lecturers is considered unimportant by male students. They attribute no great meaning to having female lecturers. Two male students even comment that they have chosen not to attend any or only parts of the classes taught by women (Alexander and Hugo).

The few men that do have something to say about the female lecturers primarily comment on them negatively. Three out of the 12 men critique the women for being poor lecturers:

'The lecturer I wasn't so crazy about was also the only female lecturer I had … it was just a coincidence [that I didn't like her], and it wasn't just me … I know girls who have said: "Listen, if I had to choose my favourite female lecturer I couldn't because I have only had one and she was lousy". So, it's just a coincidence that I didn't stick with it. It's not because I said: "She is bad *because* she is a woman".' (Benjamin)

Benjamin tries to make sure that his negative evaluation is not categorised as discriminatory. He does this by claiming that many of his fellow female students agree and by explicitly rejecting the idea that his dislike is because of the lecturer's gender. He fails to consider that his fellow female students might have internalised the male norms from the culture, and that his dislike for the female lecturer might be gendered, even if he is not conscious of this.

Hugo offers the following critique:

'X [female lecturer's name] was really nice, but I think she confused herself at times … . In my study group we ended up not attending the last four lectures. We just sat and discussed it on our own. … Almost every lecture she would say: "Oh, it's just one of those days", and she would make excuses for herself. I don't feel she was very confident about what she was doing and that was unfortunate.' (Hugo)

Hugo starts out complimenting her for being nice (a female stereotypical trait), but then moves on to being highly critical of her teaching skills. Importantly, he interprets the problem as a matter of deficiency – she is not good enough at her job. Again, this is an interpretation which aligns well with a need to 'fix the women' rather than the organisation. But as we shall see later in this chapter, there are several gender-discriminatory dynamics in play here which contribute to her 'confusing herself' and her 'lack of confidence'.

The women in the degree programme on the other hand *do* notice the lecturers of their own gender and they attribute great meaning to their presence. However, half of them (five) end up being disappointed:

'I had looked forward to getting [a female lecturer] I was so [clapping her hands excitedly]: "I'm getting her for my next lecture". I was *so* pumped! … And then she came and lectured with PowerPoint slides and a bad structure on the board, and I was like: "I can't work with this".' (Alberte)

'I feel a bit like I'm denigrating my own gender. But I don't mean it in that way, because I think women can be as good as men. It's just that my experience is that at least some of the women I have come across – the researchers – I have not thought of them as highly as the men. And I don't know what the reason is.' (Hannah)

Alberte has extremely high expectations of her first female lecturer, expectations which are not met, while Hannah's quote captures a more subtle devaluing of the female lecturers that she cannot quite place. One possible interpretation of this could be internalised sexism – her study environment devalues women, and she might have internalised that. Another possibility is that gender stereotypes affect the students' expectations. Heilman's model of fit shows us that gender-stereotypical expectations shape our evaluations of others (Heilman, 2001): we attribute gender stereotypes to both people *and* occupations – and we assume that people who have aligned their gender with their occupation are better qualified for their job (and reward them accordingly in our evaluations). Simply put, we perceive people as more competent at their job if they fit gender stereotypes. Therefore, women taking on STEM degrees or jobs are more likely to have their qualifications questioned and undervalued.

Dora offers a structural explanation for why the few female lecturers might be a disappointment to them:

'I didn't feel I learned much … but from what I remember she was an x [mentions field of physics] physicist who was thrown into this topic like: "Now, this is what you will be teaching" and it didn't seem like she had the same passion for teaching … and that rubs off on you. … If you are not allowed to teach a topic you research, then it might not be as exciting. The topic was highly y [another field of physics] and she was x [field of physics].' (Dora)

This quote suggests that the mere presence of women on the staff is insufficient. When students are only offered access to semi-integrated female lecturers, it sends the message that women do not belong in the department. When female staff members are primarily offered courses outside their research field, it ends up sending an exclusionary message to the (female) students. The message becomes: women who work here must fill in teaching gaps which the male staff do not wish to take on.

Furthermore, the male students' reception of and talk about the female lecturers matters for a sense of belonging among the female students. Alberte offers her experience after having had her first female lecturer:

'I was so disappointed, but also I remember that the boys were disappointed with her too – and *they* blamed it on her *gender* … . I remember I got so angry and frustrated, because it was the first time we had had a female lecturer.' (Alberte)

Alberte's quote captures that a gender-essentialist interpretation of the female lecturer's perceived lack of ability made the situation worse for her. She must live with her own disappointment, as well as her fellow male students' interpretation of the female lecturer as failing *because* of her gender – painting females as essentially ill-fitted for the degree she herself has embarked on.

Issac offers an additional explanation as to why the female lecturers might be lacking in confidence in teaching situations: explicit gender discrimination in the classroom:

'I have observed … a difference between the degree of trust some students have in a female compared to a male lecturer. They … sit in the front row and ask questions about it all. They raise their hand every time the [female] lecturer makes a mistake to point it out. My experience is that they are harder on the two female lecturers we have had compared to all the others. … I think they hound the female lecturers – that's my experience.' (Issac)

Isabella and Barbara elaborate on the same discriminatory classroom dynamic:

'Sometimes in lectures I feel there are more questions about whether something is correct if it's a woman showing it, compared to a male lecturer … . And I wonder: don't you trust that your lecturers know what they are doing?' (Isabella)

'When we had lecturer X [female name], I think she was really good at it. But she did seem a bit new or at least uncertain as a lecturer. Every time someone would be like: "You missed a minus" or something like that – those small kinds of corrections, where you would be like: "Okay, we could figure that out", and she would say it out loud when she wrote the equation. She was affected by this and had a hard time getting back on track to where she was. And I felt sorry for her. I didn't think it was her fault. It was the same three guys doing it every time.' (Barbara)

These examples suggest that Hugo's interpretation of their female lecturer as internally insecure or confused might be too simplistic. The full picture is not captured by understanding the lecturer as having an individual or inherent 'deficiency' expressed in a lack of confidence or qualifications. Their lecturer is not 'confusing herself' or 'lacking confidence', but rather responding to the male students who are positioning her as an illegitimate lecturer, simply because of her gender. These male students' hounding techniques cast their female lecturer as an illegitimate lecturer who is less qualified to disseminate knowledge about physics than the male Bachelor's degree students themselves. In other words, the female lecturer is thrown by working in a sexist and hostile environment in which the power imbalance between the genders is so great that even low-ranking Bachelor's degree students feel more entitled to be there than the female staff. Importantly, these male students' entitlement is so great that they intentionally humiliate their lecturer to cast her as an illegitimate academic within her own field.

Unwanted sexual attention

None of the students were asked explicitly about unwanted sexual attention, and none of the male students commented on it as a problem. However, a few of the female students introduced the topic on their own and called it out as a problem in their degree programme. Isabella and Alberte comment on having changed what type of clothes they wear or having stopped wearing make-up to minimise the spotlight they had been placed under due to their gender:

'I feel like I get too much attention if I wear … I used to wear make-up, but I definitely don't do that anymore … . I get the sense that if I make an effort to look nice in the everyday then I will be made to feel that I'm not smart enough. [The interviewer follows up: 'That you are assessed on your looks rather than on your brain?'] Yes exactly, I don't know if it's a general societal thing or I was just made to feel this during my degree.' (Isabella)

'In the beginning I really felt I had to dress down because I felt bad about standing out because I was already a girl. So, I felt like I had to dress in black and grey clothes to hide in some way.' (Alberte)

This ties in well with the former finding that some of the female students strove to shed their femininity or female stereotypical characteristics to fit into the male-defined environment. However, these quotes have a more explicit sexualising undertone. Another study based on interviews with physicists found similar comments and concluded: 'This [to allude to themselves as sexual beings] would be unthinkable in a Danish context because it is perceived as triggering a sexualization of the body, which in the Danish context is connected with a lack of scientific abilities' (Hasse and Trentemøller, 2008, p 202). One must downplay one's gender to be perceived as a competent academic. The message seems to be that belonging to the female gender stands in the way of being perceived as a competent academic. If you happen to be female, you ought to tone down your gender to increase your perceived fit as an academic.

Alberte also describes how she has received so much unwanted sexual attention (a sub-category of sexual harassment) that she has had to give up on attending any classes:

'On the intro trip there were always some boys that were like: "Oooh, there is a girl over there" and then they would always make passes at me really aggressively. Where I'm like: "That's not okay, I'm a fellow student of yours, you shouldn't." I tried to explain that I'm like everyone else – I would just like to enjoy the trip with my friends and my team. But they kept at it ... . It happened several times and they didn't get it.' (Alberte)

It is obvious that Alberte feels that her fellow male students went too far in their sexualising of her – and that she has made it explicit *that* they were overstepping a line, and *why* it was wrong. However, it is also obvious that the male students were not respecting her as an equal, but rather marking her as an outsider who is only interesting as a sex object.

She adds yet another experience:

'I have had some unfortunate experiences with guys from physics, who I thought were my friends and then it turned out they just wanted a relationship with me, and when I said no they didn't want to be friends with me anymore.' (Alberte)

Both these two cases are classic examples of unwanted sexual attention, where women are reduced to being sex objects in their workplaces. In contrast to being treated like a person, a sex object's opinions or preferences are not registered (or overruled if registered). In this way, Alberte is reduced to a prop for her fellow male students to use to mark their own position of power. At the end of the scale of this behaviour is sexual assault (see the Sexual Experiences Questionnaire for a sense of the continuum in Fitzgerald et al, 1999). Any dehumanising behaviour is, of course, highly problematic for anyone in a study or work environment, but sexualised dehumanisation is particularly problematic because it taps into a long culture of extreme power asymmetries between women and men.

Conclusion

I started out by showing that female and male students were equally passionate about physics. The women were just as interested (if not more) in their STEM degree as their fellow male students. However, what does differ between the two genders is the amount of sexist and sexual harassment hurdles which are placed in front of them when they embark on a physics degree. Throughout the analysis, these hurdles have been shown to be intimately linked with gender-stereotypical perceptions of people as well as of the physics culture itself. Furthermore, gender-essentialist interpretations of the gender asymmetries are entangled with the Danish 'fixing the women' approaches to gender equality. This entanglement unfortunately seems to feed into male privilege blindness.

Pratto and Stewart (2012) sum up privilege blindness as: 'Powerful groups are culturally and mentally normalized, which disguises their privilege as "normal" while highlighting inferiority and stereotypes about other groups' (p 28). This also sums up our study quite well; the male students and the male study environment are considered the norm which casts the female students as 'deviant'. This has the effect that being female ends up standing in the way of being perceived as a legitimate academic. In this way, our findings reiterate many of the gendered elements in Hasse and Trentemøller's (2008) study regarding 'the ideal Hercules type' – including that this 'ideal type' is male, individualistic, nerdy, and sexist. Because of this male norm, female students are encouraged to shed their femininity or tone down their gender and embrace the male geek norms of their chosen degree programme. The only alternative to this unidirectional adaptation to the male culture and norm – at least according to the men – seems to be to withdraw from physics altogether.

Summing up, the marginalisation of women in this physics degree programme starts out by interpolating women as marginal to the degree simply because of their gender but ends up dehumanising them as sex objects. While the first steps of defining the degree as male might seem innocent or harmless to the untrained eye, it is in fact these first steps that legitimise the next. O'Connor et al (2021) describe it as follows: '[T]o understand the nature of GBVH [gender-based violence and sexual harassment], it is necessary to see it as involving a continuum of behaviours to demean, isolate and marginalise, with rape and sexual assault being part of a larger spectrum' (p 2). When being male is defined as the norm of the degree programme, this casts female students as not belonging – or even 'deviant' – while shifting the focus away from the normative advantage which is bestowed on the male students. What our study captures is that, if there is no structural or normative intervention when a degree programme is cast as belonging to a particular gender majority, then this can become a slippery slope towards more and more demeaning attitudes and behaviours directed at the minority.

Labelling sexist and harassment hurdles

To unpick this slippery slope further, next I run through our findings while drawing attention to the labels which most accurately capture the different discriminatory processes. We see the entanglement of gender stereotypes with gender discrimination – in the form of sexist/sexual hostility and sexual harassment – expressed throughout our study. Concretely, I have documented that the physics degree programme is associated with male geeky stereotypes and male geeky sexist behaviour. That is, men have been defined as the normatively legitimate gender in this degree programme, and men function as the yardstick against which others are measured. I have also shown that this definition of the degree programme as male is a mindset which the female students are expected to assimilate to. Furthermore, I have captured that this male norm – expressed in gender representation – goes almost unnoticed by the male students but sends a powerful message to the female students about who belongs in the degree programme and who has a future in STEM.

We have seen multiple examples of what can be categorised as sexual harassment in the Sexual Experiences Questionnaire (SEQ) developed by Fitzgerald et al, (1995). First, we have seen how female lecturers are demeaned in class because of their gender. This is a classic example of 'sexist hostility' (measured on the SEQ scale, Fitzgerald et al, 1999). Second, we have heard how female students have experienced a need to tone down their femininity or their gender to be perceived as legitimate physics students. This is an example of a response to sexist hostility (Fitzgerald et al, 1999). Finally, the female students have been exposed to unwanted sexual attention, which has reduced them to sex objects or props for their fellow male students. In fact, one of the female students has had to turn her study into self-study (avoiding attending classes altogether) because of the unwanted sexual attention she was subjected to. This type of dehumanisation also falls within the purview of the Sexual Experiences Questionnaire, (Fitzgerald et al, 1999). Summing up, this clearly classifies as a hostile study and work environment.

While the optimal solution to these challenges – at an individual level – is to shed one's female gender or the gender stereotypes that one's gender is associated with (as we see in our study), complying with this demand has the unfortunate effect that it reinforces the male norm and privilege yet again. While the individual women have very few other options than to assimilate to the male-normed culture that is enforced in their degree programme, this has no long-term positive effect on the study environment. On the contrary, it enforced the male norm which served to marginalise the women in the first place.

A recent and comprehensive review of the literature on gender-based violence and sexual harassment in higher education (O'Connor et al, 2021) suggests two structural interventions instead: 'reducing HEI's [higher education institutions] male dominance and increasing the gender competence of those in positions of power' (p 10). We need to challenge and change the male norm in universities and educate the people in power to see and address gender inequalities.

In contrast, applying the Danish approach of 'fixing the women' only adds fuel to the sexist and sexual harassment flames by casting gender equality as a problem of the 'deficient' minority, rather than the structural and normative challenge that in fact it is. This is best captured by Hugo's interpretation of a female lecturer's 'lack of confidence' in teaching and her ability 'to confuse herself' in class as an individual problem. In fact, Dora reveals that the lecturer has been allocated a topic which does not map well with her research area, suggesting a form of structural marginalisation. Alberte adds to this perspective that the female lecturers are assessed on gender-essentialist terms by the male students — where one poor performance, by one woman, is generalised to prove that all women are 'deficient' physicists in all contexts. Issac, Isabella and Barbara capture the concrete demeaning and belittling processes set in play in class by some of the male students. These demeaning and belittling actions directed towards the female staff reveal that the lecturer is in fact not 'confusing herself' — as Hugo interprets it — but rather is openly being discriminated against in front of an auditorium full of her students.

In our study, we find several examples of male students who have internalised the typical Danish perception of discrimination as the minority's own problem. Gordon explicitly states that women who do not feel comfortable with the male-dominated environment should leave. Daniel recognises that it might be hard for women to feel at home in the degree programme with all the 'locker room talk' but still maintains that it must be up to the women to assimilate to this hostile environment (rather than vice versa). Frederik offers a gender-essentialist interpretation and assumes that women and men are born with fundamentally different interests. His gender-essentialist assumptions are *not* supported in our study in which the women are no less passionate about their physics studies than the men. But importantly, holding such gender-essentialist attitudes is positively correlated with support for gender discriminatory practices (Skewes et al, 2018). That is, explaining away gender asymmetries with gender essentialism is yet another way of maintaining male privilege blindness in a male-normed environment.

If we wish to implement effective gender equality interventions, then we need to draw our attention away from individualistic interpretations that are fuelled by both the Danish 'fixing the women' approach (Nielsen, 2017; O'Connor et al, 2021) and gender-essentialist interpretations of gender difference as expressed in academia (Skewes et al, 2018). Both the 'fixing the women' approach and the gender-essentialist interpretations of gender differences uphold male privilege blindness. To overcome this privilege blindness, we need to facilitate identification with the women, as well as ensure an awareness of the constraints imposed on the women by the privileged male group (Pratto and Stewart, 2012; O'Connor et al, 2021). In other words, the dominant group needs to practise taking on the perspective of the subordinate group. Maintaining a male norm — or a culture which privileges men — draws the attention to the women as 'deficient' *because* they stand out from the male norm (Pratto and Stewart, 2012). This is illustrated in our study. However, if we maintain our focus on the minority as deviant *without* drawing attention to what they are supposedly deviating *from*, we will keep reproducing the male norm. If on the other hand we wish to challenge the male privileges in order to make STEM degrees more inclusive for *all* the students, then we need to direct our interventions towards the majority group's blind spots. That is, to ensure that we remove sexist and sexual harassment hurdles from women's career paths, we need to ensure that male students and male staff are made aware of the asymmetrical workload which is currently placed on female students and staff (O'Connor et al, 2021). We need to make everyone understand that these hurdles are unjust and unacceptable. *We need to stop prioritising the dominant group's comfort, derived from fitting into the male norm, over the subordinate group's wellbeing and safety.*

In other words, we need to hold the people in power – particularly the ones who belong to the majority group – accountable for detecting and fighting the gender discrimination which the minorities are exposed to. If we do set such structural interventions in motion, then the current generation of women in STEM can become positive role models for the next generation. Because with such structural interventions, women will be able to say that they were facilitated by their study and work environment to the extent that it became possible for them to thrive and reach their full academic potential.

Notes

[1] The Global Gender Gap Index captures four dimensions: (a) Economic Participation and Opportunity, (b) Educational Attainment, (c) Health and Survival, and (d) Political Empowerment (Gender Gap Index, 2021, p 5).

[2] These numbers capture individuals' experiences with sexism and sexual harassment in a 2–5 year period prior to the COVID-19 lockdown.

[3] Why 'Hercules'? "We chose this name because it carries connotations of an individual fighter, who never gives up, who is always engaged in a struggle, who is completely devoted to his labour and who strives for immortal fame" (Hasse and Trentemøller, 2008, p 100).

[4] I use the terms *female* and *male* even though I do not intend to refer to any biological essence of any sex. Hopefully, the chapter will make it clear that gender discrimination is not understood as arising from gendered biological essences, but rather from gender-stereotypical assumptions or associations attributed to people and environments.

[5] The type of masculinity the women align themselves with is the geeky physicist. See Hasse and Trentemøller (2008) for more information on the 'Hercules' type of physics nerd, and see Mendick et al (2021) for a detailed analysis of a new form of geeky masculinity.

[6] Daniel uses the Danish word *drenge-fnidder*. *Pigefnidder* is more typical, which most directly translates as bickering among girls. The connotation of the term is that girls create unnecessary conflict among themselves and that this type of conflict should not be taken seriously.

[7] Here Hannah used the term *pigefnidder* in the traditional sense of the word.

[8] I use the term gender representation in the sense of numerical presence. But the concept is primarily relevant because it marks the majority as belonging, in contrast to the minority.

[9] All female staff with a postdoctoral fellowship or above are referred to as 'lecturer' to ensure anonymity.

References

Ahmed, S. (2012) *On Being Included – Racism and Diversity in Institutional Life*. London: Duke University Press.

Ahmed, S. (2015) 'Introduction: Sexism – A Problem with a Name'. *New Formations 2015* (86): 5–13.

Ahmed, S. (2017) *Living a Feminist Life*. London: Duke University Press.

Baron-Cohen, S. (2003) *The Essential Difference*. London: Penguin Books.

Borchorst, A. and Dahlerup, D. (2020) *Konflikt og konsensus – det danske ligestillingspolitiske regime*. Frederiksberg: Frydenlund Academic.

Easteal, P. and Judd, K. (2008) '"She Said, He Said": Credibility and Sexual Harassment Cases in Australia'. *Women's Studies International Forum*, 31, pp 336–44.

Einersen, A.F., Krøjer, J., MacLeod, S., Muhr, S.L., Munar, A.M., Myers, E.S., Plotnikof, M. and Skewes, L. (2021) *Sexism in Danish Higher Education and Research: Understanding, Exploring, Acting*. Department of Organization, Copenhagen Business School.

Fitzgerald, L.F., Gelfand, M.F. and Dragow, F. (1995) 'Measuring Sexual Harassment: Theoretical and Psychometric Advances'. *Basic and Applied Social Psychology*, 17(4), pp 425–45.

Fitzgerald, L.F., Magley, V., Drasgow, F. and Waldo, C.R. (1999) 'Measuring Sexual Harassment in the Military: The Sexual Experiences Questionnaire (SEQ-DoD)'. *Military Psychology*, 11(3), pp 243–63. DOI: 10.1207/s15327876mp1103_3.

Gender Gap Index (2021) https://www3.weforum.org/docs/WEF_GGGR_2021.pdf.

Hasse, C. and Trentemøller, S. (2008) *Break the Pattern! A Critical Enquiry into Three Scientific Workplace Cultures: Hercules, Caretakers and Worker Bees*. Estonia: Tartu University Press.

Heilman, M.E. (2001) 'Description and Prescription: How Gender Stereotypes Prevent Women's Ascent up the Organizational Ladder'. *Journal of Social Issues*, 57(4), pp 657–74.

Illies, R., Hausman, N., Schwochau, S. and Stibal, J. (2003) 'Reported Incidence Rates of Work-related Sexual Harassment in the US: Using Meta-analysis to Explain Rate Disparities'. *Personal Psychology*, 56, pp 607–18.

Margolis, J. and Fisher, A. (2002) *Unlocking the Clubhouse – Women in Computing*. Cambridge: MIT Press.

McCabe, M. and Hardman, L. (2005) 'Attitudes and Perceptions of Workers to Sexual Harassment'. *Journal of Social Psychology*, 145, pp 719–40.

Mendick, H., Ottemo, A., Berge, M. and Silfver, E. (2021) 'Geek Entrepreneurs: The Social Network, Iron Man and the Reconfiguration of Hegemonic Masculinity'. *Journal of Gender Studies* (ahead-of-print): pp 1–13.

Nielsen, M.W. (2017) 'Scandinavia Approaches to Gender Equality in Academia: A Comparative Study'. *Scandinavian Journal of Educational Research*, 61(3), pp 295–318.

O'Connor, P., Hodgins, M., Woods, D.R., Wallwaey, E., Palmen, R., Van Den Brink, M. and Schmidt, E.K. (2021) 'Organisational Characteristics That Facilitate Gender-Based Violence and Harassment in Higher Education?' *Administrative Science*, 11(138), pp 1–13.

Pratto, F. and Stewart, A.L. (2012) 'Group Dominance and the Half-Blindness of Privilege'. *Journal of Social Issues*, 3(68), pp 28–45.

Pronin, E., Steel, C.M. and Ross, L. (2004) 'Identity Bifurcation in Response to Stereotype Threat: Women and Mathematics'. *Journal of Experimental Social Psychology*, 40, pp 152–68.

Skewes, L., Fine, C. and Haslam, N. (2018) 'Beyond Mars and Venus: The Role of Gender Essentialism in Support for Gender Equality and Backlash'. *PLOSone*, 13 (7), pp 1–17.

Skewes, L., Skewes, J.C. and Ryan, M.K. (2019) 'Attitudes to Sexism and Gender Equality at a Danish University'. *Women, Gender & Research, special issue on Gender and Academia*, 27 (1–2), pp 71–85.

Skewes, L., Skewes, J.C. and Ryan, M.K. (2021) 'Attitudes to Sexism and the #MeToo Movement at a University in Denmark'. *NORA – Nordic Journal of Feminist and Gender Research*, 29 (2), pp 124–39.

Swim, J.K., Aikin, K.J., Hall, W.S. and Hunter, B.A. (1995) 'Sexism and Racism: Old-Fashioned and Modern Prejudices'. *Journal of Personality and Social Psychology*, 68(2), pp 199–214.

Willness, C., Steel, P. and Lee, K. (2007) 'A Meta-analysis of the Antecedents and Consequences of Workplace Sexual Harassment'. *Personnel Psychology*, 60, pp 127–62.

8

Some ten years ago, I started writing a novel

Sigbjørn Skåden

Some ten years ago, I started writing a novel. What I knew at the time was that I wanted it to be about power relationships: an exploration of how the majority's supremacy in the Scandinavian countries might have weighed down on the indigenous Sámi population at different times, and what it does to a people to be weighed down on for generations.

My approach was to look at my own family and trace it three generations back, to my great grandparents' time. My great grandparents were born in the late 1800s. All of them on my mother's side were descendants of reindeer herders who historically migrated with their reindeer in a yearly cycle between the winter grazing lands in the hinterland and the summer grazing lands by the coast. In 1751, a state border was drawn in the middle of their migratory route. Their winter grazing land was now in Sweden and their summer grazing land was in the Dano-Norwegian Realm. For the generations to come, this life of reindeer herding would become increasingly difficult, due to both the border issue and the increasing number of Norwegian and Swedish settlers in northern Scandinavia. During the 1800s, a huge number of Sámi reindeer-herding families thus had to give up their migratory life of reindeer herding and settle on their summer grazing land on the Norwegian side. They cleared farmland in the woodlands some distance away from the Norwegian settlers who had inhabited the coast, and started raising cattle and growing grain and potatoes.

This was the life my great grandparents were born into: children of small-scale farmers in secluded villages up in the woods. During the 1800s, the rule of Norway had changed hands from the Danish king in Copenhagen to the Swedish king in Stockholm, and in my great grandparents' youth their ruler changed again. In 1905, Norway gained its independence, and was now ruled by a king in Oslo. During the time my great grandparents started raising their own children, Norwegian state nationalism and the assimilation pressure on the country's minorities were at an all-time high.

It was during this period that Norway laid the foundations for crushing the Sámi language. My grandparents – raised on these same farms in post-independence Norway – grew up in a village where Norwegian was not

117

spoken as an everyday language. As non-Norwegian-speaking children, their encounters with the Norwegian school system were brutal. So were their interactions with Norwegian civil society in general. They learnt that they were people of an inferior race belonging to an inferior culture.

The discrimination against the Sámi people can, of course, be traced through well-documented collective processes led by nation states. The mentioned use of the school system as a tool to assimilate the Sámi was collectively effective, and in Norway the law prohibiting the use of the Sámi language in schools that was passed in 1851 was enhanced after Norwegian independence in 1905, among other things by organising a huge proportion of the Sámi pupils into special boarding schools. The prohibition by law of using the Sámi language in schools remained in force until 1959. In addition, one could mention other traceable collective processes, like the Norwegian land sales act of 1902 stating that only people with Norwegian names who used Norwegian as their primary language were allowed to own land in the north, or the ongoing human genetics (racial biology) research that targeted the Sámi and used the measurements of Sámi skulls and other physical characteristics as proof that the Sámi belonged to an underdeveloped and inferior race.

But then there are also the stories in every Sámi family and in every Sámi village: narratives telling how they felt badly treated and discriminated against, fragments of their lives that shaped how they saw themselves and their heritage. I so often heard the same sentence repeated in different contexts by people in my grandparents' generation in my village: "We who were considered of less worth". It was an echo that kept ringing in the mouths of old people in my youth, often said in a sort of amazement over how the tables had turned, when they witnessed the self-confidence and pride with which the Sámi in my generation worked with Sámi issues, a kind of 'Imagine that we used to be considered of less worth, and look at you now'.

I often think that it was during my grandparents' generation that my village was broken beyond repair. They were treated so brutally because of their Sámi background that they felt that the only way to try save their own children from the same brutality was to do as they were told, adapt to the majority culture, leave the Sámi culture behind. This was the generation that unanimously broke the Sámi language chain in my home village. When they themselves had children, round about the time of WW2, they chose Norwegian as the language for bringing up their children, even though they kept on speaking Sámi among themselves and with their relatives and neighbours.

So, it becomes more complicated after this. Different families have navigated this situation in different ways, and they continue to do so. On a grand scale, one can say that most Sámi families and villages at some point in history have left their Sámi culture and identity and gone into hiding, posing as majority people because the stigma of being singled out as inferior people became too heavy to bear. Some families and villages one can similarly say have come back out from hiding during the changed climate of the last couple of decades and reclaimed their Sámi identity, but most have not. Some have retained their Sámi identity for the entire ride, some even with the language intact.

In my village, knowledge about our Sámi background never left us, but whether this heritage was something we should enhance and show pride in or rather just throw on the trash heap of history and pretend never happened has been an internal quarrel in my village my whole life. Now in 2022, most families in the village are okay with saying and showing that we are Sámi. But if you go back just two decades in time, the majority still weren't. It's been a slow shift, from being almost totally crushed under the boot of Norwegian colonialism in my early childhood, until today where we have managed to revive a positive attitude towards Sámi culture and to preserve and redevelop our cultural knowledge.

What has this got to do with sexual violence and harassment? One could claim that history has turned us into a traumatised people. What a generational trauma like this might entail was one of the truths I wanted to explore in the novel. Is there an invisible line from generation to generation where the good and the bad of one's ancestors gets imprinted in the flesh of a newborn? And what happens to the collective mentality of a people who experience shaming and persecution for their family background and culture for generation after generation, and even today still experience that the marginalised culture we have been left with is under constant pressure?

I'm a novelist. That entails seeking truth in a way that differs from the source-based truth-seeking of an academic. I have no intention of trying to end up with an answer to the questions that drove me through the writing process. Instead, I try to expand on them and test their flexibility and breadth.

My novel *Våke over dem som sover* (*Watch Over Those Who Sleep*) (2014) is a book that I think ends up wanting to expand on many things. One of the things it is trying to explore is a possible connection between being collectively oppressed and the formation of a culture of silence, where the oppressed within an oppressed collective have limited scope for bettering their situation by speaking up.

Almost 20 years ago, after having finished my university degree, I was offered a teaching job at the Sámi High School in Guovdageaidnu. Guovdageaidnu, or Kautokeino in Norwegian, is on the northern tundra and is arguably the municipality in the Sámi territories where Sámi culture has been best preserved; a huge majority of the inhabitants are native Sámi speakers. It was both exciting and rewarding to get to know a place better where Sámi culture is the majority culture.

Coinciding with my two years in Guovdageaidnu, the municipality was struck with what later would come to be known as the vice scandal of Guovdageaidnu. It started with a whistle-blower, and then swiftly went very deep. The snowball that was set in motion unravelled a culture where it was reasonably common that underage girls had sexual relations with older men, a revelation that also implicated the then vice mayor of Guovdageaidnu, a man in his mid-forties. The cases exploded in the national media, and all of a sudden Guovdageaidnu was the top story in the national press with teams of journalists swarming to the place for a hot couple of weeks.

By the time the dust had settled, the Norwegian criminal police had charged twenty or so men in Guovdageaidnu in relation to illicit sexual relations with underage girls. During their investigation, they had also uncovered a relatively large number of rapes and other sexual assaults. As commonly is the case in matters like these, one must also assume that the numbers of unreported cases were big in both those categories.

Like all Sámi municipalities, Guovdageaidnu is a small place with a tightly woven web of families. The scale and also aggressiveness that was part of the vice problem that was brought to the surface must probably have come as a surprise to many inhabitants, but it also must be fair to say that a very large proportion of the population must have had some knowledge of, and even accepted parts of, what was going on. It stank of a culture of silence.

This phenomenon is known in Sámi society, that Sámi villages and milieus have had a tendency to develop a sort of inner solidarity culture that has sometimes resulted in keeping difficult internal issues under wraps instead of speaking up and thus involving external forces that could intervene. In recent decades, large-scale sexual abuse cases that partly could be attributed to a culture like this have exploded in Sámi communities in Guovdageaidnu and in Divtasvuodna/Tysfjord.

However, cases like these have complex causes. In the individual process that is novel writing, it felt both interesting and somehow also important to include one of these modern cases of abuse within a Sámi community in a novel that starts with historical scenarios of colonial oppression of the Sámi people. In short, *Váke over dem som sover* is a novel that, through fragments, spans approximately one hundred years from the early 1900s up until the present day, and follows people belonging to the same Sámi family through four generations along five different timelines. Through the novel, I have attempted to offer scenarios that can shed light on how the state abuse of power over the Sámi people might have affected Sámis at different times; in the most recent timeline of the novel, it is then no longer a scenario that shows state abuse of power over the Sámi people, but a scenario of power relations and abuse within Sámi society. It is, of course, a way of pointing out a line that might exist between these scenarios. And this last scenario of the novel is fuelled by the vice cases in Guovdageaidnu, where most of the events in this scenario take place, although it does not describe the cases directly.

In the present-day timeline of the novel, a young Sámi artist, resembling myself, identifies and abuses the internal power structures that are forged by the culture of silence to create an artwork where he himself takes advantage of his position within this power structure and uses it to victimise and abuse people further down in the hierarchy. I don't aspire in the novel to give a clear answer to the questions that might arise, and I won't try that here either. But, like in the novel, this chapter may ask those questions that ponder on whether there is a line between this abuse and that abuse. What *does* happen to the collective mentality of a people who are victims of oppression and persecution for generations? What happens to that people's trust in public services constructed by their oppressors, and thus their willingness to reach out to those services to help solve problems? What happens to the individual's ability to make internal problems public, which might further stigmatise their community when that community is already weighed down by centuries of heavy stigmatisation?

This is in no way an attempt to excuse the abuse of power that might take place within Sámi society, nor is it a way to try to fully explain why these things happen. The causes for things like these will always be complex, no matter what the context. Matters like sexual violence, abuse and harassment must of course be promptly dealt with also when they occur in a Sámi context. But I do believe that when matters like the cases in Guovdageaidnu and Divtasvuodna do surface in a Sámi context, these questions *also* need to be on the table. They are part of our map. If not imprinted in our flesh.

References
Skåden, S. (2014) *Våke over dem som sover*, Oslo: Cappelen Damm.

PART II

Violence, knowledge and imagining justice

9

ON THE PROMENADE

Mads Ananda Lodahl

Translated by Paul Russell Garrett and Nielsine Nielsen

It's one of those really hot summer days in Copenhagen. There's no breeze, the air feels heavy and dry, and I've headed out to Svanemøllen to swim off the big rocks by the sailing club, when I run into Monica and Anna. We have a few friends in common but don't know each other that well. Still, they invite me to sit with them on their plaid blanket. They've brought a picnic basket full of food and drinks. All I have is a bottle of water and an apple. We talk about our mutual friend, Anette, who has just been hired as a consultant by one of Denmark's main political parties.

"Crazy, isn't it", Monica says.

"Yeah", Anna says. "But it's so her. I could never imagine her having a normal job."

I smile and nod. That's the Anette I know and love.

Another young woman arrives. She is holding her phone in one hand, a takeaway coffee in the other, and has a shoulder bag dangling from her elbow.

"This place is crawling, I nearly didn't find you!" she says. She had tried to call, but Monica's and Anna's phones were on silent. The newcomer lets out a beleaguered sigh.

"Would you hold this for a sec?" She hands Monica her coffee, slips the phone into her bag, and puts it down on the grass. When she's finally settled, I hold out my hand.

"Jannick", I say.

"Liv", she says.

"Is everything all right?" Monica asks, smiling.

"Well ... argh ... I have to tell you what happened on the way here. Today has been bad enough as it is. Sorry, I am fuming right now."

She'd stopped by the little coffee van on the promenade, and when it came time to pay, the young man who was serving her asked for 28 kroner "and your phone number".

While telling the story, she imitates the guy's smile, which he'd probably considered charming, but which Liv had deemed rude and inappropriate. The other two sigh and shake their heads.

"What is wrong with people", Monica says.

"Seriously!" Liv says.

"You shouldn't have to put up with comments like that, just for trying to buy a coffee."

"The heat does something to people", Anna says.

"That doesn't give them the right to be rude to other people", Liv replies.

They continue for a while in the same vein. Agreeing with each other that it was an unpleasant experience for Liv.

"But you're here now", Monica says. "You've got your coffee. And you've found us. The sun is shining and soon we'll be out in the water."

"Yes", Liv says, gesturing as if trying to force something out and away from her.

They start talking about something else. I'm not really involved in their conversation. They seem to know each other pretty well, and I only know two of them, and only a little.

Nobody has ever said anything like that to me.

"That'll be 28 kroner ... and your phone number."

I've never said that to anyone either, but I wish someone would say it to me one day. A young man on the promenade. Smiling at me in a cheerful and charming kind of way, I return his smile but don't give him my number. I play hard to get. It could never lead to anything. It's just a game. A bit of harmless flirtation.

I know it's not the same for women. They hear it constantly, which must be exasperating. Liv is young and beautiful. She probably gets comments like that all the time, while she's off in her own world, going about her business. It must be frustrating. It's never happened to me. And I've never hit on a guy I didn't know in public.

When I was 17, I went to a New Year's Eve party at my friend's, and for some reason or other her older brother was also there. He was a big guy, kind of rough looking, and gave off a weird vibe, but later that night everyone was really drunk, and I was sitting next to him on the sofa, and somehow, we got to talking about me being gay.

"Couldn't care less", he said. "As long as you lot don't get too close. I don't want any of that in my face."

"Is this too close?" I asked.

I had a strange urge to provoke him, but I also felt I needed him to say – convincingly – that I was perfect the way I was, and that he was all right with it.

"I hadn't really given it much thought, but now that you mention it, yes. You're sitting too close", he replied.

I moved back a few centimetres.

"Better?"

I could see the revulsion in his eyes.

"When you put it like that, if I can hear your voice, I think you're too close."

I moved as far away from him as the sofa would allow.

"I just don't understand why it's such a big deal", I said.

"It disgusts me, that's why I don't want you getting too close."

The sofa wasn't very big. I could easily reach him.

"What would happen if I put my hand on your leg right now."

"I would take my elbow and drive it through your skull."

He pointed his elbow in the direction of my face to show how he'd do it. He looked me right in the eyes, like he was really serious.

I went quiet, long enough to notice how drunk I was. Now he was staring straight ahead. He seemed relaxed but primed at the same time. Like a guy in a film. My urge to provoke him and my need for his acceptance were still there, jostling for position inside me.

"I want to do it", I said. "To see if you're really serious."

"Go on then."

Apart from one of the girls who had fallen asleep on the other sofa, everyone else was in the kitchen. We were alone. The music was extremely loud.

"Have you never kissed another man?" I asked.

Putting the moves on a strange guy in a place that isn't gay-friendly is completely out of the question for me. Not only is it possible that any such declaration of love would be met with physical violence, it is probable.

If just once I had to pay a smiling stranger 28 kroner "and my phone number" for a cup of coffee, I'd be on cloud nine for months.

All right, all right, I know it's different for women. I read the papers and talk to friends about it. I know. I'm not an idiot. The problem is that some men just see red if they're rejected. It's as though they only have two emotions, and if they don't find an outlet for their sexual urges, they turn straight to violence. Those are their two default settings. Horny. And angry. What a strange little life it must be, not being able to feel or express other aspects of yourself. It must be hard on them, too, not that it makes it okay.

When there's a lull in the conversation, I bring up the situation with the guy on the promenade again. I ask Liv if there was any appropriate way the coffee guy could have flirted with her if he genuinely thought she was nice.

"Just let me know if you don't want to talk about it anymore", I say.

She struggles to form a proper response to my question.

"I'm not even sure he should be trying to chat me up in the first place. Maybe I would just like to order a coffee without having to deal with some man's need for attention."

She tells us about this time she was at a nightclub, and a stranger came up to her and offered her a drink.

"I thought it was a bit old-fashioned, and not a particularly nice way of trying to pick someone up, but hey, why not get a free drink out of it", she says.

Monica and Anna nod and laugh.

They'd talked for a while as she sipped her drink, she might even have flirted a bit to see where it would lead, but then she lost interest, thanked him for the drink, and went back to her friends.

"A little later I'm out on the dance floor with a girlfriend, and I've forgotten all about this guy, but then suddenly, he's standing right there, pressing in between us, wearing this stupid grin and it's like ..."

Her eyebrows move all the way up her forehead and she gives an exaggerated smile.

"He's in a right state."

Then he puts one arm around Liv and the other around her friend. The situation isn't exactly ideal, but they can't really get out of it. Then out of nowhere, he grabs them both by the back of the neck and slams their heads together. Forehead to forehead.

Liv uses her hands to illustrate, and we all grimace as if we'd just been headbutted.

"What the fuck!" Monica says.

"It was really painful", Liv says.

"Did nobody do anything?"

"I don't think anyone saw it. It happened so quickly. We were just dancing. I don't think anyone realised something was wrong."

"The guy just disappeared. It was a big club."

"Experiences like that, they resurface whenever a stranger makes a pass at me", Liv says to me.

Anna and Monica nod.

I nod too, slowly, to show that I understand. The strange thing is that in a way I can relate to what she's saying one hundred per cent, but in other ways I can't relate at all.

10

Sextortion: linking sexual violence and corruption in a Nordic context

Silje Lundgren, Åsa Eldén, Dolores Calvo and Elin Bjarnegård

Introduction

Many acts of sexual harassment, violence and abuse include quid pro quo (this for that) elements: a teacher demands 'sex for grades', a civil servant offers a job candidate an internship in exchange for sex, a coach offers positions in a sports organisation in exchange for nudes. These are examples of 'sextortion'. Sextortion occurs when a person with entrusted power abuses this power to obtain sexual favours in exchange for a service or a benefit that is within their power to grant or withhold. Thus, sextortion entails the abuse of power, and it is simultaneously an act of sexual violence and of corruption: sexual conduct involving a coerced quid pro quo and a corrupt form of conduct in which the currency is sex.[1]

Sextortion is clearly a form of corruption, but is often not acknowledged as such precisely because the currency of the transaction is sex instead of the more widely recognised money or material benefits (IAWJ, 2012; Feigenblatt, 2020; Eldén et al, 2020; Bjarnegård et al, 2022). Recognising the abuse of entrusted power is key to revealing the corruption component of sextortion. The absence of corruption means that people entrusted with positions of authority stand for equal treatment and distribute services fairly, according to pre-established criteria. When this entrusted power is instead abused for personal gain – be it of a sexual or monetary nature – it fits the definition of corruption.[2] Just like with other forms of corruption, power imbalances and relative dependency are common facilitators in cases of sextortion (Eldén et al, 2020; Bjarnegård et al, 2022).

But sextortion is also clearly a form of sexual violence. Power imbalances and vulnerabilities are exploited and, although physical force may not be involved, psychological coercion is used to obtain sexual favours. With a sexual violence lens, however, the relative absence of force combined with the transactional aspect of sextortion – quid pro quo – can be misinterpreted to imply consent on the part of the victim. Thus, sextortion should be seen as *both* sexual violence and corruption. Its properties and ramifications cannot be properly understood without acknowledging the intersectional power structures underpinning sexual violence, nor can responsibility be properly attributed unless the abuse of entrusted authority is adequately considered (Eldén et al, 2020; Bjarnegård et al, 2022).

Sextortion as a concept has gained increasing attention in international research and policy discussions (Chêne, 2009; IAWJ, 2012; UNDP-Huairou Commission, 2012; Towns, 2015; Amnesty International, 2016; Transparency International, 2016; Merkle et al, 2017; UNDP-SIWI, 2017; IBA, 2019; Eldén et al, 2020; Feigenblatt, 2020; UNODC, 2020). In a Nordic context, however, the concept remains relatively unknown, and the phenomenon is still unexplored. This chapter is the first to examine documented empirical cases of sexual harassment, violence and abuse that include the abuse of entrusted power and quid pro quo aspects: that is, cases of sextortion in Sweden and Norway. The chapter shows how applying a framework of sextortion permits an analysis that sheds light on important corruption aspects in cases of sexual harassment, violence and abuse that may otherwise remain invisible. In particular, a sextortion lens necessitates a shift in focus from the question of the consent of the victim to the perpetrator's abuse of entrusted power. To understand why sextortion is not reported, however, we must also analyse the vulnerability and stigmatisation involved.

Materials and method

Sextortion as a concept has hitherto not been used in the Nordic countries. This means that there are no public stories nor available previous research on sextortion as such. No one has been sentenced for committing 'sextortion' as an act of both sexual violence and corruption. Thus, there are no available empirical cases that explicitly refer to 'sextortion'.

This does not mean, however, that sextortion as a phenomenon is absent in the Nordic context. Many of the #MeToo movement's hashtags from 2017 and beyond gathered testimonies about sexual harassment, violence and abuse from different professions that included quid pro quo aspects. There were examples of testimonies about: judges and prosecutors demanding sex for judicial favours; police officers and senior physicians offering jobs to female colleagues in exchange for sex; patients sexually abused to obtain medical certificates; and university professors passing students' exams in exchange for sex (#nödvärn, #medvilkenrätt, #akademiupproret, #vårdensomsvek, see also Lundgren et al, 2020). The sexual favours in these examples span a continuum of harassment and sexual violence – from a suggestion to sit in someone's lap in exchange for a necessary signature to a request for sexual intercourse in exchange for a medical certificate. Sometimes the expectation could be implicit, and in other cases there was an implicit threat of violence if the victim did not comply with the suggested quid pro quo. Therefore, it is not the gravity of the sexual offence which is the common denominator in these cases. Instead, these cases are all examples of the abuse of entrusted power in exchange for personal gain in the form of sexual favours, that is: sextortion.

Moreover, the lack of recognition of sextortion does not mean that there are no legal cases in the Nordic countries regarding acts of sextortion. For the purposes of this chapter, we have chosen two judgments that describe acts of sextortion in detail, one from Norway and one from Sweden. Both the Norwegian and Swedish cases have attracted wide media attention, and the Norwegian case has also been mentioned in international reports as an example of sextortion (IBA, 2019; Feigenblatt, 2020). These legal cases, unlike the testimonies in the #MeToo movement's hashtags, give detailed descriptions of both the acts of sextortion and of the contexts in which they took place. As such, they are used here as empirical cases of sextortion that allow for an in-depth analysis.

In both the cases analysed in this chapter, we use judgments from the District Courts (*Tingsrätt* in Swedish and *Tingrett* in Norwegian) as our primary source material.[3] Both cases were brought to the relevant Court of Appeal (*Hovrätt* in Swedish and *Lagmansrett* in Norwegian), and in the Swedish case we also analyse the judgment from the Court of Appeal.[4] In the Norwegian case, the appeal was withdrawn.

The judgments are public documents in both Sweden and Norway. The victims are protected by confidentiality in the judgments, while the perpetrators are named. In this text, we refer to the perpetrators' positions, since these are key to our analysis of the abuse of power, but do not use their names or the name of their specific organisations.[5]

The judgments are texts written with the purpose of presenting the arguments for and against a person being found guilty of a crime. We approach them with a different purpose: to analyse them as stories about acts that we identify as sextortion, produced by Swedish and Norwegian institutions, and as their interpretations of the stories told (compare: Westerstrand, 2017; Wallin et al, 2021). Therefore, the reasonings put forward in the judgments offer clues for understanding how acts of sextortion are handled in a Nordic context.

The two empirical cases analysed in this chapter both concern male perpetrators and male victims. Even though reliable statistics on sextortion remain scarce (see, however, Transparency International, 2019a, 2019b), documented cases from all over the world paint a somewhat different picture. All documented international cases of sextortion include male perpetrators (see for example IAWJ, 2012; IBA, 2019; Eldén et al, 2020; Feigenblatt, 2020), and women and girls, regardless of context, are overrepresented as victims of sextortion, due to gender norms and gendered power relationships (Bjarnegård et al, 2022). However, in international reports about sextortion, examples of young men and boys being exposed to sextortion by other men are not uncommon. Regardless of the sex of the victim, gender norms and gendered power relations – intertwined with other hierarchisations – are key to understanding the dynamics of sextortion. Also central to situations of sextortion is a relationship of dependency, in which the victim is dependent on the favours or services of the perpetrator. Previous research (Eldén et al, 2020) shows that such dependency is conditioned by different forms of asymmetrical power relationships and strengthened in situations of insecurity and vulnerability such as migration processes (Merkle et al, 2017; Feigenblatt, 2020).

Next, we present the two empirical cases in more detail. We unpack the two cases, applying a framework of sextortion that we have developed in previous research (Eldén et al, 2020). We then turn to a discussion about what a framework of sextortion – that is, a focus on the abuse of entrusted power in exchange for sexual favours – adds to an analysis of sexual violence and how it relates to imaginaries of Nordic exceptionalism.

Two cases of sextortion

In Sweden, a former employee of the local division of a national organisation for LBGTQI rights was charged with rape and sexual molestation of four members of a sub-group of the organisation in spring 2021. This sub-group brought together persons who were newly arrived in Sweden: asylum seekers, undocumented immigrants or persons who had received a residence permit in the preceding two-year period. When committing the crimes analysed in this chapter, the employee was working as a migration advisor for the sub-group of the organisation.

In the District Court, the migration advisor was convicted of several cases of rape and sexual molestation perpetrated in 2018 and 2019, and sentenced to four years in prison. The migration advisor confessed that he had been involved in sexual acts with the victims, but claimed that they had consented to have sex with him. The District Court argued that the victims were in a 'particularly vulnerable situation', and the sexual acts constituted 'undue exploitation' of this situation, and therefore the question of consent was considered irrelevant. The Court found him guilty of five cases of rape and of sexual molestation and sentenced him to four years in prison (ST, 2021, p 2).

The Court of Appeal, however, dismissed the District Court's reasoning. The Court of Appeal claimed that the victims were not in a 'particularly vulnerable situation' and therefore examined whether they had consented to the sexual acts or not. The migration advisor was acquitted in two of the five cases of rape, and the sentence was reduced to three years and four months in prison (SH, 2021, p 2).

The Norwegian case concerned a former cabinet minister of the Norwegian Government and former county governor. In 2018, he was charged and convicted for abusing his position as county governor to obtain sex from three young men, one of them a minor when the abuse started, during the period 2011–17. He was sentenced to five years in prison for abusing his position of power as a county governor and for exploiting the vulnerable situation of the victims (NTT, 2019, p 41).

The victims of the former county governor's abuse were three young men who had previously obtained asylum in Norway. One of them had been granted Norwegian citizenship in August 2009, another was granted citizenship in February 2015, and the third had had a temporary residence permit since 2004 (NTT, 2019, pp 2–3, 11, 20, 26).

The judgment from the District Court in the Norwegian case presents as central elements both the asymmetrical power relationship between the former county governor and his victims and the vulnerable situation of the victims. The former county governor was convicted of 'exploiting' the subordinate position and lack of resources of 'particularly vulnerable' young, unaccompanied former asylum seekers to obtain sexual favours (NTT, 2019, pp 2–3, 41).

Next, we first analyse the judgments from the District Courts in Sweden and Norway. The District Court's findings in both these cases, we will argue, emphasise the abuse of both power and an entrusted position, and the quid pro quo aspects of the crimes. We then turn to the judgment from the Court of Appeal in the Swedish case, and examine the implications of focusing on consent instead of on the undue exploitation of the particularly vulnerable situation of the victims for understanding the crimes committed.

We start by analysing the two cases, focusing on the perpetrator and the impact of power and position on sextortion. Subsequently, we focus on the victim and the vulnerabilities that do not just facilitate sextortion, but also contribute to stigmatisation and silence.

Perpetrator and power: the abuse of an entrusted position

The abuse of entrusted power is central to the definition of sextortion (Eldén et al, 2020). A sextortion lens brings about a focus on how the perpetrator uses their entrusted position of power as a tool for obtaining personal sexual favours. From a corruption perspective, this implies that services are not distributed according to protocol such as need or merit. Instead, the perpetrator abuses the position of trust and responsibility that comes with their entrusted power, disregarding criteria and regulations that stipulate how services should be distributed, or permits given.

In the cases presented in this chapter, the perpetrators used their formal positions to explicitly or implicitly indicate that they had the formal power to withhold or offer services that were important to the victims. It was in their capacity as persons with entrusted power that the sexual acts were requested.

The first step of the analysis of the two cases will focus on this abuse of power.

The Swedish case

Part of the role of migration advisor at the organisation for LGBTQI rights was to keep in contact with the members of the sub-group that brought together newly arrived persons in Sweden and give them psychosocial support and advice regarding health, including HIV and other sexually transmitted diseases (ST, 2021, p 8). The role of migration advisor also included providing information about migrants' rights and obligations in Sweden and supporting them in their process of seeking asylum. This included informing the members of the sub-group about the migration process for LGBTQI persons, writing affidavits, and keeping in contact with the Swedish Migration Agency and the lawyers provided by the LBGTQI rights organisation (ST, 2021, p 8).

The victims in this case were at different stages of the asylum-seeking process. None of them had a residence permit in Sweden. The crimes that the migration advisor was prosecuted and sentenced for were all committed in his office at the organisation, under circumstances in which the victims were seeking his advice to help them in their migration process. The victims believed that the migration advisor in his position 'had a decisive influence over their asylum-seeking process' (ST, 2021, p 60). In the judgment, one of the victims is quoted as stating that: '[He] thought that [the accused] could speak for him at the Swedish Migration Agency so that the Swedish Migration Agency could reopen his case and re-examine his application for asylum which had previously been rejected' (ST, 2021, p 29).

Another victim is quoted as stating that he believed that it was in the migration advisor's power to 'call the police' and 'have him deported' (ST, 2021, p 18). This was not necessarily the case: the migration advisor had a position in a civil society organisation and had presumably no influence over any public authority decision. Part of his role was to write affidavits to the Swedish Migration Agency, a task, however, that other employees at the LBGTQI rights organisation could also have done (ST, 2021, p 43).

Thus, all victims believed that the migration advisor had extensive power over their asylum cases, and more power than he actually had. They also expressed great fear of the migration advisor, and were afraid of the consequences if they did not comply with what he required them to do. Given the circumstances, the District Court argued that the victims had good reason to believe so, and the fact that his actual powers were more limited was not considered relevant when evaluating the migration advisor's responsibility for his acts.

The migration advisor made the four men perform different sexual acts in his office, either alone with him or in some cases with one of the other victims present. The door was locked in some situations, but only closed in others. In none of these situations did the sexual abuse involve physical violence or explicit threats. However, it was clear that the victims believed that having sex with the migration advisor was a prerequisite for receiving his help:

> When [the accused] was on his knees he [the victim] thought that [the accused] would never help him if he refused to have sex with [the accused]. He then decided that he would agree to have sex if [the accused] demanded this because he needed help from [the accused] and thought that he needed to give something in order to receive help. (ST, 2021, p 30)

> [The accused] had taken him by surprise with sexual advances and there and then he felt that he could not deny [the accused] sex because if he did, he would risk not getting help and/or that [the accused] would call the police and tell them that he was an undocumented immigrant. (ST, 2021, p 24)

The District Court quotes a witness as stating that the demands from the migration advisor were common among the members of this sub-group in the LBGTQI rights organisation.

> He [the victim] told [the witness] what had happened when he came out [of the office], and [the witness] then said that it was common that [the accused] did that and that 'he is doing this to everyone, not just you, I am sure he is doing this to everyone'. (ST, 2021, p 29)

Thus, the migration advisor gave the victims the impression that he could determine the results of their asylum processes. Physical force was unnecessary; the victims were terrified, as they believed their future was in his hands. He exploited their fear and abused his position of power by implying that his help was conditional on sexual favours.

In the judgment, the District Court connects the particularly vulnerable situation of the victims with the position of the migration advisor, and states that his acts constituted undue exploitation of their situation.

> According to the District Court, it has been proved that the plaintiffs had little or no possibility to preserve their sexual integrity because they were lacking knowledge of Swedish, did not have residence permits in Sweden, and believed that [the accused] had a decisive influence over their asylum-seeking process, and [the accused] has abused both his position as a migration advisor and the fears of the plaintiffs. (ST, 2021, p 60)

The Norwegian case

In the Norwegian case, the former county governor was charged with and convicted of abuse of a position of power, and abuse of a relationship of dependency or trust to obtain sexual favours from three victims. His position as county governor was a key element in the prosecutor's argument and in the ensuing judgment (NTT, 2019, p 36).

Importantly, the position as county governor gave him access to his victims in the first place:

> In his capacity [as county governor], [the accused] sought out [the victim] at institutions under the county governor's supervision and could bring [the victim] on trips to *inter alia* his cottage and his home. (NTT, 2019, p 2)

His position as county governor also allowed him to make his victims believe he had the power to grant them jobs, housing, and even residence permits. Regarding one of the accusations, the District Court argued that: 'As a former county governor and central politician, he deceived [the victim] into believing that, through his position, he could help [the victim] with housing as well as obtaining a permanent residence permit in Norway' (NTT, 2019, p 3).

One of the victims stated in court that the former county governor had said that 'he could help him with everything, and that he did not have to worry about anything in Norway' (NTT, 2019, p 17). He had also said that 'he knew a number of important people including the King, the Chief of Police in Oslo and [the County], and people at the UDI [Norwegian Directorate of Immigration] that were responsible for his asylum case' (NTT, 2019, p 17).

Similarly to the Swedish case, the former county governor exploited his position of power and the victims' vulnerable position by making his victims believe he had more power than he really had. In the Norwegian case, the District Court emphasised this. In the judgment, the Court pointed out that the former county governor made his victims believe he had the power to decide or influence whether they got to stay in the country or not. The Court then argued that the fact that he did not actually have that power and authority: 'has no significance in this context as long as the victim had been convinced that this was the situation. The defendant understood that the victim believed that he had the power to, among other things, influence [the victim's] residence permit, and used this consciously to obtain sexual intercourse' (NTT, 2019, p 18).

One of the victims received Norwegian citizenship in a ceremony led by the former county governor in 2009: '[The accused] had delivered Norwegian citizenship to [the victim] in a ceremonious capacity and deceived [the victim] into believing that he had the power and authority to give and deprive him of his citizenship' (NTT, 2019, p 2).

The case of this victim is particularly illustrative. The former county governor first met the victim thanks to the access he had to the institution where the victim was placed, then by virtue of his position as county governor at a ceremony where the victim was awarded his citizenship. When they met again some years later, he used his position of power to exploit the victim sexually. The judgment states: 'The accused has deliberately exploited his position to obtain sexual intercourse. He knew that the offended party thought that he, as the county governor, was able to revoke his citizenship, and he knew that this was the reason he obtained sexual intercourse' (NTT, 2019, p 34).

The nature of the sexual exploitation varied and only one of the victims referred to physical violence (NTT, 2019, p 13). The former county governor mainly used psychological coercion, taking advantage of the vulnerable position of the victims, which was referred to by the District Court as 'psychological influence' that he used to 'deceive' the three victims (NTT, 2019, p 18).

In connection with his sexual advances, the former county governor would always ask about the residency situation of his victims and mention that he had powerful friends and acquaintances. The District Court concluded that this 'conduct and procedure' was used in relation to all three victims (NTT, 2019, pp 23, 31). The pattern of this conduct and procedure was systematic, which according to the Court added to the 'cynical and serious' nature of the exploitation (NTT, 2019, p 36). The District Court concluded: 'The defendant's actions were characterised by building trust with the complainant through showing care and interest in their challenging situation, to then exploit that trust for his own sexual gratification' (NTT, 2019, p 36).

Victims and vulnerability: quid pro quo

Previous research shows that the combination of fear and shame that is often experienced by victims of sextortion means that most cases of sextortion pass unreported and remain unknown (Eldén et al, 2020, p 11). In the cases presented in this chapter, the victims had 'fear of deportation' (NTT, 2019, p 40), fear that if they did not comply, they would not receive the help they needed, and 'felt strong concern about reporting' (ST, 2021, p 38). Also, they expressed strong 'feelings of shame' (NTT, 2019, p 23; ST, 2021, pp 38, 79).

Fear and shame are key aspects of all forms of sexual harassment, violence and abuse. In cases of sextortion, however, the quid pro quo aspect adds to the fear and shame, as it may be used to frame the sexual acts as consensual. This has the effect of portraying the victim as 'complicit' and thus legitimises the sexual favours obtained (Bjarnegård et al, 2022). This, in turn, can add to the difficulty of the victim coming forward and reporting sextortion (Eldén et al, 2020). Therefore, the quid pro quo aspect of sextortion can be understood as a risk-reducing strategy on the part of the perpetrator. By portraying the victim as 'complicit', and by using offers of quid pro quo in lieu of physical coercion, the risk of being reported is minimised for the perpetrator (Eldén et al, 2020).

The Swedish case

In its internal policy, the national organisation for LBGTQI rights acknowledged that many of the members of the sub-group for newly arrived members were in a particularly vulnerable situation. The people working with the sub-group of the organisation were not all employees; many were volunteers. The volunteers had to sign an undertaking where they 'promised not to initiate sexual relations with the members, since [the organisation] considered that there was a pressing risk of undue exploitation due to the desperate situation that most of the members were in' (ST, 2021, p 23). At the time when the crimes were committed, this undertaking did not apply to employees of the organisation – a fact used by the defence in the Court of Appeal (SH, 2021, p 4). However, this undertaking clearly illustrates an awareness on the part of the organisation of the potentially vulnerable situation of the members of this sub-group.

The District Court made a point of stating that the members of the sub-group for newly arrived members were not vulnerable per se: that it could not be argued that 'the group "migrants", "refugees", and "asylum seekers" are by default in a particularly vulnerable situation and therefore can never be said to consent to sexual acts' (ST, 2021, p 11). In the case of the four victims in this case, however, the District Court argues that their situation when the migration advisor raped and sexually molested them was just that: a particularly vulnerable situation. The court refers to their situation as a whole, which they argue should be the basis of the assessment (ST, 2021, p 57): '[They] lacked knowledge of Swedish, they did not have residence permits in Sweden, they believed that [the accused] had a decisive influence over their asylum processes, and [the accused] abused his position as a migration advisor and exploited the fear of the complainants.' (ST, 2021, p 60).

Therefore, the District Court concludes, the victims had 'little or no possibility to protect their sexual integrity' (ST, 2021, p 60). Moreover, the District Court stated that the migration advisor was fully aware that the victims were not consenting to the sexual acts:

> Apart from the general knowledge and insights that [the accused] had about the vulnerability of [the victim], the District Court's assessment is that [the accused] more or less made a habit of having sex with [the

victim] when he sought his help and advice. Therefore, the District Court's assessment is that [the accused] knew that [the victim] did not participate in these acts voluntarily. (ST, 2021, p 58)

The District Court's judgment refers to several witnesses from different professions (psychotherapists, counsellors, and so on) who stated that the victims had feelings of shame about the abuse and feared reporting it:

[The victim] was feeling very bad, had difficulty talking about the abuse. After the first visit, [the victim] had not reported it to the police and was very concerned about reporting. He [the psychotherapist] recalls [the victim] as frightened, depressed and that he had lost hope. ... He [the psychotherapist] remembers that [the victim] had a strong feeling of disappointment ... [the victim] had difficulties sharing his story and he felt shame. (ST, 2021, p 38)

Witnesses and the lawyers testified that the victims felt 'fear of being assaulted again in similar situations' and had 'feelings of shame due to the crime' (ST, 2021, p 79), and felt 'shame and anxiety' when talking about what had happened (ST, 2021, p 19). The fear that was already strong before the sexual abuse seems to have increased in the wake of these acts.

The Norwegian case

In the Norwegian case, the vulnerable situation of the victims is key in the reasoning presented by the District Court. In the case of one of the victims, the Court points out that the former county governor 'took advantage of [the victim]'s position as a particularly vulnerable young, unaccompanied asylum seeker who lacked resources' for his 'own sexual purposes' (NTT, 2019, p 3).

Another of the victims had problems related to his mental health (NTT, 2019, p 20) and was in a particularly desperate situation when he met the former county governor in 2014:

[The victim] had no permanent job, had inadequate living conditions, and no permanent residence permit in Norway. ... In this situation, he would do anything to obtain a permanent residence and a dignified life in Norway, so much so that he was brought into an abusive situation with an older man who exploited the deception of the complainant: that the accused *inter alia* could facilitate residence in the country. (NTT, 2019, pp 25–6)

In examining whether the accused had abused the vulnerable situation of the victims, the District Court concluded that:

The accused has exploited and deceived persons who lacked resources and who were in a vulnerable situation into engaging in sexual intercourse by making them believe that he had *inter alia* the power and authority to influence their right to residency in Norway. There was a significant power relationship between the accused and the victims, and there was nothing in their relationship that can explain the sexual intercourse independently of the power relationship and the deception on the part of the accused. (NTT, 2019, p 5)

Also important in this context is that the Court clearly establishes that real consent cannot exist when the perpetrator exploits the vulnerable situation of the victim:

it is not relevant in this case whether the victim did or did not resist engaging in sexual intercourse, or whether violence, coercion or the like was used. There is no real consent when the element of exploitation in the case of abuse of a vulnerable situation is satisfied. (NTT, 2019, p 19)

All three victims of the former county governor's abuse expressed fear and feelings of shame: fear of losing the right to stay in the country, but also fear of others finding out about the sexual abuse, such as their families and communities. The District Court refers to the reports from a psychologist who attended one of the victims:

The victim has told [the psychologist] about the exploitation and the background for why he let it happen, and why he did not manage to put a stop to it. He has shared the feeling of being in debt, of having 'promised himself' to a man of high status who could offer him benefits, but the status could also be used against him if he did not comply, and he was bitter about not putting a stop to it before. (NTT, 2019, p 16)

Thus, it is clearly stated in the judgment that the former county governor acted knowingly and intentionally when creating a 'fear of deportation' to obtain sexual favours (NTT, 2019, p 40). The victims also expressed fear that their community would find out what had happened, and all the victims had feelings of shame and guilt about the sexual abuse.

Consent or abuse of power?

In both the Swedish and Norwegian cases, the perpetrators abused their position of entrusted power to obtain sex from their victims. In both cases, sexual acts were obtained by making promises of benefits or making the victims believe that they would receive these benefits (help with an asylum process, a job, residence permit, and so on) in exchange for sex, or that these benefits would be denied them if they did not agree to sex. The presentation of the judgments here shows that it was not necessarily relevant whether the perpetrator had the actual power to provide these services or benefits. The important point is that the perpetrators made the victims believe – and that the victims had reason to believe – that the perpetrators held the power to decide or facilitate the victims' migration processes.

As previously discussed, the District Courts in both Sweden and Norway recognise many of the aspects embedded in sextortion. The judgments from both District Courts take into consideration the abuse of an entrusted position and power, and illustrate how the combination of a power imbalance, dependency, and shame, fear and stigma for the victims enable improper exploitation of their particularly vulnerable situation. This was done by utilising the available legal frameworks for rape and sexual molestation in the Swedish case; and abuse of position, dependency and trust in the Norwegian case.

Does this mean that, in a Nordic context, there are already sufficient tools available to recognise the specificities of sextortion? Is it possible to avoid impunity for perpetrators in cases that combine corruption (abuse of power and quid pro quo) and sexual violence? In order to answer these questions, we now turn to the judgment from the Swedish Court of Appeal in the Swedish case, and then connect our discussion to a feminist theoretical discussion that problematises consent.

Shifting responsibility from perpetrator to victims

While the Swedish District Court argued that the victims were in a particularly vulnerable situation in relation to the migration advisor, and that the sexual acts thus constituted 'improper exploitation of a person in such a situation', the Court of Appeal handled the case differently. In their judgment, the Court of Appeal stated that they agreed when the District Court argued that all the victims had been in a difficult situation when they had turned to the organisation for LBGTQI rights and the migration advisor. The Court of Appeal also agreed that all the victims 'believed among other things that they would risk not receiving help and advice if they did not participate in the sexual acts' (SH, 2021, p 7) and that the circumstances had placed the victims in a 'somewhat disadvantaged position' and under 'some pressure' (SH, 2021, p 8). However, the Court of Appeal argued that the course of events was not so sudden that the victims were not able to comprehend what was going on and make a decision in order to avoid being exploited, nor were they in an inferior position in relation to the migration advisor due to their age or physical appearance (SH, 2021, p 8). The Court of Appeal concluded that:

> Even if we consider the fear of the complainants and how they perceived the risks if they did not agree to be involved in the sexual acts, there is insufficient evidence to support the conclusion that the circumstances implied that any of them had very limited possibilities to protect themselves from exploitation. (SH, 2021, p 8)

Importantly, the new Swedish sexual offences legislation which focuses on consent (Govt Bill, 2017/18) stipulates specific conditions under which a person is not considered capable of consenting to sex. These conditions include fear or coercion through gross abuse of their position of dependence (Gunnarsson, 2020, pp 13f). In such cases, a sexual act will be considered rape and not consensual, as it is argued in the District Court's conclusions in the Swedish case. The Court of Appeal, however, concluded that the victims had not been in a particularly vulnerable situation and the migration advisor should not be sentenced for improper exploitation of a person in such a situation. Since the Court of Appeal could not rule out that the victims were voluntarily involved in the sexual acts, the Court instead examined whether or not they consented to the sexual acts (SH, 2021, p 8).

In this case, the Swedish Court of Appeal did not consider the context and the situation of the victims in relation to the perpetrator, but instead focused on the acts of the victims in relation to potential consent. As a consequence, the perpetrator's liability for abusing his position of power disappears from the picture.

The Court of Appeal found that on three of the indictments, the migration advisor was still guilty of rape, arguing that it was clear that the victims did not consent to have sex. In coming to this conclusion, the Court of Appeal focused on the details of the situation: the unexpectedness and suddenness that was proposed to have made it difficult for the victims to refuse, and their passiveness during the sexual act (SH, 2021, pp 10f, 12, 16).

On the other two charges of rape, the migration advisor was acquitted. The Court of Appeal does not doubt that the victims did not want to have sex with the migration advisor and states that they were 'uncomfortable' in the situation and badly affected psychologically because of the act (SH, 2021, pp 14, 18). Nevertheless, the Court of Appeal argued that the victims were actively involved by not resisting the sexual act but instead enabling the rape. In both these acquittals, the Court of Appeal referred to the fact that the victims needed the migration advisor's help with their migration cases.

> The fact that he unbuttoned his trousers and got to his feet to let [the accused] undress him should be considered voluntary participation to some extent. Moreover, it appears from [the victim's] own account that he chose to accept sexual acts with [the accused] for the purpose of receiving his help in contacts with the Migration Agency ... The

Court of Appeal finds credible [the victim's] declaration that his motive for participating was to receive help from [the accused] and that the incident made him feel very bad afterwards. (SH, 2021, p 18)

From his account, it has become clear that his acts were a result of his decision to accept being involved in sexual acts with [the accused]. Under these circumstances, the Court of Appeal finds that according to the law nothing else is shown than that the acts of [the victim] should be regarded as consensual. (SH, 2021, p 14)

In the judgment from the Court of Appeal, the abuse of power is completely absent from the Court's reasoning. As the Court of Appeal did not consider the victims to be in a 'particularly vulnerable situation', it embarked on a discussion of potential consent, and how the perpetrator might have interpreted signs that potentially communicated consent. The context, situation, and position of dependence of the victims was erased, and through this, the power relationship between the perpetrator and the victim was made irrelevant. Instead, the Court's reasoning turns to the details in the specific situations, such as the suddenness of the situation, if the victims had time to leave the room, if they were 'helpful' in unbuttoning their trousers, and so on. The focus of the reasoning in judgment is on the acts of the victims, not the criminal liability of the perpetrator.

'Coerced consent'

The Swedish sexual offences legislation does not stipulate what an expression of consent entails; this is up to the Court to determine (Wallin et al, 2021). The District Court in the Swedish case decided to take into consideration the situation as a whole – including the power imbalance and relationship of dependence – while the Court of Appeal took into account only the details in the situation and what could be assumed about the victims' intentions. Although the Court of Appeal in the Swedish case acknowledges that the victims did not want to have sex with the perpetrator, that they were physically uncomfortable during the act, and were badly affected psychologically afterwards, the Court argued that they still could be considered to have consented to the sexual acts because they were depending on help from the perpetrator.

A broad body of literature problematises the concept of 'free consent', arguing that consent is always 'saturated with normative ideas and power relations' (Linander et al, 2021, p 112). Many scholars argue that laws which focus on consent, such as the new Swedish sexual offences legislation, do not necessarily address these complexities, and 'there is a need to consider the role of power and gendered discourses in shaping consent' (Linander et al, 2021, p 110).

Within a framework of consent, it is presumed that consent is expressed through communication between the parties involved in a sexual encounter (Gunnarsson, 2020, pp 16ff, see also Wallin et al, 2021). However, it is also argued that people may 'consent' ('say yes') while 'lacking desire or willingness because they are exposed to interpersonal forms of power, ranging from violence and clear violations of consent' (Linander et al, 2021, p 121; see also Gunnarsson, 2020, p 20f). Consent understood as communication between autonomous subjects risks missing the importance and complexity of the gendered power relations underlying sexual relations (Gavey, 2013; Linander et al, 2021). Whether 'saying yes' can be translated as consent in situations of coercion or threat is also questionable (Beres, 2010; Linander et al, 2021).

When defining sexual violence, the Civil Society Declaration on Sexual Violence states that one of the factors that is relevant to take into consideration when determining 'whether an act of a sexual nature was committed without genuine, voluntary, specific and ongoing consent' is the existence of an unequal power relationship, including the perpetrator being 'a person in a position of authority' or the victim 'having any type of dependency on the perpetrator' (The Hague Principles on Sexual Violence, 2020, p 11). The International Association of Women Judges (IAWJ) argues that there are situations 'in which the disparity in power is so great that the "consent" is, in fact, coerced and not true or meaningful consent' (IAWJ, 2012, p 15). IAWJ therefore uses the term 'coerced consent' in their definition of sextortion to capture, for example, psychological coercion, threats, or abuse of authority 'that would invalidate a sextortion victim's apparent "consent" to the sexual conduct' (IAWJ, 2012, p 15). Similarly, Gitlin argues that 'legal consent cannot exist in contexts where the power imbalances are extreme', and that therefore, 'all cases involving a sexual quid pro quo should be deemed per se coercive' (Gitlin, 2016).

In the cases of sextortion discussed in this chapter, the quid pro quo took place in the context of an extreme power imbalance in which the victims were in a position of dependence, in need of the favours or services of the perpetrator (for example, help with asylum processes, jobs, and/or residence permits). In these cases, the sexual acts are a condition for access to such favours or services, and could hence be deemed 'coerced consent'.

Liability for abuse of power

The Court of Appeal in the Swedish case could be said to have used a 'reverse sextortion logic': *because* the victims needed the help of the perpetrator, they effectively consented to the sexual acts. The Court of Appeal thus portrays the victims as 'complicit' which legitimises the sexual acts – a logic that, as we argued earlier in the section 'Victims and vulnerability', contributes to impunity for the perpetrator.

Our argument is that it is precisely the extreme power imbalance, together with the victims' need for the benefit or service offered as a quid pro quo, that reinforces a relationship of dependence between victim and perpetrator, and therefore invalidates any meaningful form of consent.

This insistence on focusing on liability for the abuse of power is the main contribution of an analytical framework of sextortion. Liability in cases of sextortion always lies with the actor who abuses their entrusted power for personal gain.

As illustrated, the argument in the judgment from the Swedish Court of Appeal differed strikingly from that of the District Courts in both the Swedish and Norwegian cases, which presented reasoning that focused on the abuse of power, abuse of an entrusted position, and hence made it possible to hold the perpetrators to account for improper exploitation of the particularly vulnerable situation of the victims. The Court of Appeal instead focused on the acts of the victims, and whether these might have been interpreted by the perpetrator as expressions of consent.

Therefore, there are evidently ways to prosecute sextortion – that is, violence/harassment that includes the abuse of power and quid pro quo elements – within the framework of sexual offences legislation *without* losing sight of power imbalances and improper exploitation of a type of dependency. Still, there are obvious risks when applying a logic of consent, for instance by redirecting focus from the liability of the perpetrator for their abuse of power to the actions and intentions of the victims, even using their position of dependence as an argument for consent.

Nordic self-image and sextortion

The migration advisor and the former county governor sexually exploited their victims for a long period of time before action was taken against them. To varying degrees, people around them knew of or suspected the sexual abuse while they continued to abuse the victims. Their formal positions gave them access to the victims. We can only speculate on whether or not acknowledging the abuse of power – instead of focusing on the gravity of the sexual offence, or evidence of the sexual offences committed – prevented these cases from being brought to court sooner.

But did the perpetrators' positions as an employee of a civil society organisation working with discrimination and human rights (the organisation for LBGTQI rights) and as a representative appointed by the Norwegian government (county governor), along with their well-known engagement with the plight of immigrants, also prevent the disclosure of their abuse? Did the Swedish and Norwegian societies' views and expectations of persons in these positions possibly add to the invisibility of and impunity for their crimes?

To try to answer these questions and further develop our arguments in this chapter, we will conclude by turning to a critical strand of scholarly work that challenges a Nordic self-image characterised by 'exceptionalism'. This strand examines underlying 'notions of the Nordic countries as global "good citizens", peace-loving, conflict-resolution orientated and "rational"' (Loftsdóttir and Jensen, 2012, p 2, making references to DeLong, 2009, pp 368–9 and Browning, 2007, pp 27–8), and as progressive 'human rights champions' (McEachrane, 2014).

Corruption plays an important, but often implicit, part in imaginaries of Nordic exceptionalism. From an international perspective, social trust is very high in the Nordic countries and has been referred to as 'the Nordic gold' because it tends to extend to trust in public authorities and to low levels of corruption (Andreasson, 2017). The Nordic countries consistently end up at the top of international rankings of non-corrupt countries (see, for example, Bergh et al, 2016). Many of these rankings, however, use a narrow conceptualisation of corruption, and critical voices have been raised claiming that the self-image of Nordic countries as non-corrupt can be dangerous and lead to complacency (see, for example, Forsberg, 2019; Wahlberg, 2021). A recent report by Transparency International found that when broader conceptualisations of corruption are used, the picture painted is somewhat different. While only one per cent of Swedes have paid bribes, 20 per cent have used personal connections to gain different types of benefits (Transparency International, 2021). Thus, if the abuse of entrusted power for private gain is at the centre of the analysis, this Nordic self-image may, at least in part, be questioned. This image of exceptionalism is grounded primarily in the idea that the country is a 'moral superpower' in a number of different areas (Jansson, 2018, p 86; see also Loftsdóttir and Jensen, 2012, p 2), which 'makes it harder to deal with various problems that directly impinge upon democracy' such as corruption (Jansson, 2018, p 90; see also Bergh et al, 2016).

Gender equality also plays a very specific role in the Nordic self-image of 'exceptionalism'. Recent research on nation-branding in the Nordic countries shows that gender equality is 'essential to the self-understandings of the Nordic countries, serving as a source of pride and national identity' (Larsen et al, 2021, p 2; see also de los Reyes and Mulinari, 2005), and is also referred to as 'gender exceptionalism' (Larsen et al, 2021, p 2). The idea of gender equality as a Nordic or national trait has also become central in racist hierarchisations through being ' "implicated in a new inequality": the hierarchical categorisation of "Swedes" and "immigrants"' (Towns, 2002, p 157).

Gendered violence is central in imaginaries that connect gender equality to national pride or ideas of exceptionalism. In both the Swedish and

Norwegian cases, decades of research have shown that gendered violence in general, and sexual violence in particular, challenge the national self-images of the Nordic countries as havens of gender equality (see, for example: Jeffner, 1997; Larsen et al, 2021; Skilbrei, 2021). Sexual violence is used by right-wing extremists to make 'rape a matter of national identity and protection' (Skilbrei, 2021, p 79). Research about honour-based violence from Sweden, Norway, Denmark and Finland has shown that this form of gendered violence is used to create a contrast between a gender-equal 'us' and a violent 'them' (see, for example: Eldén, 2003; Bredal, 2014; Lund-Liebmann, 2015; Keskinen, 2012).

A Nordic self-image characterised by ideas of exceptionalism, centring gender equality and protection against sexual violence, is thus clearly implicated in processes of othering. Violence – specifically sexual violence – is attributed to 'others' that are excluded from national belonging. This, in turn, makes it difficult to acknowledge, let alone work against, violence. It prevents an understanding of (sexual) violence as an extensive and fundamental problem that permeates all spheres of society in the Nordic countries, and makes it difficult to acknowledge underlying cultural patterns and social and legal structures that legitimise rather than protect from or prevent sexual violence.

Conclusion

In this chapter, we have shown how the Court of Appeal in the Swedish case did not recognise that the victims had been in a 'particularly vulnerable situation', and therefore discussed the extent to which the victims could be said to have consented to the sexual acts. Even though the Court acknowledged that the victims did not wish to have sex with the perpetrator, in the judgment it was argued that the victims had still 'consented' since they needed the help of the perpetrator in their individual migration cases. When understood in terms of a logic of consent, and centring the actions and intentions of the victims, the Court of Appeal in the Swedish case lost sight of the context, power imbalance and dependency characterising the situations.

We argue that an analytical framework of sextortion prevents a shift in focus from the actions of the perpetrator to the actions of the victim. By recognising the corruption aspects of the sexual violence in these cases (the abuse of power and quid pro quo elements), liability is instead placed on the perpetrator: the one who abuses a position of power. Applying a framework of sextortion, the question of consent becomes irrelevant, since the focus is on the abuse of the power of the perpetrator.

In the two cases of sextortion discussed in this chapter, the specific conditions of the migration process, and the vulnerability and fear engendered by the insecure migration status of some of the victims, created an extreme power imbalance and relationships of dependence that enabled the abuse of power and sexual exploitation.

In addition, we argue that a Nordic self-image characterised by exceptionalism regarding both sexual violence and corruption makes it harder to acknowledge abuse of power within legal structures that are presumably designed to protect victims and prosecute perpetrators of sexual violence.

Moreover, the perpetrators in the two cases discussed in this chapter held positions that not only entailed entrusted power in general, but also made them 'good Nordic men': positions from which they worked against discrimination, for human rights, and engaged with the plight of immigrants belonging to a particularly vulnerable group. Through their formal and informal positions in these Nordic societies characterised by a self-image that actively 'others' sexual violence, they became unlikely as perpetrators (compare: Jeffner, 1997; Livholts, 2007). Thus, the Nordic self-image of exceptionalism in this sense protects perpetrators that operate from the centre of national belonging, contributing to the invisibility of and impunity for their crimes.

To sum up, we argue that the broader self-image of Nordic exceptionalism – including ideas of gender equality, protection from sexual violence, and an anti-corruption culture – helps to obscure rather than expose conditions that enable the abuse of power, and hence contributes to impunity for perpetrators. Our suggested framework of sextortion has great implications for the rather forced reasoning by the Court of Appeal in the Swedish case that it was in the victims' 'self-interest' to have sex with the perpetrator since they needed his help. With this 'reverse sextortion logic', the victims' position of dependence was used to argue that they effectively 'consented' to the sexual acts and that these acts could therefore not be considered rape. A framework of sextortion instead insists on centring abuse of power and thus the responsibility of the perpetrator for abusing their position of power – not the potential consent of victims of exploitation.

Notes

[1] The term sextortion was coined by the International Association for Women Judges (IAWJ) in 2008 (IAWJ, 2012). The conceptualisation of sextortion that we build on in this chapter was developed in the report *Sextortion: Corruption and Gender Based Violence* (Eldén et al, 2020). We want to acknowledge the important contributions of our report's co-author Sofia Jonsson in this early work on sextortion.

[2] See, for example, https://www.transparency.org/en/what-is-corruption.

[3] The translations of quotes from the judgments from Swedish and Norwegian to English are ours.

[4] One of the victims in the Swedish case brought the case to the Supreme Court (Högsta Domstolen), but the appeal was denied.

5   We have not included references to the media debate (in the Norwegian case, also extensive international media coverage) due to considerations of maintaining anonymity. Nevertheless, analysing material about sexual violence raises a number of important ethical concerns. The confidentiality of victims is of the utmost importance, as well as recognising the dangers of revictimisation or sensationalism (Jewkes et al, 2012). However, there are also risks associated with silencing experiences of sexual violence (Ellsberg and Heise, 2002). Against this background, we analysed quotes from the judgments, but have made an effort to exclude details of the acts of violence.

References

Amnesty International (2016) 'Female refugees face physical assault, exploitation and sexual harassment on their journey through Europe' [online]. Available from: https://www.amnesty.org/en/latest/news/2016/01/female-refugees-face-physical-assault-exploitation-and-sexual-harassment-on-their-journey-through-europe/ [Accessed 18 January 2022].

Andreasson, U. (2017) *Trust – The Nordic Gold*, Nordic Council of Ministers, Analysis Report.

Beres, M.A. (2010) 'Sexual miscommunication? Untangling assumptions about sexual communication between casual sex partners', *Culture, Health & Sexuality*, 12(1): 1–14.

Bergh, A., Erlingsson, G., Sjölin, M. and Öhrvall, R. (2016) *A Clean House? Studies of Corruption in Sweden*, Lund: Nordic Academic Press.

Bjarnegård, E., Calvo, D., Eldén, Å. and Lundgren, S. (2022) 'Sextortion: Corruption shaped by gender norms', in I. Kubbe and O. Merkle (eds) *Corruption and Gender: The Role of Norms*, Cheltenham: Edward Elgar Publishing.

Bredal, A. (2014) 'Ordinary v. other violence? Conceptualising honour-based violence in Scandinavian public policies', in A.K. Gill, C. Strange and K. Roberts (eds) *'Honour' Killing and Violence. Theory, Policy and Practice*, New York: Palgrave Macmillan.

Browning, C. (2007) 'Branding Nordicity. Models, identity and the decline of exceptionalism', *Cooperation and Conflict*, 42(1): 27–51.

Chêne, M. (2009) 'Gender, corruption and education' [pdf], *Transparency International/U4*. Available from: https://www.u4.no/publications/gender-corruption-and-education.pdf [Accessed 18 January 2022].

de los Reyes, P. and Mulinari, D. (2005) *Intersektionalitet: kritiska reflektioner över (o)jämlikhetens landskap*, Malmö: Liber.

DeLong, R.D. (2009) 'Danish military involvement in the invasion of Iraq in light of the Scandinavian international relations', *Scandinavian Studies*, 81(3): 367–80.

Eldén, Å. (2003) *Heder på liv och död: Våldsamma berättelser om rykten, oskuld och heder*, Uppsala: Acta Universitatis Upsaliensis.

Eldén, Å., Calvo, D., Bjarnegård, E., Lundgren, S. and Jonsson, S. (2020) *Sextortion: Corruption and Gender-Based Violence*, Report for the Expert Group for Aid Studies (EBA) 2020: 06, Sweden.

Ellsberg, M. and Heise, L. (2002) 'Bearing witness: Ethics in domestic violence research', *Lancet*, 359(9317): 1599–604.

Feigenblatt, H. (2020) *Breaking the Silence around Sextortion. The Links between Power, Sex and Corruption*, Berlin, Germany: Transparency International.

Forsberg, B. (2019) 'Svenskars självbild stämmer inte med verkligheten', *Svenska Dagbladet* [online], 20 April. Available from: https://www.svd.se/svenskars-sjalvbild-stammer-inte-med-verkligheten [Accessed 10 October 2021].

Gavey, N. (2013) *Just Sex? The Cultural Scaffolding of Rape*, London: Routledge.

Gitlin, S. (2016) 'Sextortion victims are not guilty of bribery', *The Global Anti-corruption Blog: Law, Social Science, and Policy* [blog]. Available from: https://globalanticorruptionblog.com/2016/07/22/sextortion-victims-are-not-guilty-of-bribery/ [Accessed 28 September 2021].

Govt Bill (2017/18) (177) *En ny sexualbrottslagstiftning byggd på frivillighet*, Stockholm: Justitiedepartementet.

Gunnarsson, L. (2020) *Samtyckesdynamiker: Sex, våldtäkt och gråzonen däremellan*, Lund: Studentlitteratur AB.

IAWJ (International Association of Women Judges) (2012) *Stopping the Abuse of Power through Sexual Exploitation. Naming, Shaming and Ending Sextortion. A Tool Kit*, Washington: IAWJ.

IBA (International Bar Association)/Sara Carnegie (2019) *Sextortion. A Crime of Corruption and Sexual Exploitation* , London: IBA.

Jansson, D. (2018) 'Deadly exceptionalisms, or, Would you rather be crushed by a moral superpower or a military superpower?', *Political Geography*, 64: 83–91.

Jeffner, S. (1997) *Liksom våldtäkt, typ*, Uppsala: Acta Universitatis Upsaliensis.

Jewkes, R., Dartnall, E. and Sikweyiya, Y. (2012) *Ethical and Safety Recommendations for Research on Perpetration of Sexual Violence*, Pretoria, South Africa: Sexual Violence Research Initiative, Medical Research Council.

Keskinen, S. (2012) 'Transnational influences, gender equality and violence in Muslim families', in K. Loftsdóttir and L. Jensen (eds) *Whiteness and Postcolonialism in the Nordic Region. Exceptionalism, Migrant Others and National Identities*, London: Routledge.

Larsen, E., Moss, S.M. and Skjelsbæk, I. (eds) (2021) *Gender Equality and Nation Branding in the Nordic Region*, Routledge Studies in Gender and Global Politics, Abingdon, Oxon: Routledge.

Linander, I., Goicolea, I., Wiklund, M., Gotfredsen, A. and Strömbäck, M. (2021) 'Power and subjectivity: Making sense of sexual consent among adults living in Sweden', *Nordic Journal of Feminist and Gender Research*, 29(2): 110–23.

Livholts, M. (2007) *"Vanlig som vatten". Manlighet och normalitet i mediernas berättelser om våldtäkt*, Malmö: Gleerups.

Loftsdóttir, K. and Jensen, L. (201[2]) 'Introduction: Nordic exceptionalism and the Nordic "others"', in K. Loftsdóttir and L. Jensen (eds) *Whiteness and Postcolonialism in the Nordic Region. Exceptionalism, Migrant Others and National Identities*, London: Routledge.

Lundgren, S., Eldén, Å. and Jonsson, S. (2020) 'Metoo as sextortion: Approaching testimonies from metoo through a corruption lens', *Long-term Global Perspectives on Preventing Sexual Harassment in the Workplace: Policy and Practice*, International Conference at The Museum of Work, Norrköping, Sweden 8–10 March 2020.

Lund-Liebmann, L. (2015) 'Æresrelateret vold: en gen-anvendelig selvfortælling', *Tidskrift for kjønnsforskning*, 1(39): 39–59.

McEachrane, M. (ed) (2014) *Afro-Nordic Landscapes: Equality and Race in Northern Europe*, New York: Routledge.

Merkle, O., Reinold, J. and Siegel, M. (2017) 'A gender perspective on corruption encountered during forced and irregular migration', *Deutsche Gesellschaft für Internationale Zusammenarbeit (GIZ) GmbH* [online]. Available from: https://www.giz.de/de/downloads/giz2017_eng_Gender-pers pective-on-corruption-encountered-during-migration.pdf [Accessed 26 September 2021].

NTT (Nord-Troms Ting[]rett) (2019) DOM 18-194021MED-NHER.

SH (Svea hovrätt) (2021) Dom 2021-07-16. Mål nr B 5848-21.

Skilbrei, M. (2021) 'Keeping Sweden on top: Rape and legal innovation as nation-branding', in E. Larsen, S. Moss and I. Skjelsbæk (eds) *Gender Equality and Nation Branding in the Nordic Region*, Routledge Studies in Gender and Global Politics, Abingdon, Oxon: Routledge.

ST (Stockholms tingsrätt) (2021) Dom 2021-04-21. Mål nr B 5388-20.

The Hague Principles on Sexual Violence (2020) *Published by the Women's Initiative for Gender Justice* [online]. Available from: https://4genderjustice. org/test1/ [Accessed 26 September 2021].

Towns, A. (2002) 'Paradoxes of (in)equality: Something is rotten in the gender equal state of Sweden', *Cooperation and Conflict,* 37(2): 157–79.

Towns, A. (2015) 'Prestige, immunity and diplomats: Understanding sexual corruption', in C. Dahlström and L. Wängnerud (eds) *Elites, Institutions and the Quality of Government*, Basingstoke, Hampshire: Palgrave Macmillan, pp 49–65.

Transparency International (2016) 'Sextortion: Undermining gender equality' [online]. Available from: http://www.transparency.org/news/feat ure/sextortion_undermining_gender_equality [Accessed 18 January 2022].

Transparency International (2019a) *Global Corruption Barometer for Latin America and the Caribbean* [online]. Available from: https://www.transparency.org/files/content/pages/2019_GCB_LatinAmerica_Caribbean_Full_Report.pdf.

Transparency International (2019b) *Global Corruption Barometer for Middle East and North Africa 2019* [online]. Available from: https://www.transparency.org/files/content/pages/2019_GCB_MENA_Report_EN.pdf.

Transparency International (2021) 'Citizens' views of and experiences of corruption', *Global Corruption Barometer. European Union 2021* [online]. Available from: https://www.transparency.org/en/publications/gcb-european-union-2021 [Accessed 21 January 2022].

UNDP-Huairou Commission (2012) *Seeing Beyond the State: Grassroots Women's Perspectives on Corruption and Anti-corruption* [pdf], New York, USA: United Nations Development Programme. Available from: https://www.undp.org/content/dam/undp/library/Democratic%20Governance/Anti-corruption/Grassroots%20women%20and%20anti-corruption.pdf [Accessed 18 January 2022].

UNDP-SIWI Water Governance Facility (2017) *Women and Corruption in the Water Sector: Theories and Experiences from Johannesburg and Bogotá*, WGF Report No. 8. Stockholm: SIWI.

UNODC (United Nations Office on Drugs and Crime) (2020) *The Time is Now. Addressing the Gender Dimensions of Corruption,* Vienna, Austria: UN.

Wahlberg, S. (2021) 'Sverige har en väldigt naiv självbild när det gäller korruption', *Dagens Juridik [online]*, 17 September. Available from: https://www.dagensjuridik.se/nyheter/sverige-har-en-valdigt-naiv-sjalvbild-nar-det-galler-korruption [Accessed 10 October 2021].

Wallin, L., Uhnoo, S., Wettergren, Å. and Bladini, M. (2021) 'Capricious credibility – legal assessments of voluntariness in Swedish negligent rape judgements', *Nordic Journal of Criminology*, 22(1): 3–22.

Westerstrand, J. (2017) 'Kontextualiseringens svåra konst. Kunskap, kön och förbindelselinjer i en förundersökning om "hedersvåld"', *Sociologisk forskning*, 54(3): 209–32.

11

I have always thought a lot about the nature of violence: carceral feminism and sexual violence in the neoliberal state

Silas Aliki

Translated by Katherine Stuart

I have always thought a lot about the nature of violence.

As a child, I grew up in a military family. My father attended the Swedish Armed Forces School for Secondary Education in Uppsala, became a career officer and was very loyal to the Armed Forces. When I was six years old, we moved abroad. My father was taking up a foreign posting, and we were going to be away for just over two years – one year in Israel, and one year in Syria.

Before we left, I got to go with my father to buy a second-hand Audi that had air conditioning, an unusual feature in the 1990s. We were going to drive the car to Damascus; my parents had not travelled much in their lives and wanted to take the opportunity to see Europe.

When we left the ferry from the Greek port city of Piraeus, my father told me and my little brother that when we arrived in Lebanon, he was going to lock the doors to the car, because it could be dangerous for us to go out. He did not say why, but well inside the country I have a memory of us stopping on a gravel road, surrounded by a vast field. This was at the beginning of the 1990s, only a few years after the civil war. From inside the car, my father pointed out the red skull signs and explained that the road we were travelling on went through a minefield, left after the civil war. If I or my brother saw signs like this anywhere else, we were to stand still, and call out for help from an adult.

It was my first encounter with the type of state violence that war represents. As a child, it was difficult to understand that grassy fields could be death traps, but it was even more difficult to understand why someone had wanted to make them death traps in the first place.

Since I was a child, the question of violence and what it means has followed me, even staking out my political convictions and choice of profession. I have previously worked within the Swedish Armed Forces and the Swedish

Prison and Probation Service. Now my work with the state is as the opposite party in the majority of my cases – the state I previously served in uniform. This is not a contradiction, but my previous experiences, in parallel with the increasingly repressive times in which we live, has led me to a position where I do not see that I have any other choice than to stand on the side of the individual.

I have practised as a lawyer since 2016. I have my own firm, Folkets Advokatbyrå, which I founded after my degree. The firm represents asylum seekers, victims of crime, and people subject to preventive detention. I also work a lot with the messy administrative law that often affects transgender people and other minorities.

In my work, I see people being deprived of their dignity every day. 'Public power shall be exercised with respect for the equal worth of all and the liberty and dignity of the individual', says one of the introductory articles in our Instrument of Government, part of the four fundamental laws that make up Sweden's constitution (Regeringsformen, 1974, p 52). In reality, this is not the case.

Carceral feminism

'Rapists should not get a cent in damages.'

These words come from a well-known lawyer in Sweden, who often represents victims of crime in the role of counsel for the injured party and who seldom miss an opportunity to call herself the 'victim's lawyer' (Massi Fritz, 2021a). Representing people who have been victims of sex offences has made her known and celebrated in some feminist circles. In the name of feminism, her Instagram account shows hashtags such as #kvinnokraft, #upprättelse (female power, redress) and #ladyjustice side by side with demands for an increase in the number of expulsions of immigrants, and more and longer prison sentences.

The quote that begins this section comes from the title of an article in the evening newspaper *Expressen*, published in connection with a debate that raged in Sweden in the autumn of 2021 after a highly publicised case in which a boy, a minor, raped a woman in a particularly brutal way. The rape, which was described as torture-like, went on over several days, and the woman was deprived of her liberty in a cellar during this time. In the article a number of suggestions for preventing such acts are presented: higher damages paid to victims of crime and the right to legal counsel in all cases, but also the abolition of both reduced sentences for juveniles and of rights to compensation to those who have committed crimes, regardless of what they are being compensated for. Other suggestions in line with this repressive policy, sharing the same feminist discourse, are: that life imprisonment for all deaths by shooting should be a matter of course, that anonymity for witnesses should be introduced, and that 'expulsion is an obvious cause of action and should be accompanied by a re-entry ban for all time' (Massi Fritz, 2021b).

These suggestions would greatly increase the power of the state to punish individuals. For example, the link between scrapping the compensation paid to children wrongly detained by the state, and women, transgender persons and children being able to live safe and meaningful lives free of violence, is treated here as something self-evident despite there being few arguments to substantiate this link.

How did we end up in a situation where it is feminists who are arguing for tougher penalties, the removal of procedural safeguards for detainees, more expulsions, and the abolition of more lenient treatment of young offenders?

The rape case mentioned caused outrage in Sweden. The boy received compensation, but this was not actually related to him having committed an offence, but to something quite different, namely that he was shown to be a minor (a child under the law) at the time of his arrest. Sweden has rules governing the detention of children, and since the boy had been detained for longer than is permitted for children in Sweden, the compensation he received was high. However, it was lower than would otherwise have been the case, because, in its decision, the Office of the Chancellor of Justice wrote, 'the deprivation of liberty and verdict referred to particularly serious offences'.[1]

Even though the compensation he received was due to Sweden having locked up a child unlawfully, in the autumn of 2021, many people describing themselves as feminists exploited the case as a springboard to link defending the rights of certain women and children with arguing for more state repression.

Criminologist and feminist Nina Rung may serve to illustrate this drift. In April 2021, she said to *Aftonbladet* (another evening newspaper), referring to the issue of men's violence against women, that 'we must make sure that we increase the penalties' in order to prevent this violence (Emnéus Ekström and Cecilia Vaccari, 2021). The fact that her basic assumption – that there is a direct link between higher penalties and reduced intimate partner violence against women – is not critically interrogated at all by the interviewing journalist is a clear sign that the public conversation has changed.

People who argue in this way represent a movement that in previous writings I have chosen to call 'prison feminism' in Swedish (Aliki, 2019). It relates to the term 'carceral feminism' that was coined by sociology professor, Elizabeth Bernstein. In *The Sexual Politics of the 'New Abolitionism'*, she describes carceral feminism as feminist advocacy for 'a law and order agenda and … a drift from the welfare state to the carceral state as the enforcement apparatus for feminist goals' (Bernstein, 2007, p 128).

I see the emergence of carceral feminism in the Swedish context as occurring in parallel with two fundamental changes in society: the triumph of neoliberalism in public administration and the society in general, and the normalisation of racism in the public conversation.

Law and order

The central concept of law and order was launched as part of the game of politics in the West by US President Richard Nixon, who held the highest office in the land during the politically turbulent years of 1969–74. At that time, 'law and order' was above all a way of demonising the US civil rights movement, the anti-Vietnam War movement and the LGBTQ struggle, and also, to a certain extent, the women's movement. In practice, this demonisation consisted of painting these movements as those of drug addicts disturbing the peace, who were a threat to middle-class Americans who had recently become a bit better off.

A quote from President Nixon's adviser at the time, a lawyer called John Ehrlichman, is illuminating:

> The Nixon campaign in 1968, and the Nixon White House after that, had two enemies: the anti-war left and black people. You understand what I'm saying? We knew we couldn't make it illegal to be either against the war or black, but by getting the public to associate hippies with marijuana and blacks with heroin, and then criminalizing both heavily, we could disrupt those communities. We could arrest their leaders, raid their homes, break up their meetings, and vilify them night after night on the evening news. Did we know we were lying about the drugs? Of course we did. (DuVernay, 2016)

Since Nixon's time, the concept of law and order has been picked up by an increasing number of people. Today, it is not only conservative parties and commentators who pursue policies under that flag. Even Sweden's Social Democrats and the Green Party are exploiting both the concept and its historical meaning – tougher measures.[2] Many years after his death, despite being the only US President to date to resign before he was removed from office, Nixon therefore remains one of the politicians who exerts a great influence on the present. But for a society to agree to increasingly repressive policy, as the Nixon administration so skilfully realised, requires both identified enemies and issues that unite. The Nixon administration, and later the Reagan administration, used both the war on drugs and the war on crime to unite the White American population in particular and to get it to accept ever increasing repression. However, throughout history, the issue of sexual violence, who perpetrates it, who is subjected to it, and how it should be dealt with, has also been a similarly politicised issue.

This is, of course, due to the issue being complex and highly charged – sexual violence is often traumatising, and criticising people or movements who are fighting to combat such abuses is rarely politically viable. For that reason, the issue has often been hijacked. For example, claiming that Black men raped White women was a common weapon used to target the movement working to abolish slavery in the US. This is despite the fact that, during the period of slavery, it was far more common for White men to rape Black, enslaved women. In modern times in the US, some movements working for women's rights and against sexual violence have advocated for, in particular, mandatory arrest in cases of domestic violence and tougher penalties for sex offences, which, together with economic vulnerability, the police's racial profiling and the war on drugs for example, has resulted in the US today having a very high rate of incarceration in relation to its population. In her recent book *The Feminist War on Crime: The Unexpected Role of Women's Liberation in Mass Incarceration*, Aya Gruber, professor of law at the Colorado Law School, has shown how parts of the US feminist movement have gradually become focused on the prosecution of criminals as the paramount issue for feminism; and how, in particular, the question of mandatory arrest when the police receive a report of domestic violence has led to an increase in the number of arrestees (Gruber, 2021). A disproportionately large number of those arrested and in custody are Black Americans.

Sweden's legal history

In order to understand contemporary carceral feminism, we need to look back into Sweden's political and legal history. A couple of decades ago, things were quite different in Sweden.

In the late 1960s and early 1970s, punishment and correctional care were debated intensely in Sweden. The issue of general prevention – that is, whether locking up people who commit crimes has a general deterrent effect on others – as well as individual prevention – the idea that a prison sentence discourages the individual from committing new offences – was hotly debated. Intense pressure from civil society – such as from the *Riksförbundet för kriminalvårdens humanisering* or KRUM (the national association for humanising correctional care) and *Förenade Fångars Centralorganisation* (FFCO, the united prisoners' central organisation), which pointed out that criminality was not a personality trait, but that a person's economic and social position strongly influences the probability that they will commit offences – led to the Correctional Care Inquiry (*Kriminalvårdsberedningen*, 1972) being launched.

This Inquiry, which completed its work in 1972, noted, among other things, that:

For its part, the Inquiry wishes to limit itself to emphasising that a custodial sentence as such does not generally improve the individual's chances of adapting to a life of freedom. ... From the perspective of the individual, better preventive results (can) be achieved through correctional care on probation than institutional care. In addition, probation is a more humane and cheaper form of care than institutional care. (Kriminalvårdsberedningen, 1972, p 15)

It was also emphasised that a custodial sentence rarely leads to the person who is locked up becoming better adapted to a law-abiding and peaceable life when released into the community again. In addition, the Inquiry emphasised that locking people up is not humane.

The Inquiry subsequently led to the Correctional Care Reform (*Kriminalvårdsreformen*) in 1974. This reform was strongly influenced by civil society's view that in order to combat crime, regardless of the type of offence involved, social disparities needed to be reduced. Later in the 1970s and early 1980s, the liberalisation of correctional care as well as Swedish criminal law in general continued. Some indefinite-term forms of punishment, such as reformatories, were removed. This was done in addition to reduced sentences for juveniles, introduced back in 1965, which meant taking into account the fact that the capacity to understand consequences is not fully developed in young offenders, and that it is therefore particularly inappropriate to impose long sentences on people up to 21 years of age. But the tide turned. In 1989, the penal value principle was introduced in Sweden as a guide to how long the sentence imposed should be. This new principle emphasised that the length of the sentence ought to be proportional to the seriousness of the offence, rather than, as had been the case previously, the individual's chances of reintegrating into the community being central when determining the length of a prison sentence.

For a long time, developments in criminal law have been linked to changes in how the role of the state is seen, and the influence of the market in the society. In the 1980s, the social reforms that the labour movement had built up in Sweden started being rolled back as neoliberal ideas gained more and more ground.

A clear shift could be seen in the 1990s. Sweden suffered a raging financial crisis in the years 1990–94. The crisis was mainly due to the fact that more and more of the rules that restricted the market and kept it in check had been gradually repealed during the neoliberal 1980s. In parallel with these quite revolutionary changes in the relationship between the state and the market, the women's movement in Sweden had been pushing for a long time to increase the number of criminalised acts, and to use the state's legislative power to prevent violence against women by introducing more offences. The result of their efforts was the commission of inquiry into violence against women (*Kvinnofridsutredningen*), which was initiated with the purpose of combating violence against women (Kvinnovåldskommissionen, 1996).

One of this inquiry's many proposals was to introduce the offence of gross violation of a woman's integrity into Chapter 4 Section 4a second paragraph of the Swedish Criminal Code. It was argued that the introduction of this class of crime was in fact a gender equality measure to combat men's violence against women . The offence of violation of a woman's integrity was thus one of the first offences specifically established to address a social problem. Here too, one of the tendencies in the neoliberal ideological construction that is most contradictory can be seen. Neoliberalism is often described as an ideology that aims to abolish all regulation, and have complete freedom for the individual – a kind of anarcho-capitalism. In practice, however, neoliberal nation-building has resulted mainly in the liberalisation of the financial markets and of the state's capacity to control how organised capital operates. In parallel with this development, more and more regulation of individuals has emerged. High walls have been erected in countries across Europe, migration rules have become increasingly complex, and the state's capacity to intervene in the lives of its citizens through the police and the judiciary, and to impose stiff penalties, has steadily grown. It is important to understand this trend in order to understand the increasing popularity of carceral feminism within feminist movements in Sweden, which tends to call for criminalisation and punishment over redistribution of resources.

There is, of course, a plethora of different theories about the function of punishment. For many people, it seems obvious to have a social order in which the state has the right to punish those who are within its jurisdiction. But the legitimacy of this – from where the state gets its legal and moral right to punish, so to speak – has been a matter of heated debate throughout history. In Sweden, because our Instrument of Government establishes that the Kingdom of Sweden is to be governed by the principle of democracy, implemented in an elected legislative assembly in the form of the Riksdag, we have solved the problem of legitimacy by simply saying that Swedes themselves have decided on the right to punish. The idea is that, because our elected representatives make the laws, from this flows a legitimacy for the courts' imposition of penalties: so to speak, we ourselves have determined what is to be punishable. Swedish criminal law is primarily based on what are known as the general prevention theories of criminal justice, that is, that the purpose of criminal law is to make citizens in general avoid committing crimes. We should therefore punish ourselves in order to be reminded not to commit certain acts. However, the severity of criminal penalties – deciding how long the prison sentence will be – is instead determined in accordance with absolute theories of criminal justice, based on how reprehensible the offence as such is seen as being. In determining the sentence in a concrete case, a form of individual prevention theory is also applied where, for example, the choice between prison and probation is governed to some extent by what can induce the individual not to commit offences in the future. If deterrence in general is considered to be the basis for criminalising something, the length of the sentence will usually depend on how serious the crime is considered to be.

In her thesis Monica Burman, professor of jurisprudence and someone who has devoted her research to studying violence against women, pointed out that the way in which criminal law was used in the introduction of the offence of gross violation of a woman's integrity was in stark contrast with the prevailing view of the function of criminal law at the time (Burman, 2007). Earlier in the 20th century, the focus was on social measures that, it was hoped, would put a stop to violence, and the general view was that criminal law could not contribute to solving social problems. Since then, a great deal of water has flowed under the bridge, and criminal law is now seen by the legislator as a pathway towards gender equality, and men's violence against women is clearly seen as a matter of criminal law. In essence, therefore, the question is about how much one believes that punishment prevents the commissioning of violent offences, and about a shift in the community's view on what is most effective.

Identification with the state

It is often the absolute theories of criminal justice that are highlighted by feminist movements that have moved towards a carceral feminism when it comes to criminalisation and the punishment of various forms of sexual and domestic violence offences. The argument is that the criminalisation of these acts, and severe punishment for certain acts, sends a message that the state takes offences against women seriously. However, this argument assumes that people fundamentally identify with the state's power, a feeling that it is there for you when you need support and protection, and that you are included in the community that the state's monopoly on violence is said to safeguard and protect. It also assumes that the value of the message from the state is more important than other measures, such as: more and cheaper housing so that the victims of violence can leave their perpetrators; better pay in female-dominated occupations so that women are not financially dependent on violent men; or a fairer legal framework for migration so that recently arrived migrant women are not forced to remain in violent relationships in order not to jeopardise their and/or their children's residence permits.

This reasoning serves to illustrate that the women who are primarily served by the police are, on the one hand, women with financial resources in the form of income, housing and networks large enough to survive without an additional income and, on the other hand, women who are citizens or hold residence permits and who are only in domestic relationships with other people who also hold citizenship or residence permits. They are also women who do not run the risk of having their children removed from their custody if the police were to visit their home and conduct an analysis of the children's situation, for example, which could lead to a report of concern to social services. Women who can safely call the police know that they are not in danger of being expelled, racially profiled or reported to social services. The dichotomy on which Bernstein based her definition of carceral feminism is clearly apparent here: 'A drift from the welfare state to the carceral state as the enforcement apparatus for feminist goals' (Bernstein, 2007, p 128). The fact that punishment has become a more common feminist argument thus illustrates that those who argue for it are people who are less dependent on the redistribution functions of the welfare state per se.

This is a matter of a shift in certain parts of multifaceted feminist movements concerning the role that the state should play in a society, and, by extension, the role that the state should play in the market. This shift within parts of the feminist line of argument naturally reflects a shift in the entire community. The role that the state has played for a long time in Sweden under social democratic governments is to attenuate the most extreme expressions of ruthless capitalism through, for example, progressive taxation policy and the redistribution of wealth from those who have the most to those who have less. We have quite simply had a relatively functional social democratic welfare state. Since the 1980s, however, this model has slowly but surely been eroded as part of Sweden's neoliberal transformation. Much of what used to be our communal property in the form of infrastructure for providing healthcare, energy and public transport has been privatised and sold off at bargain basement prices. Inheritance tax, the national defence tax, real estate tax and wealth tax have all been abolished. Less and less of our communal resources go directly to healthcare, schools and social care, and more and more is going to private profits, even in Sweden's central welfare services.

The areas in which the state has increased its presence are instead in areas of oversight, border controls and penalties. "Since we took office, we have introduced some 60 tougher penalties", said the Swedish Minister of Justice Morgan Johansson at a press conference on the issue in September 2021; he then went on to point out that the Swedish government had also introduced "a great increase in CCTV surveillance" and in addition introduced the possibility of secret data interception; in other words, trojan-spyware programs put by the state onto individuals' mobile phones (Aliki, 2020). With shining eyes, and just the hint of a smile, Morgan Johansson said that Sweden now has a record number of people in prison.[3]

At the same time, we are seeing the normalisation of racism in the public conversation as well as in the legislative machine. More and more parties are inviting the Sweden Democrats (the Swedish nationalist party, with roots in Nazism) to form a government with them in coalitions. There has also been a 'race to the bottom' to find out who can tighten migration legislation the most. Party leaders are no longer averse to describing immigration to Sweden as a burden, or calling people with non-European backgrounds who commit offences in Sweden 'domestic terrorists' (Svensson, 2021). Other party leaders feel confident saying that many women feel unsafe when they walk the streets of our cities, and that this fear is 'largely due to harassment by marauding groups of young men, often recent arrivals from parts of the world where women are not expected to be able to move about freely' (Busch Thor, 2019).

Swedish racial profiling

A few years ago, I moved to the Stockholm suburb of Akalla, located in Järva to the north-west of Stockholm. The area is part of what is known as the 'Million Programme', and consists of a mixture of 11-storey rental apartment buildings and terraced houses. Akalla, just like other parts of Järva, is an area of great natural beauty but also a place that is often reported on negatively in the Swedish media due to the area's low socio-economic level and the incidence of crime. I live right next to the underground station, which has an exit into the middle of a small square. During the first summer I lived here, I came home one afternoon after a court hearing, dressed in a business suit and with my green briefcase on my back. When I exited from the underground station, I saw that a police squad bus was parked in the middle of the square, and that the police who had arrived in Akalla in the bus were moving around among the people. I noted that many of them did not have rank insignia, nor did they have name tags or numbers visible on their uniforms.

The patrol was in the process of lining up all the boys who usually hang out in the square against a wall. There were about fifteen boys, all of them, I believe, under 15 years of age. Most of them were Black. I stayed there to see what was going to happen. At first, it was all quite calm, but then the atmosphere became increasingly aggressive as the police started photographing each boy and asking for his name. After a few minutes, a man who lives in the neighbourhood came walking past the line of boys, and asked why the police were forcing them to stand there and why they were being photographed. The situation escalated quickly, the man was arrested and handcuffed behind his back and forced to bend forward and get into the police squad bus. When I tried to make contact with one of the officers, I was pushed hard in my chest and reeled backwards. More and more people began to gather in the square and started to question the behaviour of the police. When I asked another police officer who came to the square in his own smaller squad car, why so many of them lacked rank insignia and identification numbers, he squirmed a bit sheepishly and said that they were police cadets who were out to get a picture of reality. While this was happening, several of the boys' mothers, and a woman who turned out to be the partner of the man who had been forced into the squad bus, had come down to the square and started trying to get an explanation for why the police were there and why they were behaving this way. One of the police screamed at the woman whose partner was in the squad bus to go home.

The situation de-escalated finally, the handcuffed man was released, and what officially remained after the incident were the photographs of the boys on the police cadets' phones. The woman whose partner had been handcuffed and I discussed whether we would report the incident to the Parliamentary Ombudsman, but this would be difficult when none of the police there could be identified. But what also remained, for everyone who was in the square that day, was the experience of how the state's monopoly on violence treated those who live there.

There are many legal question marks about what happened on that summer afternoon. Why did the police not have their identification numbers visible? What legal basis did they have for photographing the children? And the decision to handcuff, a state coercive measure, the man who asked questions: how could this be understood?

Many of those who were there that day already know that the actions of the police had no basis in law and therefore were unlawful. But they also know that it was neither the first nor the last time that something like this will happen – it is part of everyday life. Many therefore do not see the police as a security resource that is welcome into the most private sphere of their lives. The police, and therefore the community, act more like a violent and unwanted perpetrator, but one against whom it is impossible to get a restraining order. A perpetrator in fact with a far greater capacity for violence than a normal man. A perpetrator who can not only demand to enter your home, photograph your children or handcuff your husband or partner, but is also part of the state border control that can ultimately expel people.

The violent face of the state

Together with human rights organisation Civil Rights Defenders, criminologist Leandro Schclarek Mulinari has carried out one of the first studies in Sweden on the extent of racial/ethnic profiling. In the study, which was published in 2017 and titled *Slumpvis utvald. Ras-/etnisk profilering i Sverige (Randomly Selected. Racial/ethnic Profiling in Sweden)*, the informants talk about the police's racial profiling having given many people a feeling of being pointed out as perpetrators (Schclarek Mulinari, 2017, p 33). In the report, a number of the informants also state that racial profiling by the police is part of their everyday lives. They are stopped several times a month, sometimes several times in the same day, without it being made clear to them why they were stopped, but that, for most of them, it is in fact just racial profiling (Eriksson, 2019).

Women who grow up seeing their fathers, brothers, friends and boyfriends, and perhaps later their sons, being stopped by the police and searched without being suspects for any crimes, or seeing them driven to remote locations to find their own way home as best they can, are not generally willing to allow society to use additional violence against these boys and men, regardless of how they behave otherwise (Zare and Sehlin, 2016). In other words, some women and children who are subjected to domestic violence by their men may have a stronger loyalty to the perpetrator, despite him being violent, than to the society as an abstract entity. The extensive police presence in certain areas of Sweden, and the police's racial profiling combined with a strong feeling that the society's support functions are not there for you, and the sub-prioritisation of the public domain in these areas, combine to create a lack of trust in general in society's institutions.

In November 2021, a clip was uploaded to the Instagram account *Polisnytt* (police news).[4] The video purported to show a 17-year-old boy waiting in a car park in the Johanneshov area of Stockholm. According to the Instagram account, the boy had ended up in a fight inside a concert venue nearby, and therefore left the venue to be picked up by an acquaintance in the car park. In the clip, a big muscular man in police uniform pushes the much smaller and less muscular boy hard in front of him while shouting at him: "Keep moving! Move!". The boy regains his balance after the push and stands still, with his hands hanging down by his sides, as the police officer approaches him again and thumps him in the chest anew. Then the police officer says: "I'm going to drop you; you understand what I'm saying?", before he forces the boy's arms up behind his back and pushes him face down into a pool of water in the car park.

The fact that the police behave in this way towards non-White children has been demonstrated again and again for decades, but has continued, nevertheless. For many, therefore, state violence against Black and Brown children is also an important feminist issue, the extent of which is a major problem in everyday life. When the person who is said to be the protector is the perpetrator, what options remain? Who will the mother of a son who has been abused by the police call for protection against violence?

In addition to the racial profiling that the police subject non-White Swedes to, another type of state racism is embedded in how migration is handled.

One issue that is highly relevant to the state's racial profiling is the migration status of both the victims of violence and the perpetrators. There are no reliable figures on how many people today live without permission in

Sweden. But we do know that it is a considerable number. We also know that there is increasing pressure on the police, the authority responsible for locating and expelling people who are in hiding, to spend time and resources on getting more of these people expelled. This means that for those people who are living without permission in Sweden, the police will be seen as anything but a security resource. In theory, it is possible to report being the victim of a crime even as a stateless person in Sweden. As a participant in a preliminary investigation and criminal trial, the prosecutor can petition for a special residence permit for the victim. But such a residence permit is always temporary, and the risk of ending up on the radar of the border police after it has expired is always there. And a person who commits an offence always risks expulsion if they are convicted. These are the kinds of people whom Elisabeth Massi Fritz refers to when she argues for 'expulsion direct from prison' (Massi Fritz, 2021a). Thus, for a person who lives with, or has children with, a person who is staying without permission in Sweden, a police report entails a risk that both the notifier and the offender, including any children, will ultimately be expelled from Sweden, with very small chance of being able to travel back, because expulsion orders are often combined with a re-entry ban. The weighing up of the pros and cons that a victim of violence has to make in such a case is extremely difficult: "We have children together. Should I contribute to contact between them and the perpetrator being cut off more or less entirely?" Moreover, with the prevailing tightening of maintenance requirements, few are able to meet the income requirement imposed to be eligible for family reunification with an expelled partner: "Should I expose the perpetrator to the violence that the risk of being expelled entails?"

Because that is how the society's actions must be understood – as violence. The increased CCTV surveillance of certain areas, the withdrawal of support systems, the racist line of argument in the public domain, migrant detention centres, the arrests and remand centres, the police presence – all of this is also an exercise of violence, which for many would appear to be far more aggressive and limiting on their everyday lives than the violence perpetrated by a man in their domestic sphere.

The state violence that the risk of expulsion entails also affects women who are victims of violence in a way that is clearly illustrated by the case of 'Betty', which attracted much attention in the Swedish media in 2021 (Ferhatovic, 2020).

Betty came to Sweden as a family reunification migrant, on the basis of a relationship she started with a Swedish man who she had met in her home country. In Sweden, the man showed his violent side. He kept her locked up and subjected her to sexual violence. Betty left him, and met a new man with whom she had children. She also applied for a residence permit on the basis of her relationship with her new partner and their children in common. But this man also subjected her and the children to violence. In the end, Betty chose to leave and report him to the police.

This jeopardised her and her children's chances to stay in Sweden. Sweden's migration legislation requires that a relationship must last for at least two years in order for the person who has applied for a residence permit on the basis of the relationship to be able to stay permanently. The purpose of the rule is said to be to avoid marriages of convenience or 'sham' marriages – marriages that have been entered into solely for the purpose of obtaining a residence permit. In practice, the rule means that many women are forced to remain in violent relationships in order not to risk expulsion. In the case of Betty, this was precisely the consequence. She was expelled, after living in Sweden for ten years, along with her three children, all of whom were born in Sweden and had fathers who were Swedish citizens or held a residence permit.

In this text, Betty may serve as an example of the many women who have to choose between being subjected to violence by a single man and being subjected to violence by the state. For many of my clients who are in situations similar to Betty's, domestic violence is preferable to the violence of expulsion. Many of the people I meet in my work have been judged by the immigration authorities to be without grounds for asylum, but that does not mean that they are in practice. For example, for asylum-seeking LGBTQ persons, the Swedish Migration Agency makes an assessment of whether the Agency believes that, as they have said, a person is a lesbian. If the Agency comes to the conclusion that the person is not gay, even though they have told the Agency in detail how they have been persecuted precisely because of being a lesbian, they risk expulsion. If for any reason the person has had children in Sweden as a lesbian woman, they can be refused asylum because of it. Because if you were actually a lesbian, how did you get pregnant? In the eyes of the authorities, biological children are seen as an unmistakable sign of heterosexuality. Expulsion.

Here, an anti-racist, queer feminism can highlight how the state is the ultimate patriarch, especially in the neoliberal reality in which we now live, where what remains of the communal is often, ultimately, the possibility to discipline.

Transformative justice

Another complexity that tends to get lost when the focus of one's argument is on higher penalties and more police officers is that not everyone, quite simply, can afford to have their perpetrators locked up. Much of the violence committed in society is perpetrated in families, where the perpetrator also contributes to the family's livelihood. Furthermore, statistics show that gaps in income in Sweden have never been higher than they are now since measurements began, while a high proportion of those who make up the working class and those who are poor in Sweden are also people who are subjected to racism (Neergaard, 2018; Statistics Sweden, 2018). In parallel with this, the rules that protect workers are being relaxed, and more and more people are in insecure jobs. This means that many people, particularly in the working class and also subjected to racism, simply have to ask themselves the question: "Can we afford to lose an income, perhaps for a long time to come, if a perpetrator were to be imprisoned?" For many, the answer to that question will be no. This means that the support measures available to victims of violence, such as access to safe house accommodation, counselling or financial assistance, will not be available to them since these measures are often predicated on a police report being made against the perpetrator. Without the police report, no access to support.

Society's clear requirements that repression must be involved in order to receive support forces people who want to work for real support for the victims of violence to think innovatively. Many people who have worked for social equity have long known that a more reasonable distribution of economic resources, where there are other ways of leaving a perpetrator than asking the community to keep them locked up, can be an important part of feminist aspirations. In the US and UK, there have been movements working with what is termed *transformative justice* for a long time. These are feminist, anti-racist, queer and anti-capitalist movements that spend their time thinking about new definitions of justice that could mean opportunities to provide real healing for victims of violence as well as opportunities to rehabilitate those who perpetrate violence. Instead of making individual perpetrators into monsters, transformative justice is about putting the perpetration of violence into context and getting violent offenders to understand how their violence affects the victim.

This way of confronting and managing violence, which has its roots in Black feminism, feminist critique of ableism, indigenous movements, anarchism and queer activism, presents a different analysis of the causes of the violence. The perpetration of violence is seen instead as part of a larger structure with its roots in capitalism, heteropatriarchy and colonialism. Those who are subjected to state-sanctioned violence, for example, often subject others to violence who are even lower down on the social ladder – 'hurt people hurt people'. Instead of the one-sided analysis that is currently being reiterated in the public domain, where violence is seen as merely something that cis men perpetrate against cis women without any connection to material structures, in transformative justice violence is instead seen as a structural problem and a communal responsibility. In a transformative justice analysis, the strongest opposition to all the structures that destroy lives, families and their dreams is not demands for even more repression.

Instead, these structures should be opposed with social care and forgiveness. Not the kind of fake forgiveness that involves always turning the other cheek or downplaying the violation of the victim that has taken place, but the kind of forgiveness that comes from jointly taking responsibility for each other, and providing the means for healing for both the perpetrator and the victim, well beyond individualised perpetrator-monsters. Here there is an awareness that insisting on social care and healing can be a powerful strategy in combating violence. This is because people who are subjected to violence and disciplinary punishment on a daily basis – by the state, by other people, by their lives – know deep down within themselves that they will not be put in a better position simply because someone else is also subjected to violence. Because prisons, police interventions, CCTV surveillance, body searches, border controls and 'restricted areas' are part of the perpetrator society (Wikén, 2019). To instead insist that our lives, to quote Judith Butler, must be liveable, and that freedom is not about choosing between fifteen different health insurance policies, but about real opportunities for equity in the distribution of resources, could be the way out of the repressive spiral that parts of the feminist movement in Sweden have fallen into (Butler, 2009).

Conclusion: Feminist futures

Because the tone in the community on racism and migration has become sharper, a shift has also occurred where the state is being reduced to a control and punishment machine. These two things are connected. Such a shift in the role of the state, from redistributor to punisher, would not have been possible without generating a feeling that certain people in Sweden do not deserve the benefits of solidarity. The greater the socio-economic gaps in Sweden, and the more the lines of these gaps are drawn along racial boundaries, the less (the hope seems to be among those who want such a development) the White middle class – which otherwise could have shown solidarity – will feel that a wide-ranging system for the redistribution of the society's wealth is a good idea. So far, those in power who have based their actions on such an analysis seem to have been right. In the public conversation today, crime is often understood as synonymous with the offences committed by poor people. Therefore, when our party leaders talk about tougher measures against organised crime, everyone knows that they actually mean tougher measures against poor and racialised perpetrators and their families. It is never the case, for example, that organised crime involving the avoidance of tax from Sweden is what is intended. The leaked Paradise, Panama and Pandora Papers, in which it was revealed that many Swedes had evaded paying billions in tax owed to the Swedish state by placing their money in tax havens, are not what the Right means when they talk about tougher measures. US feminist and civil rights activist Angela Davis, referring to the 'war on crime' discussed earlier, has described how 'crime started to stand in for race' in public debate (DuVernay, 2016). The same shift can be seen in contemporary Sweden.

It is these shifts which mean that feminism, in the guise it has in the form of carceral feminism, is reduced to a tool of organised capital and structural racism. A state that just punishes, but does not protect, is the ultimate dream of neoliberalism.

As feminists, therefore, we have everything to gain from demanding a society that opposes violence in all its forms – whether it is perpetrated by the state or the individual.

Notes

1   Dagens Juridik, 13 August 2021, www.dagensjuridik.se/nyheter/valdtaktsdomd-far-840-000-av-jk-satt-frihetsberovad-for-lange/ [Accessed: 4 January 2022].
2   Swedish Social Democratic Party, 24 September 2021, https://www.sociald emokraterna.se/nyheter/nyheter/2022-02-09-skarpta-straff-och-fler-atgarder-mot-grov-brottslighet [Accessed 15 February 2022]. Green Party, 2019, https://www.mp.se/politik/lag-och-ordning, [Accessed 7 March 2019].
3   The Swedish Government, 24 September 2021, https://www.regeringen.se/press meddelanden/2021/09/morgan-johansson-presenterar-atgarder-mot-grov-brott slighet/ [Accessed: 4 January 2022].
4   Polisnytt, 8 November 2021, https://www.instagram.com/reel/CWBPsm9o T3p/?utm_medium=copy_link [Accessed: 4 January 2022].

References

Aliki, S. (2019) 'Det våras för fängelsefeminismen', *Kontext*. Available at: https://www.kontextpress.se/politik/det-varas-for-fangelsefeminismen/ [Accessed: 1 April 2020].

Aliki, S. (2020) 'Idag införs lagen som tillåter staten att spionera i våra telefoner', *Kontext*. Available at: https://www.kontextpress.se/politik/idag-infors-lagen-som-tillater-staten-att-spionera-i-vara-telefoner/ [Accessed: 15 February 2022].

Bernstein, E. (2007) 'The Sexual Politics of the "New Abolitionism"', *Differences* (Bloomington, Ind.), 18(3), pp 128–51.

Burman, M. (2007) *Straffrätt och mäns våld mot kvinnor: om straffrättens förmåga att producera jämställdhet*. Thesis, Umeå: Umeå universitet.

Busch Thor, E. (2019) 'Nog med menskonst – en ny feminism krävs', *Aftonbladet*. Available at: https://www.aftonbladet.se/a/l1pVXy [Accessed: 16 February 2022].

Butler, J. (2009) *Frames of War: When is Life Grievable?* London: Verso.

DuVernay, A. (2016) *13TH*. Available at: http://www.avaduvernay.com/13th [Accessed: 15 February 2022].

Emnéus Ekström, J. and Vaccari, C. (2021) 'Kriminologen: Högre straff för kvinnovåld måste bli verklighet', *Aftonbladet*. Available at: https://www.aftonbladet.se/a/6zJVXW [Accessed: 15 February 2022].

Eriksson, C.-F. (2019) 'De vittnar om svenska polisens rasprofilering', *Expressen*. Available at: https://www.expressen.se/nyheter/de-vittnar-om-svenska-polisens-rasprofilering/ [Accessed: 4 January 2022].

Ferhatovic, M. (2020) 'Hennes val: Leva med en våldsam man eller riskera utvisning', *Dagens Nyheter*. Available at: https://www.dn.se/sverige/hennes-val-leva-med-en-valdsam-man-eller-riskera-utvisning/ [Accessed: 15 February 2022].

Green Party (2019) 'Alla ska kunna känna sig trygga'. Available at: https://www.mp.se/politik/lag-och-ordning [Accessed 7 March 2019].

Gruber, A. (2021) *The Feminist War on Crime: The Unexpected Role of Women's Liberation in Mass Incarceration*. Oakland: University of California Press.

Kriminalvårdsberedningen (1972) *Kriminalvård: betänkande*. Stockholm: Riksdagen.

Kvinnovåldskommissionen (1996) *Remissammanställning - Kvinnofrid* (SOU 1995: 60).

Massi Fritz, E. (2021a) 'Våldtäktsmän borde inte få ett öre i skadestånd', *Expressen*. Available at: https://www.expressen.se/debatt/valdtaktsman-borde-inte-fa-ett-ore-i-skadestand--/ [Accessed: 15 February 2022].

Massi Fritz, E. (2021b) 'Våra barn ska inte behöva växa upp i dagens Sverige'. *Expressen*. Available at: https://www.expressen.se/debatt/vara-barn-ska-inte-behova--vaxa-upp-i-dagens-sverige/ [Accessed: 15 February 2022].

Neergaard, A. (2018) *Klassamhällets rasifiering i arbetslivet*, Katalys. Available at: https://www.katalys.org/publikation/no-53-klassamhallets-rasifiering-i-arbetslivet/ [Accessed: 15 February 2022].

Regeringsformen (1974) *Regeringsformen*. Stockholm: Riksdagen.

Schclarek Mulinari, L. (2017) *Slumpvis utvald: Ras-/etnisk profilering i Sverige*. Civil Rights Defenders; Kriminologiska institutionen, Stockholms universitet. Available at: http://urn.kb.se/resolve?urn=urn:nbn:se:su:diva-176715 [Accessed: 15 February 2022].

Statistics Sweden (2018) 'Inkomsterna ökade 2005–2016, och mest för kvinnor', Available at: http://www.scb.se/hitta-statistik/statistik-efter-amne/hushallens-ekonomi/inkomster-och-inkomstfordelning/inkomster-och-skatter/pong/statistiknyhet/slutliga-inkomster-och-skatter-2016/ [Accessed: 15 February 2022].

Svensson, O. (2021) Ulf Kristersson: 'Invandringen i Sverige har blivit en belastning', *Aftonbladet*. Available at: https://www.aftonbladet.se/a/23GVnB [Accessed: 15 February 2022].

Swedish Social-Democratic Party (2021) 'Skärpta straff och fler åtgärder mot grov brottslighet', Available at: https://www.socialdemokraterna.se/nyhe ter/nyheter/2022-02-09-skarpta-straff-och-fler-atgarder-mot-grov-brott slighet [Accessed 15 February 2022].

Wikén, J. (2019) 'Skarpa förslagen mot gängen: "Goda chanser"', *Svenska Dagbladet*. Available at: https://www.svd.se/skarpa-forslagen-mot-gangen-goda-chanser [Accessed: 15 February 2022].

Zare, S. and Sehlin, A. (2016) 'Polisen dumpade 13-årig pojke i skogen', *SVT Nyheter*. Available at: https://www.svt.se/nyheter/lok alt/stockholm/polisen-dumpade-13-arig-pojke-i-skogen [Accessed: 15 February 2022].

12

Beyond restorative justice: survivors' calls for innovative practices in Iceland

Hildur Fjóla Antonsdóttir

Introduction

In the Nordic countries and elsewhere, justice for victim-survivors of sexual violence and harassment remains elusive. Few cases are ever reported to the police and the criminal justice procedure is characterised by high attrition rates and low conviction rates (Antonsdóttir and Gunnlaugsdóttir, 2013; Krahé, 2016). In this context, restorative justice is increasingly being discussed as an alternative pathway to justice for survivors of sexual violence and harassment (Ptacek, 2009; Zinsstag and Keenan, 2017; Peleg-Koriata and Klar-Chalamish, 2020). The aim of this chapter is to explore the potential of using restorative justice in cases of sexual harassment and violence based on interviews with 35 victim-survivors in Iceland. The guiding questions have been: How do survivors of sexual violence and harassment view restorative justice? How could alternative justice processes satisfy survivors' justice interests?

Restorative justice is often described in juxtaposition to criminal justice or retributive justice. In his influential article 'Retributive justice, restorative justice' from 1985, Howard Zehr juxtaposes the paradigm of restorative justice with the paradigm of retributive justice in an effort to highlight the differences between them. According to retributive justice, crimes are defined as a violation of the state, where the focus is on establishing guilt based on past actions. The relationship between the parties is conceptualised as adversarial while guided by a normative process. Retributive justice entails the imposition of pain to punish, deter and prevent, and justice is defined by intent and procedural fairness. According to restorative justice, crime is defined as a violation of one person by another, where the focus is on problem-solving, liabilities and obligations, and on future actions. The normative process is based on dialogue and negotiations. The goal is reconciliation and restoration of both parties, and justice is defined in terms of a right relationship which is judged by the outcome (Zehr, 1985).

However, it has been pointed out that this juxtaposition is misleading. Neither retributive justice nor restorative justice exist as a coherent system or type of justice. Also, retributive justice refers to the criminal justice system, which has many aims, including rehabilitation, deterrence, and incapacitation. Moreover, restorative justice lacks a fact-finding method, and therefore cannot replace the conventional criminal justice system (Daly, 2016).

Restorative justice has been used predominantly in relation to less serious crimes and to youth crimes, and usually includes the practice of mediation (Zinsstag and Keenan, 2017). Using restorative justice in cases of sexual violence has been criticised by feminist scholars, who have highlighted the risk of revictimisation (see, for example: Stubbs, 2002; Coker, 2002; Daly and Stubbs, 2006; Keenan and Zinsstag, 2014) and the inability to guarantee offender accountability and responsibility (see, for example: Stubbs, 2002; Herman, 2005; Cossins, 2008). Moreover, previous research suggests that survivors' ideas of justice do not fit well with the aims of standard restorative justice practices (Herman, 2005; Jülich, 2006; McGlynn et al, 2017).

In the Nordic countries, mediation is widely practised in Norway and Finland and to a considerable extent in Denmark, but less so in Sweden and Iceland (Nylund et al, 2018). In Denmark and Norway, mediation is conducted in all types of cases, including in cases of sexual violence. However, while there are examples of reports and books written by practitioners (see, for example: Madsen, 2005; Andersson and Madsen, 2017), Nordic research on mediation in cases of sexual violence and harassment seems to be very limited.

In Iceland, restorative justice is not used in cases of sexual violence. As emphasised in instructions no. 2/2021 issued by the Icelandic Prosecution Authority, mediation is not to be used in cases that fall under the sexual offences chapter of the General Penal Code, except for minor offences (Icelandic Prosecution Authority, 2021). However, according to the new Agreement on the Platform for the Coalition Government (2021) in Iceland, the government's intention is to consider applying mediation in cases of sexual offences. It is therefore important to gain a better understanding of how survivors of sexual violence view restorative justice.

In this chapter, I will explore the potential for using restorative justice in cases of sexual harassment and violence in the Icelandic context within a feminist socio-legal framework.[1] I will discuss the international literature and best practices on the topic and then present some findings on survivors' views of restorative justice in Iceland, based on interviews conducted between January 2015 and January 2017. Subsequently, I will discuss the implications of these findings for the development of restorative justice practices, or rather innovative justice practices, in cases of sexual violence and harassment.

Restorative justice in cases of sexual violence

While there are several definitions of restorative justice, Zehr's (2002) definition has proved to be highly popular (Gade, 2018).[2] The definition is as follows: 'Restorative justice is a process to involve, to the extent possible, those who have a stake in a specific offense and to collectively identify and address harms, needs, and obligations, in order to heal and put things as right as possible' (Zehr, 2002, p 37).

Restorative justice is comprised of many different models, but the most popular approaches include victim–offender mediation/dialogue (VOM/VOD), restorative conferences, and restorative circles. VOM/VOD generally only includes the victim–survivor, the perpetrator, a support person for each party, and one or two facilitators. In addition to the victim–survivor and the perpetrator, restorative conferences bring together members of their community and relevant professionals. Restorative circles bring together yet a broader range of participants and, in addition to those mentioned, also includes wider community members. While restorative justice has predominantly been used in relation to youth crime (Zinsstag and Keenan, 2017), in some countries restorative justice is used in all types of cases, including cases of sexual violence, such as in Belgium, Denmark, Norway, New Zealand, Canada and Australia (Keenan, 2017).

In cases of sexual violence, the benefit of restorative justice has been questioned, given that the primary focus of many such programmes is to integrate the offender back into the community, and therefore victim–survivors' needs and interests can end up in second place. Further, there is an underlying assumption in restorative justice practice that victims are angry with their offenders, while in cases of violence against women victims are often characterised by a lack of anger and a strong sense of self-blame and shame (Ptacek, 2009, pp 19–23).

Several studies have, however, found that victim–survivors' visions of justice do not fit well with either retributive or restorative ideas of justice, while containing elements of both (Herman, 2005; Jülich, 2006; McGlynn et al, 2017). Based on interviews with victim–survivors of historical child sexual abuse, Jülich (2006) found that, although survivors spoke of justice in ways that reflected the goals of restorative justice, they were 'reluctant to endorse restorative justice as a paradigm within which they would pursue justice' (p 125), particularly those who had not reported the abuse to the police. In addition, those who had reported the case to the police were not convinced that restorative justice would provide them with a sense of justice (Jülich, 2006).

Importantly, Herman (2005) found that, for victim–survivors, it is not about restoring the relationship with the offender (where such a relationship had existed), as suggested in the restorative justice literature, but about restoring the relationship with their community. For the research participants in her study, the retributive aspects centred on their wish to have their offenders 'exposed and disgraced' – not primarily for punitive reasons, but rather because 'they sought vindication from the community as a rebuke to the offenders' display of contempt for their rights and dignity' (p 597).

As already noted, feminist scholars have been critical of using restorative justice in cases of gender-based violence. Some of their concerns are that restorative justice: might risk reprivatising gender-based violence, i.e., making sexual violence a private matter again after years of struggle to have it recognised as a public concern for the criminal justice system (see, for example: Coker, 2002; Stubbs, 2002); might risk survivors' safety and allow for revictimisation due to power imbalance (see, for example: Stubbs, 2002; Coker, 2002; Daly and Stubbs, 2006; Keenan and Zinsstag, 2014); is not able to guarantee offender accountability and responsibility (see, for example: Stubbs, 2002; Herman, 2005; Cossins, 2008); is based on an assumption that community members will be supportive to survivors and contribute to holding offenders to account, which cannot be guaranteed (Niemi-Kiesiläinen, 2001; Coker, 2002; Herman, 2005); and is inadequate in addressing the broader structural inequalities of race and class in which gender-based violence is embedded (Coker, 2002).

In this context, Daly (2016) notes that standard restorative justice practices 'require major revision if they are to be victim-focused and appropriate for cases of gender violence' (p 20). For this purpose, she suggests using the term 'innovative justice' for justice practices which do not anticipate an outcome that aims for restoration or reconciliation (Daly, 2016).

Therefore, it is important to proceed with caution when applying restorative justice in cases of sexual violence, and important to address the concerns raised by feminist scholars when developing alternative, or innovative, justice options.

Specially designed restorative justice programmes

There are some examples of restorative justice programmes that have been specially designed to be victim-centred. Such programmes tend to be characterised by a strong focus on trained personnel, careful case selection, survivor safety, and the management of power imbalances. These include the RESTORE[3] Program in Arizona, US (Koss, 2014), and Project Restore in New Zealand, which is inspired by the former (Jülich and Landon, 2017). There is reason to discuss in more detail the outcomes of these programmes from the survivor's perspective.

RESTORE is a restorative justice conferencing programme adapted to prosecutor-referred adult misdemeanour and felony sexual assaults (Koss, 2014, p 1623). Importantly, components of the RESTORE conferences include 'voluntary enrolment, preparation, and face-to-face meeting where primary and secondary victims voice impacts, and responsible persons acknowledge their acts and together develop a re-dress plan that is supervised for 1 year' (Koss, 2014, p 1623). The project has undergone an empirical outcome evaluation of 22 cases. Although the sample is small, the findings indicate that victim–survivors and responsible persons (the one responsible for the injustice) generally felt safe, listened to, supported, and treated fairly in the process. The results were more mixed when it came to whether the responsible person seemed to accept responsibility according to the victim, although 66 per cent of the victims strongly agreed that they did, while 33 per cent disagreed/strongly disagreed. In terms of the responsible person feeling sincerely sorry, all responsible persons reported feeling sorry, although according to victims, only half of them seemed sincerely so (Koss, 2014).

In another study, Jülich and Landon (2017) report findings from a desk-based case review of 12 cases of sexual violence that were referred to Project Restore in New Zealand over an 18-month period between 2011 and 2012, all of which were referred by the court system for pre-sentence restorative justice. Daly's (2014) 'victimisation and justice model' was used as a framework to analyse to what degree victims' justice needs and interests were satisfied through the restorative justice programme. Daly's (2014; see also 2017) model provides a framework to determine whether a justice mechanism is effective from the victim's perspective and identifies specific victim justice interests as being prerequisites for victims to experience a sense of justice. These include: being informed of their options in order to be able to participate and ask questions throughout the justice process; having a voice and being able to tell their own truth about what happened and how it has affected them; having their experience validated, believed, and not blamed on them; being vindicated in some form, either by the legal system or their community; and offender accountability in some form, which can include offenders taking active responsibility for the wrong caused by their actions, showing regret and remorse, or receiving censure or sanction (Daly, 2014, p 388). Jülich and Landon's (2017) findings indicate that these justice interests were satisfied to a large extent, except in terms of offender accountability, which depends on the ability of the offender to understand the impacts of their harmful behaviour.

While these specially designed restorative justice programmes are operated in cooperation with the prosecution authorities, there are also examples of cases where restorative justice has been used independently of the criminal justice system with favourable outcomes for survivors. McGlynn et al (2012) conducted an exploratory study of a restorative justice conference involving an adult survivor of child rape and other sexual abuse. When asked if she would recommend restorative justice to another woman in similar circumstances, she is reported to have replied that 'if the woman was at the right stage in her recovery, sufficiently strong to undertake a conference, and after ensuring the necessary professional support and careful planning, then she should "take a deep breath and do it"' (p 240).

These studies indicate that specially designed victim-centred restorative justice programmes can, to a degree, satisfy victim-survivors' justice interests; however, the results are mixed when it comes to victim-survivors' perceptions of offender accountability. This is problematic given that a key component of victim-survivors' understanding of justice is offender accountability and responsibility, although this does not necessarily have to be in the form of punishment and incarceration (McGlynn and Westmarland, 2019). Another issue is that, in the two programmes mentioned here, cases are referred to restorative justice either from prosecutors who deem them 'provable at trial' (Koss, 2014), or from the courts, where offenders have acknowledged wrongdoing or have pleaded guilty to a crime (Jülich and Landon, 2017). Therefore, these are not representative of the majority of cases of sexual violence where those accused readily deny accusations of sexual violence, and charges are seldom raised.

Method

As a part of my PhD research on the meaning of justice for people who have been subjected to sexual violence, I conducted interviews with victim-survivors of sexual violence in Iceland (Antonsdóttir, 2020b).[4] The criteria for participation were that participants were aged 18 years or over, and self-identified as having been subjected to sexual violence. Between January 2015 and January 2017, I conducted interviews with 32 women and 3 men, focusing on participants' views and experiences of different justice mechanisms, including restorative justice (Antonsdóttir, 2020b).

Given that generally restorative justice is not used in cases of sexual violence in Iceland, none of the participants had experienced a restorative justice process. Therefore, the findings presented here pertain to participants' *views* about restorative justice. Participants' prior knowledge about restorative justice varied – while some were not very familiar with the phenomenon, others were more familiar with the process.

Participants were asked a number of questions following a semi-structured questionnaire. The first set of questions asked: if they had met the perpetrator after the assault and how they had experienced that; if there was something that they would like to tell/ask the perpetrator; how the perpetrator should take responsibility for their actions; how the perpetrator should compensate for their actions; if it was important to them that the perpetrator admits to what they did and why/why not; and, if it was important for them that such an admission would be public or made public and why/why not. I then asked if they had heard about restorative justice; if not, I briefly explained the concept as follows:

Restorative justice is a process that aims to give victim-survivors a sense of justice and for the perpetrator to take responsibility for their actions and to compensate for the harm done in some way. Restorative justice is based on the idea that crimes are not committed against the state but against people and society. Both the victim-survivor and the perpetrator have to be willing to participate in the process, which is facilitated by a neutral party. The process revolves around convening a meeting with the victim-survivor, the perpetrator, and sometimes their trusted persons, with the aim that the perpetrator understands the consequences of their actions, takes responsibility for their actions and compensates the victim for the harm. Usually, there is considerable preparation for both parties separately before a meeting is convened.

Subsequently, I asked about their views on restorative justice and if they would consider it an option for themselves.

The age of the participants ranged between 19 and 67 years, and the average age was 37. The age of the participants at the time of the sexual violence ranged from early childhood to 42 years. Participants were asked what kind of sexual violence they had been subjected to but were free to choose which experiences they wanted to talk about. Participants described a range of different types of sexual violence: rape (21), attempted rape (3), sexual abuse as children (14), sexual harassment (2), and image-based sexual abuse (such as being filmed during sex and having images of them distributed without their consent) (3). One participant talked about her experiences of prostitution, which she understood as having been subjected to sexual violence.

In some cases, participants talked about specific incidents of sexual violence, while in other cases they talked about ongoing abuse, either in terms of several incidents or over an extended period of time. The offenders responsible for the sexual violence were men and boys, except for one girl and one woman. They included family members (11), partners or boyfriends (7), friends or acquaintances (14), professionals (such as police officers and teachers) (4), and strangers (4).

To analyse the interview data, I used the tools of thematic analysis (TA) as outlined by Brown and Clark (2006; 2013). Following the TA process, I transcribed the interviews, familiarised myself with the data, and generated both semantic and latent codes which I developed into themes (see Clarke et al, 2016). The themes generated were as follows: good idea but near impossible in practice; distrust of offenders; fear of unjust exposure; conflicting processes; an offender accountability process; and, societal transformation.

Findings

Good idea but near impossible in practice

Generally, participants expressed a favourable view of the idea and aims of restorative justice as I had laid out the concept, however, most did not foresee themselves participating in such a process, let alone the offenders. A woman in her early twenties who had been subjected to sexual violence by a man she met online and whose case was still pending in the criminal justice system said:

> 'It sounds like a good solution in theory but as a victim I cannot imagine meeting him face to face and having to argue … you know. I think that roughly 90 per cent of victims would never want to do that. And there it stops. And in those 10 per cent of cases, or similar, where victims would be willing to meet the offender, then the offender would probably not want to do it. So I don't think this would work.'

A woman in her twenties, who had been subjected to sexual violence at a party in her teens by a young man she didn't know, did not see why an offender would participate in a restorative justice process. She said:

> 'The first thing that comes to my mind is, why would offenders want to go through this? Why? Based on my experience, it's difficult to get offenders, doesn't matter what kind of offences they have committed, to admit to what they have done, let alone to talk about it with the victims and compensate them for it. What is the incentive? No really, I'm asking.'

Indeed, while restorative justice is based on the willingness of offenders to want to undergo the process and take responsibility for their actions, that is usually not the case when it comes to sexual violence. Based on a review of all rape cases reported to the police in Iceland in 2008 and 2009, accused persons only confessed to the rape in four out of 189 cases (Antonsdóttir and Gunnlaugsdóttir, 2013). As already noted, restorative justice programmes designed for cases of sexual violence rely on referrals of atypical cases from the prosecution authorities, that is, cases which are either deemed provable at trial (Koss, 2014), or cases where offenders have acknowledged wrongdoing or have pleaded guilty to a crime (Jülich and Landon, 2017). These conditions, created by the criminal justice system, only apply to a minority of cases, given that the vast majority of cases are dropped by the police and the prosecution authorities.

Distrust of offenders

In most cases, participants explained that they had no reason to believe that the offenders had the capacity to participate in such a restorative justice process. A woman who, over 20 years ago, had been subjected to repeated sexual violence by her then partner, who had received a conviction, did not see restorative justice as an option. She said:

> 'I would not have been able to see this as an option in my case. Sorry. That would have had to be … no. Not at all. I just get chills. There is no way to offer … no. [Researcher: Do you think he would manipulate the process?] Yes, totally, totally. Not a chance. There is no chance that this is possible. Not in these cases. No.'

A woman in her early twenties, who had been raped by an acquaintance who had been convicted of that crime as well as others of sexual violence against other young women, said:

> 'I think he is a psychopath and that he would never take any responsibility. He wouldn't know what I was talking about. But perhaps it is enough that I tell him what I need to tell him. But I would be afraid that he would think that he was the victim in all this and then I would be even more angry with him. And I can't be having that kind of energy in my life.'

A woman in her mid-twenties who had been subjected to sexual harassment by her stepfather a few years back, and whose case had been dropped by the prosecutor, said: "There are so few of them who admit to what they have done. So, you know, I don't know how many would participate in such a process and be sincere about. I think that is the most dangerous aspect of this process."

In some cases, the perpetrator was a family member who had committed violence against participants when they were children or young persons, and had never shown any remorse or asked for an apology or forgiveness. In some such cases, family members had been told about the abuse but had not taken a stand with the survivor. A woman in her sixties, who was subjected to sexual abuse as a child by her sister, did not see restorative justice as an option as she did not trust her sister nor her family to be able to handle it. She said:

> 'These people whom I come from, which I of course know very well, are not capable of dealing with this. … [Restorative justice] is perhaps an option for others, those who are ready to do something about themselves. They are unfortunately not many.'

Similarly, a male participant in his late thirties, who had recently disclosed that he had been subjected to sexual abuse by his mother as a child, did not see restorative justice as an option. When asked if he thought it could be possible to conduct a restorative justice conference with other family members, he said:

'To put them all together would be like pouring petrol on a fire. ... to put everyone in the same room is very difficult, then the family needs to be very united. Thankfully that exists but then there are others. There are some in the family who don't want to know anything about this but still have an opinion about it.'

Most participants, therefore, had no reason to believe that offenders would be willing or have the capacity to participate in a restorative justice process and be sincere about it. This is in line with feminist critique of restorative justice, which underscores the risk of revictimisation (see, for example: Stubbs, 2002; Coker, 2002; Daly and Stubbs, 2006; Keenan and Zinsstag, 2014) and the inability to guarantee offender accountability and responsibility (see, for example: Stubbs, 2002; Herman, 2005; Cossins, 2008). Lack of offender sincerity in specially designed restorative justice processes has also been identified as a problem (Koss, 2014), as well as offenders' capacity to understand the impacts of their harmful behaviour (Jülich and Landon, 2017). In cases where the offender was a family member, some participants also did not foresee family members supporting them in holding offenders to account; feminist scholars have also identified this as a risk (Niemi-Kiesiläinen, 2001; Coker, 2002; Herman, 2005).

Therefore, offering survivors the option of participating in a restorative justice process with offenders who will manipulate the process, or are unwilling or lack the capacity to take responsibility for their actions can easily become a part of the 'continuum of injustice' (Antonsdóttir, 2020a) that characterises the experiences of most survivors in the aftermath of sexual violence.

Fear of unjust exposure

The main focus of standard restorative justice practices is convening a meeting between the offender and the survivor with the aim of restoring both parties. For many participants, the thought of meeting and talking to the offender was understood to be too risky for their mental and emotional health. One young woman, whose case had recently been dropped by the prosecution authority, had explained how the offender, whom she had been seeing for some time and who had subjected her to escalating sexual violence over a period of time, had managed to gain power over her in ways that scared her. Or, as she said: "I was starting to believe that I was mad". When asked if she would want to participate in a restorative justice process, she said:

> 'There is probably a lot that I would want to say, but I just wouldn't want to talk to him … I'm afraid of him, afraid of the influence he had over me and if he still has that hold over me. I of course hope that he doesn't … but I'm still afraid that he might still have that influence over me. … So [restorative justice] would probably not work for me.'

A young woman who had been subjected to sexual violence by a man whom she met online and whose case was still pending in the criminal justice system did not think that she would want to see him or meet him again. She said:

> 'I'm not sure I would want to talk to him or see him again. The few times that I have seen men who look like him I have had a bit of an anxiety attack … I don't think I would be able to say a word if I would bump into him. And I think it wouldn't matter what I would say to him because I don't think he would take it to heart anyway and then after the fact I would endlessly be thinking: I should have said this and I should have said that. So I don't think it would do anything for me personally.'

A man who had been sexually abused as a teenager by two different men said: "It would be so uncomfortable and then I would say something clumsy because I would want to get it over and done with. It wouldn't come out the way I would have planned it in my head."

A woman in her mid-forties, who had been raped by two men who had received convictions, said:

> 'I thought [restorative justice] was a great idea, and something I wished people would increasingly use, until it happened to me. Now the tables have turned. I wouldn't be able to sit in front of them and tell them how this has impacted me. I just can't. … If I would see them, I'm so afraid of becoming angry, I don't know, perhaps I would just say something terribly ugly, I don't know. Perhaps I would just give them a hug and wish them good luck in life. I don't know [laughs a little].'

One participant also criticised the idea of a demand for exposure, which she saw as being embedded in the restorative justice process. She said:

> 'You have to go into these circumstances because that is supposedly the way to work your way through the experience. That, therefore,

becomes a demand to expose yourself, which is supposed to be the way through. ... I think this is damned tricky.'

Therefore, many participants described a deep sense of uncertainty about their own reactions in such a setting, which highlights the power inequality that characterises these cases. As one participant pointed out, this demand for survivor exposure, which standard restorative justice processes require, in return for the uncertain promise of gaining a sense of wellbeing or a sense of justice, is deeply problematic. In addition, why should survivors risk exposure if they also do not share the aims of restorative justice, that is, to restore or reconcile the relationship with the offender (as has been pointed out in the literature; see, for example: Herman, 2005; Daly, 2016)? As I have discussed elsewhere (Antonsdóttir, 2020a), many survivors instead expressed the need for space and a guarantee that offenders would not re-enter their life space. Such a guarantee was associated with a sense of justice and freedom.

Conflicting processes

When assessing if a restorative justice process would be an option for them, many participants problematised the issue of timing in relation to their process of regaining a sense of control in the aftermath of the violence. A woman in her early twenties, who had been raped by a man who was a friend of the family and who had been convicted for the crime, said: "Today I would be ready to meet with him, but a year ago, no, absolutely not. ... Before I wouldn't have been mentally prepared, I hadn't processed the experience."

A woman in her twenties, who in her teens had been subjected to sexual violence at a party by a young man she didn't know, said:

'Perhaps some years later, but still what's it good for then? ... I would never have been able to go through this. If he or someone else would have said: can I compensate you for this? I would probably have tried to kill the man, I would have jumped across the table and tried to take his eyes out. You know, at that time, no way.'

A woman in her early thirties talked about how her ideas about justice and compensation had changed over time since the violence took place and in relation to her experiences of the criminal justice system. She said:

'Will everybody have to wait for two years or something before the meeting is held so that the person has recovered enough mentally? ... What one wants out of such a process will change over time – I don't think I'm the only one whose views change over time. So it is very difficult to know when is the right time to participate in such a process.'

A woman in her early forties, who had been subjected to sexual abuse by her stepfather and step-uncles throughout a big part of her childhood, although they had not been charged, reflected on the restorative justice process. She had already read about restorative justice and thought it was an interesting ideology. She said:

'If this is done as soon as cases come up, in particular cases within the family, and if it is done as it should be done, then I think this can deliver a good process and a good outcome. However, in my mind, it has to happen right away not 25 or 30 years later like in my case … and as long as no one is pressured.'

She proceeded to talk about the problems that arise when too much time goes by. She said that such a process would have to take place:

'before the consequences become too severe due to the denial of the offender. … I find that when offenders deny everything it compounds the consequences of the violence. Like in my case, to call a victim mad and all kinds of things is of course very common. So if that has not happened in addition to the violence itself then I think this could be a good solution, if it is done well.'

Participants' responses, therefore, highlight a tension between the importance of participating in a justice process relatively soon after the violence for it to be meaningful and to diminish the likelihood of the offender's protracted denial, which can cause added harm to survivors, and, at the same time, emphasising the importance of needing considerable time to be mentally and emotionally prepared for such a meeting. This question of timing in restorative justice practices has also been problematised in the literature. While promptness is considered important when it comes to holding offenders to account, it can take victims a long time to overcome trauma and gain a sufficient sense of re-embeddedness to feel fit to participate in a restorative justice process (Crawford, 2015).

An offender accountability process

So far, this study has shown how participants had numerous reservations about participating in a restorative justice process. These concerns are primarily related to participating in a restorative justice meeting along with the offender, which is the aim of standard restorative justice practices. Instead, many participants emphasised that offenders should undergo a professional treatment and counselling process. As I have also discussed elsewhere (Antonsdóttir, 2020c), most participants in this study emphasised offender rehabilitation as a part of their understanding of justice in cases of sexual violence and harassment.

A young woman who had been subjected to sexual violence by a man that she met online, and whose case was still pending in the criminal justice system, said:

'Wouldn't it be possible to make offenders undergo some kind of a process like this without the victim, you know, to undergo some form of treatment or counselling while they sit in prison where they have to face the consequences of their actions? ... I mean if you are going to be a part of society then you simply have to make an effort to show that you realise the consequences of your actions. I think that would be a good idea.'

A woman in her early thirties, who had been subjected to image-based sexual violence, emphasised the importance of a professional rehabilitation process for offenders. She said:

'I'm talking about a long process, long rehabilitation process where this twistedness would be tackled. That's what I would want. And then it wouldn't be a court judgment, but he wouldn't be getting off easy either, you know, just go to therapy and say sorry. It would have to be very professional and very serious.'

A woman in her late twenties said:

you need to go to a course on this, you need to sit there and just, you know, learn about human interactions or gender relations or how to behave in certain circumstances, or something to improve yourself to try to prevent this from happening again. (Antonsdóttir, 2020c, p 294)

Similarly, a woman in her late twenties said:

I don't know if rehabilitation works in these cases, but I hope so. I think it would be a better alternative than prison. I think Karlar til ábyrgðar[5] is great based on what I've heard, and it would be good if they were made to enrol in programmes like these. That's what I would be most comfortable with. (Antonsdóttir, 2020c, p 294)

Again, participants' responses highlight how, in many cases, survivors neither wish to meet with the offenders nor restore or reconcile a relationship with offenders. Instead, participants emphasised the importance of offender rehabilitation for the purposes of holding offenders to account and increasing their capacity to take responsibility for their actions. Such a process could be better described as an offender accountability process as opposed to a restorative justice process.

Societal transformation

A number of participants talked about the importance of having the right societal conditions in order for survivors to experience some form of justice. Many talked about the importance of societal support for survivors who speak out about what happened to them, but many did not feel that such support and understanding were readily available. A woman in her late twenties, who had been raped by the brother of her ex-boyfriend, said:

'Icelandic society sides with perpetrators of sexual violence. It's like it is impossible to face the fact that there are perpetrators in this society. They have to be [names two well-known serial offenders] for people to accept that these crimes take place. Icelandic society is not ready to stand with survivors. If survivors speak out or if perpetrators do something a little bit positive, then the public demand immediately that the survivor should forgive. The survivor never gets any peace.'

A woman in her early forties, who had been sexually abused by an older nephew who had never acknowledged what he did, emphasised the importance of society's participation in holding offenders to account. She said: "We need to create positive fear in society. If you commit sexual violence, then you need to face that in some way. You should not be allowed to feel safe in the society."

Others emphasised the importance of creating social space for offenders to take responsibility for their actions. A woman in her mid-twenties, who had been sexually harassed by her stepfather, said: "We need to create an environment where it is possible to admit to what you did. ... there is no room to admit to what you did ... . He would be digging his own grave." Some participants, however, gave examples of cases where offenders had taken some responsibility for their actions, which they viewed favourably. A woman in her early forties, who had been subjected to sexual abuse by her stepfather and step-uncles throughout a big part of her childhood, said:

'There is a case that came up not so long ago where a man made a public admission and said: I have committed sexual violence. Or something of the sort. The online comments were divided into two categories. On the one hand, there were people who said: "Good for you to take responsibility, that is exactly what we want to see". And on the other hand, there were people who said: "You are such a bloody looser".

If we keep doing that, then there is no chance that people will take responsibility for their actions.'

She said further:

'What we need to say is: I'm not going to accept what you did, and you have to take responsibility for it. You have to get help. You have to stop doing it. But we are not going to judge you as scum and expel you from society. ... I think the fear is that we will start to justify their actions. It's like we only have two options: you are either a monster or I'm justifying your violence. But it isn't like that. There are plenty of steps in between.'

In addition, a woman in her early twenties, who had been raped by a man who had been convicted of this crime along with other crimes of sexual violence, said:

'I read an article by a guy who had raped a girl and I thought it was really great how he simply took responsibility for it. I felt sorry for him because he now knows what he did. He hadn't fully realised it at the time but somehow knew that what he had done was not right. He has to live with having raped a girl. He felt terrible and was really sorry not to be able to tell her that. Then I realised that this guy was perhaps a bit human. He is not doomed, even if he committed this crime. But this is so complicated; how do you commit such a crime by mistake but still be a normal individual? There is another side to the matter.'

A woman in her early thirties, who had been subjected to an attempted rape as a teenager by her nephew of similar age, said.

'I understand that his mother loves him. She hasn't denied what he has done, at least not in my case. But I think people have a really hard time with this. As a society, I think we need to develop more on that front ... You can be a friend of a perpetrator ... but then people have to understand that you can support the survivor by keeping the perpetrator accountable. If you are going to be a friend to a perpetrator it becomes a societal responsibility. I feel that that is missing.'

Participants' emphasis on societal transformation reflects what Herman (2005) has noted, that is, that all justice models will fail as long as public attitudes towards crimes of sexual violence remain conflicted and ambivalent. According to participants, the necessary societal conditions entail support and understanding for survivors, as well as creating both societal pressure and space for offenders to take responsibility for their actions but, at the same time, without justifying the violence.

Conclusion

The findings of this study highlight the importance of including a feminist and survivor-centred approach to the development of alternative justice options in cases of sexual violence and harassment. While restorative justice is increasingly being discussed as a more favourable alternative to the criminal justice system in these cases, this study indicates that many survivors could experience the restorative justice process as yet another form of injustice.

First, participants generally did not share the main aim of restorative justice, that is, reconciliation and the restoration of the relationship between the parties. Instead, they emphasised the importance of holding offenders to account, offender rehabilitation, and offender accountability. Second, standard restorative justice practices usually aim to set up a meeting between the offender and the survivor for the purposes of restoration for both parties. However, participants generally had no wish to participate in such a meeting due to their legitimate distrust of offenders, fear of unjust exposure, and the conflicting processes of restorative justice on the one hand, and regaining a sense of control of their lives on the other. Third, many participants envisaged an alternative justice process – a type of offender accountability process – managed by professional counsellors and therapists.

However, offender accountability programmes, as an alternative to the criminal justice system, are not feasible unless offenders are willing to participate in them. Therefore, we are faced with the same challenge as restorative justice programmes which, in cases of sexual violence, largely rely on referrals from the criminal justice system. The question, therefore, becomes: How do we facilitate offender participation in such accountability processes? Under what kind of societal conditions do survivors receive support while offenders are held to account and supported in taking responsibility for their actions?

Since the interviews in this study were conducted, we have seen mounting public pressure on (alleged) offenders of sexual violence and harassment to take responsibility for their actions, culminating in the #MeToo movement, which continues to reverberate throughout Icelandic society. Over the course of the last 12 months, at least 31 influential men who have been publicly named and accused by survivors of indecent behaviour, harassment, gender-based violence or sexual violence have resigned from their positions, been discharged, stepped down from their positions, been refused positions of responsibility, had their events cancelled, or been blocked from participation in sporting events (Rögnvaldsson and Bárudóttir, 2022). In other cases, however, alleged offenders have threatened their accusers and their supporters with defamation suits (Ingó krefst afsökunarbeiðna og miskabóta, 2021). Nevertheless, we have increasing numbers of examples where social pressure has seemingly facilitated offender accountability, indicating an ongoing change in the social climate regarding attitudes towards survivors of sexual violence and harassment.

Although it is still unclear if and how it will unfold, it is safe to say that Icelandic society is currently undergoing a rapid societal transformation regarding sexual violence and harassment. This indicates that societal conditions are becoming increasingly favourable for alternative justice processes, independent of the criminal justice system. It is, however, important to also look beyond restorative justice when developing innovative justice practices and procedures to ensure that these are in line with survivors' justice interests.

Notes

[1] I would like to thank Gyða Margrét Pétursdóttir and the editors of this book for their helpful comments on earlier drafts of this chapter.

[2] The discussion in this section is largely based on the section 'Restorative justice' in the introductory chapter of my PhD thesis (see Antonsdóttir, 2020b, pp 37–40).

[3] The acronym RESTORE stands for Responsibility and Equity for Sexual Transgressions Offering a Restorative Experience.

[4] The aims of the thesis were first, to gain a deeper understanding of how victim-survivors of sexual violence perceive, experience, and understand justice; and second, to explore whether and how this knowledge can be used to expand and develop strategies which are capable of meeting the justice interests of victim-survivors within and outside of the criminal justice system (Antonsdóttir, 2020b).

[5] Karlar til ábyrgðar (Men Take Responsibility), now called Heimilisfriður (Domestic Peace), is primarily a programme for men who commit domestic violence. The programme model is based on a Norwegian programme called Alternativ til Vold (An Alternative to Violence). The programme is run by psychologists and men are offered individual and group counselling sessions, where men are supported to take responsibility for their violence and develop ways to tackle relational issues in a constructive way (Heimilisfriður, n.d.).

References

Andersson, H. and Madsen, K.S. (eds) (2017) Møder mellem offer og krænker. En antologi om mægling i en terapeutisk ramme ved seksuelle overgreb, Denmark: Frydenlund.

Antonsdóttir, H.F. (2020a) 'Injustice Disrupted: Experiences of Just Spaces by Victim-Survivors of Sexual Violence', Social & Legal Studies, 29(5): pp 718–44.

Antonsdóttir, H.F. (2020b) Decentring Criminal Law: Understandings of Justice by Victim-Survivors of Sexual Violence and their Implications for Different Justice Strategies (PhD Dissertation), Sweden: Lund University.

Antonsdóttir, H.F. (2020c) 'Compensation as a Means to Justice? Sexual Violence Survivors' Views on the Tort Law Option in Iceland', Feminist Legal Studies, 28: pp 277–300.

Antonsdóttir, H.F. and Gunnlaugsdóttir, S.Þ. (2013) Tilkynntar nauðganir til lögreglu á árunum 2008 og 2009: Um afbrotið nauðgun, sakborning, brotaþola og málsmeðferð, (Report), Reykjavík: EDDA – Center of Excellence, University of Iceland.

Braun, V. and Clarke, V. (2006) 'Using Thematic Analysis in Psychology', *Qualitative Research in Psychology*, 3: pp 77–101.

Braun, V. and Clarke, V. (2013) *Successful Qualitative Research: A Practical Guide for Beginners*, London: SAGE Publications.

Clarke, V., Braun, V. and Hayfield, N. (2016) 'Thematic Analysis', in J.A. Smith (ed) *Qualitative Psychology: A Practical Guide to Research Methods, 3rd edition*, London: SAGE Publications.

Coker, D. (2002) 'Transformative Justice: Anti-Subordination Processes in Cases of Domestic Violence', in H. Strang and J. Braithwaite (eds) *Restorative Justice and Family Violence*, Cambridge, UK: Cambridge University Press.

Cossins, A. (2008) 'Restorative Justice and Child Sex Offences: The Theory and the Practice', *British Journal of Criminology*, 48(3): pp 359–78.

Crawford, A. (2015) 'Temporality in Restorative Justice: On Time, Timing and Time-consciousness', *Theoretical Criminology*, 19(4): pp 470–90.

Daly, K. (2014) 'Reconceptualizing Sexual Victimization and Justice', in I. Vanfraechem, A. Pemberton and F.M. Ndahinda (eds) *Justice for Victims: Perspectives on Rights, Transition and Reconciliation*, London: Routledge.

Daly, K. (2016) 'What is Restorative Justice? Fresh Answers to a Vexed Question', *Victims & Offenders*, 11(1): pp 9–29.

Daly, K. (2017) 'Sexual Violence and Victims' Justice Interests', in E. Zinsstag and M. Keenan (eds) *Restorative Responses to Sexual Violence: Legal, Social and Therapeutic Dimensions*, London and New York: Routledge, Taylor & Francis Group.

Daly, K. and Stubbs, J. (2006) 'Feminist Engagement with Restorative Justice', *Theoretical Criminology*, 10(1): pp 9–28.

Gade, C.B.N. (2018) '"Restorative Justice": History of the Term's International and Danish Use', in A. Nylund, K. Ervasti and L. Adrian (eds) *Nordic Mediation Research*, Switzerland: Springer.

Heimilisfriður (n.d.) 'Lýsing á verkefninu', Heimilisfriður, meðferðar–og þekkingarmiðstöð um ofbeldi í nánum samböndum [online]. Available from: https://heimilisfridur.is/verkefnid [Accessed 6 February 2022].

Herman, J.L. (2005) 'Justice From the Victim's Perspective', *Violence Against Women*, 11(5): pp 571–602.

Ingó krefst afsökunarbeiðna og miskabóta (2021) *Mbl.is* [online] 14 July. Available from: https://www.mbl.is/frettir/innlent/2021/07/14/ingo_krefst_afsokunarbeidna_og_miskabota/ [Accessed 6 February 2022].

Jülich, S. (2006) 'Views of Justice Among Survivors of Historical Child Sexual Abuse: Implications for Restorative Justice in New Zealand', *Theoretical Criminology*, 10(1): pp 125–38.

Jülich, S. and Landon, F. (2017) 'Achieving Justice Outcomes: Participants of Project Restore's Restorative Processes', in E. Zinsstag and M. Keenan (eds) *Restorative Responses to Sexual Violence. Legal, Social and Therapeutic Dimensions*, London and New York: Routledge, Taylor & Francis Group.

Keenan, M. (2017) 'Criminal justice, Restorative Justice, Sexual Violence and the Rule of Law', in E. Zinsstag and M. Keenan (eds) *Restorative Responses to Sexual Violence. Legal, Social and Therapeutic Dimensions*, London and New York: Routledge, Taylor & Francis Group.

Keenan, M. and Zinsstag, E. (2014) 'Restorative Justice and Sexual Offenses: Can "Changing Lenses" Be Appropriate in This Case Too?', *Monatsschrift für Kriminologie und Strafrechtsreform*, 97(1): pp 93–106.

Koss, M.P. (2014) 'The RESTORE Program of Restorative Justice for Sex Crimes: Vision, Process, and Outcomes', *Journal of Interpersonal Violence*, 29(9): pp 1623–60.

Krahé, B. (2016) 'Societal Responses to Sexual Violence Against Women: Rape Myths and the "Real Rape" Stereotype', in H. Kury, R. Sławomir and E. Shea (eds) *Women and Children as Victims and Offenders: Background, Prevention, Reintegration*, Switzerland: Springer International.

Madsen, K.S. (2005) *Hvor ku' du gøre det?: Konfliktmægling ved seksuelle overgreb*, (Report), Denmark: Center for Voldtægtsofre Rigshospitalet.

McGlynn, C., Westmarland, N. and Godden, N. (2012) '"I Just Wanted Him to Hear Me": Sexual Violence and the Possibilities of Restorative Justice', *Journal of Law and Society*, 39(2): pp 213–40.

McGlynn, C., Downes, J. and Westmarland, N. (2017) 'Seeking Justice for Survivors of Sexual Violence: Recognition, Voice and Consequences', in E. Zinsstag and M. Keenan (eds) *Restorative Responses to Sexual Violence: Legal, Social and Therapeutic Dimensions*, London and New York: Routledge, Taylor & Francis Group.

McGlynn, C. and Westmarland, N. (2019) 'Kaleidoscopic Justice: Sexual Violence and Victim-Survivors' Perceptions of Justice', *Social & Legal Studies*, 28(2): pp 179–201.

Niemi-Kiesiläinen, J. (2001) 'Criminal Law or Social Policy as Protection Against Violence', in K. Nousiainen, Å. Gunnarsson, K. Lundström and J. Niemi-Kiesiläinen (eds) *Responsible Selves: Women in the Nordic Legal Culture*, Aldershot: Ashgate Dartmouth.

Nylund, A., Ervasti, K. and Adrian, L. (2018) 'Introduction to Nordic Mediation Research', in A. Nylund, K. Ervasti and L. Adrian (eds) *Nordic Mediation Research*, Switzerland: Springer.

Peleg-Koriata, I. and Klar-Chalamish, C. (2020) 'The #MeToo Movement and Restorative Justice: Exploring the Views of the Public', *Contemporary Justice Review*, 23(3): pp 239–60.

Ptacek, J. (2009) 'Resisting Co-optation: Three Feminist Challenges to Anti-violence Work', in J. Ptacek (ed) *Restorative Justice and Violence Against Women*, Oxford: Oxford University Press.

Rögnvaldsson, F. and Bárudóttir, H.U. (2022) 'Mennirnir sem viku vegna ásakana', [online] 4 February, *Stundin*, Available from: https://stundin.is/grein/14700/mennirnir-sem-viku-vegna-asakana/ [Accessed 6 February 2022].

Stubbs, J. (2002) 'Domestic Violence and Women's Safety: Feminist Challenges to Restorative Justice', in H. Strang and J. Braithwaite (eds) *Restorative Justice and Family Violence*, Cambridge, UK: Cambridge University Press.

The Agreement on the Platform for the Coalition Government (2021) Agreement on the Platform for the Coalition Government of the Independence Party, the Left Green Movement and the Progressive Party, Stjórnarráðið [online], Available from: https://www.government.is/library/05-Rikisstjorn/Agreement2021.pdf [Accessed 6 February 2022].

The Icelandic Prosecutor Authority (2021) 'Sáttamiðlun. Fyrirmæli: 2/2021', Ríkissaksóknari [online], Available from: https://www.rikissaksokn ari.is/fyrirmaeli/sattamidlun-3 [Accessed 6 February 2022].

Zehr, H. (1985) 'Retributive Justice, Restorative Justice', *New Perspectives on Crime and Justice*, Issue 4. Akron, PA: Mennonite Central Committee Office of Criminal Justice.

Zehr, H. (2002) *The Little Book of Restorative Justice*, Intercourse, PA: Good Books.

Zinsstag, E. and Keenan, M. (2017) 'Restorative Responses to Sexual Violence: An Introduction', in E. Zinsstag and M. Keenan (eds) *Restorative Responses to Sexual Violence: Legal, Social and Therapeutic Dimensions*, London and New York: Routledge, Taylor & Francis Group.

13

I write to tell myself it wasn't my fault

Sumaya Jirde Ali

Translated by Cathinka Dahl Hambro

'I write to you from another world.' This is how Andrzej Tichy begins his novel *Kairos* (2013, p 1). I write to make the world real again. I write from our time, from the incident that gave my body a different story.

A late summer night last year, a tight grip around my throat, a hand touching me.[1]

I write to tell myself it wasn't my fault. I write from a place within me, a place in which the broken is not weak. I write to say that the naivety that has been missing since I became a public figure, which has exposed me to various people's wrath, cannot be used to excuse or explain the assault.

I write to understand why we look within when it is what's on the outside that shakes one's world. I was alone among strangers for the first time since 2016. For a long time, I have used those close to me as a lifebuoy, but that evening I felt free and safe among friendly strangers. And that's when it happened. My initial thought afterwards was: Why didn't I leave with my friends? And the next: What was it about me that made this possible? My language, my walk, my smile, what was it? Why did I sit down next to him?

I write to say: I might have been weak at the time of the incident, but I was brave after. It takes strength to disappoint an audience. I ran into a room filled with people who, like me, considered parties a natural place of escape from the everyday, and I said: This happened to me.

The conversation that followed took place as if I were not there. My gaze rushed back and forth between those who believed me and those who did not. Was this what I had initiated – a discussion? A man much, much older than me had tried to kiss me on the balcony. He tried to choke me three times afterwards. And as we stood there now, he denied everything. So calm and experienced. In hindsight, I have asked myself why I did not leave there and then.

That evening I experienced something I have always known: distress is like a prop. It is to be felt, not discussed or problematised. I dismissed the social situation the moment I said out loud what had happened. By taking myself seriously, I had placed myself above the requirement of keeping up the great atmosphere. I ended up being thrown out of the party.

Staggering towards the city centre, I resembled a child. I felt my body blaming myself, as it refused to cooperate. And it was pouring with rain, so I felt that God blamed me too. I finally called my younger sister Sagal, who picked me up in a taxi. What you wouldn't do when your big sister comes crying!

The day after, my youngest baby sister Hayat suggested that I should report it. I looked at her as if that was the stupidest thing I had ever heard. Neither she nor I realised at the time, but now I know. In order to report a situation like this, you need to own it. And before you can own it, you must fight your own internal battle: to realise that your very being has been violated.

And I did not want to do that. I did not want to acknowledge that I had been harassed. I was so ashamed; felt that everything was my own fault. I thought that if I avoided the incident, the physical traces on my body, the shame, the fear – it would all go away. The only thing I wanted was for the evening to become part of memory's infinite ocean as quickly as possible.

The poet Felicia Mulinari writes, 'here is no soil for our bodies'[2] in her collection *Det som inte kan utplånas (What Cannot Be Obliterated)* (2019, p 56). The first week I isolated myself. The only people I saw were my two baby sisters and my boyfriend Per. My home felt like a strange place. I had to check that the front door was locked several times a day. I saw shadows where there were none. Deadlines for various texts, lectures, social plans and other commitments were soaring above my head. Shapeless, dispirited, speechless. With my eyes closed, I saw the tight grip coming towards me. It ached around my throat. The fear I was feeling, it was not mine.

A week after the incident I went out. I was with Irene and Sagal; we were at an opening; it was so good to be out among the living and it was the first time I had been out since the incident.

The universe did not want the best for me. On our way home, we saw him, he came cycling. I was paralysed, whispered to my little sister and she led me away. He stopped in front of Irene and started talking to her. Irene told me afterwards what he had said. The man was angry and frustrated, she said. He said that if I talked about the incident to friends or to the police, then … I could not then, nor can I today, perceive what he said as anything other than a threat. And I can still remember the unfathomable anger I felt. I thought, *now I'll report it!* But the next morning, I was not angry or brave anymore, just very, very scared. I got up early after an almost sleepless night to double-check whether the front door was locked.

When the poet Aimé Césaire first met his friend Leopold Sedar Senghor, he asked: 'Who am I, Who are we? What are we in this white world?' (Césaire, 2005, p 23). When I am not a Muslim, I am Black, and when I am not Black, I am a young woman bleeding within. In retrospect, I see everything more clearly: not doing anything about the incident was the beginning of a decline. I hardly slept or ate, and I often had difficulties breathing. One night, I cried hysterically and told Per there was a figure standing in front of the bed. I could not take the bus without anxiously looking around me, and the neighbour, who walks his dog every evening, appeared hostile. I stopped visiting places I like in fear of bumping into him. It became obvious to the people around me that I was not doing well. I initiated a meeting with the crisis centre in order to learn more about their work, but forgot the meeting, and remembered it again two weeks too late. Where was I, what was I doing? It all came to a pretty pass when I put on the wrong pair of shoes on two different social occasions. The banal is often the most suggestive. Both my friends and I laughed the first time it happened. The second time, I had a panic attack.

Autumn passed. Unwillingly, by chance, I saw the man another three times. Each time, I found myself back inside the dark silence afterwards. Shivering and with difficulties breathing; all signs of progress seemed to have vanished.

He appeared completely unaffected. How could an incident that affected me so much have so little effect on him? The third encounter became a turning point. Some friends and I were out on a Thursday night when he appeared and sat down at our table. He only left when my friends asked him to leave. The fact that the man came so close made me extremely upset. That is when I finally did it, I called the police. I cried and said they had to come, you need to do something now, this cannot go on any longer. In my report, I wrote: 'Without this encounter with the police, I would probably not have contacted the support centre for victims of crime and found the courage to write this report.'

It was October, and it only took a few days until I received an e-mailed letter from the police. The man had been issued with a restraining order. It said that the man is forbidden 'to visit, pursue or in any other way contact Sumaya Jirde Ali, either personally or via phone, SMS, e-mail or other electronic messaging, letter, postcard or other written communication or through a third person'. It said that there was reason to believe that the man might 'otherwise violate another person's peace'. The ban was set to last until 3 January 2021.

I was completely speechless. And so grateful. Grateful for the fact that there was a point in reporting the incident. That I had been taken seriously. This is it, I thought, you finally have an opportunity to save yourself.

From that moment, the autumn changed. I gradually managed to relax. I stopped feeling so exposed and my surroundings no longer appeared hostile. Things began to look brighter. I gave the incident less space each day. I filled my time with friends and family.

In November, I received a new letter. It was titled 'Termination of restraining order'.

The man's defence attorney had applied for a judicial examination of the restraining order. And the man had been interrogated. 'It does not appear as a likely risk that * will expose you to any future violations', it said.

I was on my way out the door, going to a café to study for an exam. I stood there with the letter in my hand for about half an hour. The silence began to creep back. I felt so much, too much. I called the investigator in order to understand. A legal advisor had made the determination on the basis of my report and an interview with the man. The investigator said I did not sound like someone who wanted anything to do with the man, yet she nevertheless advised me to stay away. And if he did anything more to me, I was to contact the police, she said.

The case was dismissed six days later.

What do I do now? Friends have told me to make a complaint. Said I should find a lawyer. But I am exhausted, so tired of his name, the memory of his hands and the incident. Tired of feeling like a victim, a child. Of being forever bound to other people's capacity to understand.

So instead, I write. I write from this world, from your time and mine. I write not to get ill, I write to move forward, I write to live without fear.

Notes

[1]   This is a translation of a text that Jirde Ali published in the Norwegian newspaper *Morgenbladet*, 14 January 2021.

[2]   The translator's own translation.

References

Césaire, A. (2005) *Nègre je suis, nègre je resterai. Entretiens avec Françoise Vergès*, Paris: Albin Michel.

Mulinari, F. (2019) *Det som inte kan utplånas*, Stockholm: Bonnier. Print.

Tichý, A (2013) *Kairos: Roman*, Stockholm: Bonnier. Print.

14

One step forward and one step back: sexual harassment in Norwegian equality and non-discrimination law

Anne Hellum

Introduction

For a long time, criminal law was the only legal instrument that dealt with sexual harassment. In the 1980s, it became a labour law and equal rights issue.[1]

Today, the perception of sexual harassment as an equality and non-discrimination law issue is firmly rooted in international human rights law, EU law and the law in the Nordic countries. On paper, the equality and non-discrimination law approach represents a more accessible and effective legal tool to combat sexual harassment than the criminal law approach.

This dynamic legal development stands on the shoulders of feminist jurisprudence from the 1970s and 1980s. Sexual harassment, feminist legal scholars like Catharine MacKinnon argued, was an equal rights issue because it created and upheld women's inferior position in law and society (MacKinnon, 1979). This perception of sexual harassment influenced Nordic scholars in the field of women, gender and the law (Petersen, 1988). In 1988, it made its way into the jurisprudence of the UN Committee that monitors the Convention on the Elimination of All Forms of Discrimination against Women (CEDAW) (Hellum and Ikdahl, 2019). The CEDAW Committee's statement that gender-based violence constitutes a violation of women's right to equality and non-discrimination was a milestone in international law.[2]

Fifteen years later, the EU adopted a new Equal Treatment Directive (2002/73/EC) that saw sexual harassment as a combined violation of the right to equality and the right to dignity, often termed the 'dual violations of equality and dignity' approach (see subsection 2 in this chapter). This prompted changes in the gender equality and anti-discrimination laws in all the EU member states, including the Nordic countries (Numhauser-Henning, 2022; Hellum et al, 2023). The Directive's definition of sexual harassment as a gender equality and dignity issue set the scene for the development of a civil law approach aiming for a more effective and accessible protection than had been provided under criminal law. Equality and non-discrimination law, unlike criminal law, does not require that the perpetrator is found to be at fault. It is enough that the sexual attention is unwanted and violates the woman's dignity. Under equality and non-discrimination law, it is the woman who decides whether or not to sue the alleged offender. In criminal law, the public prosecutor decides whether to prosecute or not.

The Norwegian prohibition, which was included in the Norwegian Gender Equality Act (GEADA) in 2002, was prompted by EU law. As member of the Agreement on the European Economic Area (EEA), Norway is bound by EU's gender equality directives.[3] Norwegian law defines sexual harassment as unwanted sexual attention that is 'troublesome'. On paper, it provides stronger protection than the other Nordic countries that have adopted EU's 'dual violations of equality and dignity' approach. Unlike EU law, Norwegian law does not demand that the unwanted sexual harassment has caused damage to dignity. It is enough that the sexual attention, from the perspective of the woman, is 'unwanted' and 'troublesome'.

In Norway, the #MeToo movement's making visible of the widespread incidence of sexual harassment stood in grim contrast to the low number of sexual harassment cases handled by the civil courts. To enhance access to justice, in 2020 the Discrimination Tribunal, which is a low-threshold alternative to the courts, was given power to enforce the Equality and Anti-Discrimination Act's (EADA) prohibition on sexual harassment. The change was a response to the long-standing quest for enforcement reform from women's rights organisations, the Gender Equality Commission, the Equality and Anti-Discrimination Ombud, experts in the field of equality and non-discrimination law, and the CEDAW Committee. In 2020, the Norwegian Supreme Court heard its first case concerning sexual harassment.

These developments make Norway an interesting case to explore the opportunities and limitations of equality and anti-discrimination law as a means to combat sexual harassment. As a scholar in the field of women's law and equality and non-discrimination law, I have followed the development of the Norwegian equality approach to sexual harassment since the enactment of the first Gender Equality Act in 1978 (Hellum and Blaker Strand, 2022). In this chapter, I explore the relationship between the Norwegian equality approach, the criminal law approach and the EU's damage to equality and dignity approach. How Norwegian lawmakers, courts and the Discrimination Tribunal have handled tensions and conflicts between coexisting and overlapping understandings of sexual harassment is the overall theme. The overall aim is to discuss the strengths and weaknesses of this approach as a means of combatting sexual harassment.

The chapter has seven parts. The second part describes and discusses the EU's damage to equality and dignity approach to sexual harassment. The third part provides an overview of the Norwegian equality approach, with a focus on how sexual harassment is defined, sanctioned and its prohibition enforced. The fourth part describes developments in the law in the pre #MeToo phase. Focusing on the disjuncture between the strong normative protection standard and the weak enforcement system, tensions and conflicts between different perceptions of sexual harassment are explored. The fifth and sixth parts describe the post #MeToo phase, with a focus on how the prohibition in the EADA has been interpreted and put into practice by the courts, the Discrimination Tribunal, and the Equality and Anti-Discrimination Ombud. The seventh part discusses why so few women, in spite of recent reforms, use equality and anti-discrimination law as a means of holding perpetrators to account.

The EU's combined harm to equality and dignity approach

In 2002, the EU adopted a new Equal Treatment Directive (2002/73/EC) that defined sexual harassment as an issue of damage to gender equality and dignity. It followed up the Council of the European Union's active role in the preparations for the UN Fourth World Conference on Women that took place in Beijing in 1995. The new Directive was also influenced by the CEDAW Committee's definition of sexual harassment as a violation of women's right to equality.

In line with earlier directives, the Gender Equality Directive (2006/54/EC) (recast) in its introduction states that sexual harassment constitutes a violation of the right to equality and non-discrimination:

> Harassment and sexual harassment are contrary to the principle of equal treatment between men and women and constitute discrimination on grounds of sex for the purposes of this Directive. These forms of discrimination occur not only in the workplace, but also in the context of access to employment, vocational training and promotion. They should therefore be prohibited and should be subject to effective, proportionate and dissuasive penalties.

Article 2.1 (d) of the Directive defines sexual harassment as when: 'any form of unwanted verbal, non-verbal or physical conduct of a sexual nature occurs, with the purpose or effect of violating the dignity of a person, in particular when creating an intimidating, hostile, degrading, humiliating or offensive environment.'

On paper, the EU's combined equality and dignity approach provides a wider and more accessible protection than the criminal law approach. According to the Gender Equality Directive (recast), sexual harassment is unwanted sexual attention that violates a person's dignity. Unlike criminal law, it does not require that the offender is found to be at fault. Furthermore, the Gender Equality Directive (recast) requires that EU member states put in place legislation empowering the offended person to take the offender to court. In criminal law, the public prosecuting authority decides whether to prosecute or not.

Another important difference between EU equality law and criminal law is the burden of proof rules. In equality matters, the reversed burden of proof rule applies. Criminal law, on the other hand, gives the offender the benefit of the doubt. In the Coleman case, the European Court of Justice (ECJ) set out the provision of the reversed burden of proof in harassment cases so that:

> in the event that (the claimant) establishes facts from which it may be presumed that there has been harassment, the effective application of the principle of equal treatment then requires that the burden of proof should fall on the defendants, who must prove that there has been no harassment in the circumstances of the present case. (p 62 of the judgment)[4]

The recast Gender Equality Directive's construction of sexual harassment has been termed the 'dual violations of equality and dignity' approach (Numhauser-Henning, 2022).[5] On the one hand, the Directive states that sexual harassment is a violation of the equality principle. On the other hand, it requires that the unwanted sexual attention has 'the purpose or effect of violating the dignity of a person'. A criticism against this approach is that it does not fully recognise sexual harassment as a matter of unequal power relations that is deeply rooted in social institutions. The critique is based on an empirical study of the implementation of the Directive in a number of EU member states showing that sexual harassment is often *hidden* behind more general regulation against victimisation (Numhauser-Henning and Laulom, 2013). According to this study, the discrimination prohibition often competes with bullying. As a consequence, the scope of the discrimination prohibition tends to focus on the perpetrator in terms of being guilty of a criminal misdemeanour and not a violation of the offended woman's right to equality.

The Norwegian equality approach on paper

The Norwegian Equality and Anti-Discrimination Act's prohibition on sexual harassment is the outcome of a long political and legal process. As a backdrop for the analysis of past and present contests between different conceptions of sexual harassment, I will give an overview of today's legislation.

The current prohibition on sexual harassment is rooted in Section 13 of the Equality and Anti-Discrimination Act (EADA), which was enacted in 2017. It is a single Act that replaced the Gender Equality and Anti-Discrimination Act (GEADA) and the previous anti-discrimination acts. The enforcement of the ban is regulated by the Equality and Anti-Discrimination Ombud Act (EADOA) which was passed the same year. The EADA, unlike the EU's Gender Equality Directive, applies in all areas of society.

This legal framework has three characteristics that, on paper, make it appear to be a well-suited legal tool to combat sexual harassment. First, it provides wider protection than the EU law's dual violation of equality and dignity approach. Second, it provides protection against both individual actions and institutional power structures. Third, it is made accessible through a low-threshold enforcement system that coexists with the ordinary courts. To ensure effective enforcement and access to justice, the Discrimination Tribunal has the power to award remedies to the offended person.

Protection against individual acts

The prohibition on sexual harassment is rooted in Section 13, first paragraph of the EADA, which states: 'Harassment on the basis of factors specified in section 6, first paragraph, and sexual harassment, are prohibited.'

Unlike EU law, the EADA's prohibition on discrimination and sexual harassment applies in all areas of society.

The prohibition targets sexual harassment as such. It does not require that the harassment is related to the gender, sexual orientation or gender identity of a person.

The wording of the EADA, in line with earlier legislation, provides wider protections than the Gender Equality Directive. Section 13, third paragraph of the EADA, defines sexual harassment as: 'any form of unwanted sexual attention that has the purpose or effect of being offensive, frightening, hostile, degrading, humiliating or troublesome'.

An individual act or utterance constitutes sexual harassment if it fulfils the following three criteria. First, the act or utterance must constitute 'sexual attention'. Second, the attention must be 'unwanted'. Third, the sexual attention must have one of the following effects: being 'offensive', 'frightening', 'hostile', 'degrading', 'humiliating' or 'troublesome'.

The 'troublesome' criteria, which defines the lower level of protection, implies that violation of dignity is not required. It suffices that the unwanted sexual attention, from the perspective of the offended person, is troublesome. By broadening the scope of the protection, the Norwegian equality approach is less likely than the EU's dual violation of equality and dignity approach to focus on the perpetrator's motives and not a violation of the offended person's right to equality.

An advantage of the Norwegian equality approach to sexual harassment, in comparison to the criminal law approach, is the application of the reverse burden of proof rule. The aim of this rule, which takes the unequal power relations between the harasser and the harassed into consideration, is to ensure accessible and effective protection. According to the first paragraph in Section 37 of the EADA: 'Discrimination shall be assumed to have occurred if circumstances apply that provide grounds for believing that discrimination has occurred and the person responsible fails to substantiate that discrimination did not in fact occur.'

The purpose of the equality approach to sexual harassment is both restoration and a deterrent. A person who is subject to treatment in breach of the prohibition may, in accordance with Section 38, first paragraph, claim compensation from the offender for economic losses and non-economic loss. In working relationships, the employer's liability for sexual harassment, according to Section 38, second paragraph of the EADA: 'exists irrespective of whether the employer can be blamed'.

Structural protection

The Norwegian equality approach to sexual harassment is not limited to individual actions.

The structural character of sexual harassment is recognised in Section 13, sixth paragraph of the EADA, which places a duty on employers and managers of organisations and educational institutions to: 'preclude and seek to prevent harassment and sexual harassment in their area of responsibility'.

These institutional duties go back to the 2002 reform, where sexual harassment was defined as a social problem that required action at the institutional level.[6]

In addition, Chapter 4 of the EADA entails a duty to make active efforts to promote substantive equality and prevent discrimination, sexual harassment, harassment, and gender violence. In 2019, it was made clear that public authorities' duties to make active efforts to promote equality and prevent discrimination included an obligation to 'preclude harassment, sexual harassment and gender-based violence, and to counter stereotyping' (EADA, Section 24). The same year, it was made clear that the employer's duty to make active efforts to promote equality included a duty to prevent 'harassment, sexual harassment and gender-based violence' (EADA, Section 26). These specifications of the duty to take active steps to promote equality and prevent discrimination were prompted by Norway's obligations under the Istanbul Convention.[7]

Access to enforcement and sanctions

An accessible and effective enforcement system is necessary to put the EADA's protection against sexual harassment into practice (Hellum and Blaker Strand, 2022). In 2019, the Discrimination Tribunal, which is a low-threshold alternative to the ordinary courts, was granted the power to handle sexual harassment cases. This change, which sets out to ensure both individual and institutional accountability, was a legal breakthrough for the equality approach to sexual harassment.

An individual who has been subject to sexual harassment can sue the offender for breach of the EADA's prohibition on sexual harassment in a court or make a complaint to the Discrimination Tribunal. In cases concerning sexual harassment in the workplace, the Discrimination Tribunal has the power to handle claims for compensation and damages from employers.

To ensure institutional accountability, the Discrimination Tribunal also has the power to handle cases where employers, educational institutions and managers of organisations have breached their duty to 'preclude and seek to prevent' sexual harassment under Section 13, sixth paragraph of the EADA. There are, however, limitations on this power. First, the special burden of proof rule in Section 37 of the EADA does not apply in such cases. Second, the right to compensation and damages on objective grounds in the workplace does not apply. Individuals or groups who want compensation for breach of the duty to prevent or seek to stop sexual harassment will thus have to take their case to the ordinary courts. In such cases, the claimant must show that the institution is guilty of violations of these duties by means of the ordinary burden of proof rule.

The proactive obligations embedded in Chapter 4 are monitored by the Equality and Anti-Discrimination Ombud in accordance with Section 5 of the EADOA which gives the following description of the Ombud's tasks:

> The Ombud shall supervise the activity duty and duty to issue a statement pursuant to sections 24, 25, 26 and 26a of the Equality and Anti-Discrimination Act, as well as the duty to report on equality and non-discrimination pursuant to section 3–3 c of the Accounting Act. The Ombud's supervision may include preparation by the Ombud and an employer of a joint strategy for compliance with the activity duty by the undertaking. The Ombud may also review equality statements, analyse the findings and propose improvement measures and strengthened initiatives for inclusion in the undertaking's equality work. The Ombud may also make follow-up visits to undertakings.

The Ombud has the power to take on cases concerning an employer's breach of the reporting duty to the Discrimination Tribunal.

Pre-#MeToo: tensions between the equality and criminal law approach

The EADA's prohibition on sexual harassment and the Discrimination Tribunal's power to enforce it is the endpoint of a long and twisted path that epitomises the tense relationship between different approaches to and conceptions of sexual harassment, particularly the equality approach and the criminal law approach.

The Norwegian equality approach to sexual harassment has been in the throes of change since the 1980s. The first Gender Equality Act, enacted in 1978, did not explicitly address sexual harassment. However, the Gender Equality Ombud, who supervised enforcement of the Act, received a number of complaints from women who had been exposed to unwelcome sexual attention in the workplace (Brantsæter and Widerberg, 1992). Due to the unclear legal situation, the Ombud referred such complainants to the organisation Free Legal Advice for Women or the trade unions. The need to harmonise protection under the Working Environment Act and the Gender Equality Act was pointed out by research in the growing field of women's studies and women's law (Andreassen, 1997).

In 2002, an explicit prohibition on sexual harassment was included in the Gender Equality Act. The reform was prompted by the proposed revisions to the EU's Gender Equality Directive (76/207/EØF) and Norwegian empirical studies showing how sexual harassment undermined women's right to equality in areas like education, work and public participation.

The prohibition embedded in Section 8 of the 2002 Gender Equality Act had the following wording: 'Sexual harassment is prohibited. By sexual harassment is meant unwanted attention which is troublesome for the person who is affected. Sexual harassment constitutes differential treatment on the basis of gender.'

The legislative history emphasised that, to be effective, the protection must take the woman's perception of what 'has the effect of being troublesome' as the starting point. According to the legislative history: 'the assessment of whether the attention must be considered troublesome must rely on a "woman's norm", and not a gender-neutral norm. A guideline may be what a reasonable woman would have perceived as troublesome.'[8]

The Gender Equality Act's construction of sexual harassment was a legal milestone. It prohibited sexual harassment because it was a barrier to equality. Sexual harassment was defined by its negative effect on the recipient. It included both intended and unintended effects and did not require a violation of dignity. As such, the equality approach offered broader protection than criminal law, requiring that the offender was found to be at fault for sexual harassment's negative effects. It also offered stronger protection than EU law, which required violation of a person's dignity.

In spite of this, in many respects sexual harassment was seen as of a different character than discrimination. An example is the EADA's special right to claim compensation on objective grounds in employment situations. According to the Ministry of Children's and Family Affairs, this right should not be extended to victims of sexual harassment because it: 'is of a different character than other types of gender discrimination, because it is perceived as particularly burdensome to be found guilty of sexual harassment.'[9] Thus, the criminal law approach's fault-based definition of sexual harassment took precedence when it came into conflict with the objective equality approach.

The lack of sanctions did not sit well with the EU's Gender Equality Directive's (2002/73/EF) call for effective enforcement. In 2005, the Gender Equality Act's rules concerning compensation on objective grounds for discrimination in the workplace were extended to include victims of sexual harassment.[10] With reference to the EU law's demand for effective sanctions, the Ministry stated: 'It is not unreasonable that an employer who has behaved in a way that results in harassment is held liable, even though there was no intention to harass. To be effective, sanctions must ensure that the person whose rights are violated is compensated.'[11]

Another area of contention was whether victims of sexual harassment should have their cases heard by the Discrimination Tribunal or have to go to court. Powerful actors like the Ministry of Justice and the Attorney General argued that sexual harassment had more in common with criminal law offences than a violation of the equality principle. In their view, the Discrimination Tribunal, which was an administrative, low-threshold agency, was not suited to handle sexual harassment cases. In line with this perception of sexual harassment, the legislative history of the 2005 reform concluded that the offender's right to due process must take precedence.[12]

This idea was strongly criticised by actors like the Equality and Anti-Discrimination Ombud, the Gender Equality Commission, Free Legal Advice for Women, and the Women's Law Institute, all of whom emphasised the commonalities between gender-based discrimination, gender-based harassment and sexual harassment. In 2011 and 2017, in her Supplementary Report to the CEDAW Committee, the Ombud stated:

> It follows from the Gender Equality Act section 8 (a) that sexual harassment is prohibited, and that only the courts shall enforce this prohibition. The Ombud questions whether the current system is good enough, as the risk involved in bringing a lawsuit is high. Almost no cases are brought before the courts. The Equality Commission has proposed that the Ombud and the Tribunal be able to enforce the provision prohibiting sexual harassment.[13]

In its concluding observations to Norway's 9th periodic report in 2019, the CEDAW Committee recommended that Norway: 'extend the authority of the Tribunal to award compensation in cases other than employment discrimination, including cases of sexual harassment'.[14]

In 2019, the Tribunal was authorised to enforce the prohibition against sexual harassment in the EADA. The large number of cases of sexual harassment, which were made visible by the Norwegian #MeToo movement, was a factor that helped to tilt the power balance between those who saw sexual harassment as an equal rights issue and those who saw it as having more in common with a criminal offence.

A key question today is how these changes are translated into practice by the ordinary courts, the Discrimination Tribunal and the Ombud.

Putting the equality approach to sexual harassment into practice

For a long time, the strong protection rooted in the Gender Equality Act, which defined sexual harassment as 'unwanted' and 'troublesome' sexual attention, stood in stark contrast to the low number of court cases concerning sexual harassment. The cases that were handled by the courts were few and of a very grave character (McClimans, 2018; Egeland et al, 2020). The risk involved in bringing a lawsuit was high because of the unclear and contested character of the troublesome criteria. Whether the Norwegian prohibition should be interpreted in the light of EU's 'dual violation of equality and dignity approach' was contested.

The first Supreme Court case: one step forward and one step back

In 2020, the Norwegian Supreme Court handed down its first ruling in a sexual harassment case. In this case, the *Mechanic Case*,[15] it dealt with a series of unclear and contested issues regarding the criteria for sexual harassment. While constituting a step forward, this case was also a step back.

The litigant was a female trainee who was the only woman among 15 employees in a mechanics workshop. She was represented by a lawyer from the National Union (LO).[16] She had experienced a customer coming in from the back of the workshop and placing his hands under her sweater on the lower part of her back when she was down on her knees working. On a later occasion, the same customer had pretended to grab her crotch. Another customer had repeatedly tickled her waist and on one occasion smacked her bottom over her trousers. Finding these facts proved, the Supreme Court concluded that that the conduct of both customers was of a sexual nature, unwanted and troublesome to the woman and as such constituted sexual harassment.

The Court made clear that the 'troublesome' criteria in the EADA provides stronger protection than EU law, which is limited to violation of a person's dignity. The Court stated that: 'The Directive is a floor directive and thus does not preclude stronger protection against sexual harassment under national law, see Article 27'.[17] The Court also clarified the content of standards such as what a reasonable woman would consider troublesome sexual attention and what 'a reasonable person' would understand as unwanted sexual attention.

In its interpretation of 'troublesome', the Supreme Court confirmed that the question whether sexual attention was troublesome or not should be judged by a woman's standard, as stated in the legislative history of the Gender Equality Act.

The Supreme Court confirmed that:

> In other words, the Government Bill stresses that the assessment of what is troublesome is objective, while at the same time, it must be based on a 'woman's standard'. The argument given in favour of such a standard is that 'women generally perceive many more situations as sexual harassment than men', and that, based on relevant research, there 'will be more women than men who report sexual harassment'.[18]

Furthermore, the Court made clear that the assessment of what constitutes unwanted sexual attention must rely on what 'a reasonable person after an overall assessment would understand as unwanted'. A relevant factor in this assessment would be:

> whether there is a relative power imbalance between the parties, and whether the party should understand that the person receiving the attention fears that rejection may have negative consequences ... . It must also be of significance whether the person at whom the attention is directed is in a particularly vulnerable situation.[19]

The Court's broad definition of 'troublesome' and 'unwanted' embedded in the legislative history from 2002 and 2017 was a step forward. By undertaking a holistic assessment of the two incidents, instead of a separate assessment of each incident, the Supreme Court avoided clarifying what the lower level of what constitutes unwanted sexual attention was. Whether the 'from the rear incident', where the customer came in from behind and placed his hands under the woman's sweater on the lower part of her back, in and of itself constituted sexual harassment was left open by the Court's statement that:

> It seems fair that the 'from the rear incident' in itself did not amount to sexual harassment under section 8 of the Gender Equality Act 2013. However, I will not take a clear stand on this issue, as I consider it substantiated that the following incident outside the breakroom took place, and that both incidents must be included in the overall assessment of whether B subjected A to sexual harassment.[20]

By leaving open whether the 'from the rear incident' in and of itself constituted sexual harassment, the Court missed an opportunity to clarify the floor level of the protection standard. This lack of clarity, which creates an uncertainty that gives the offender the benefit of the doubt, was a step back.

In addition to its ruling in the actual case, the Supreme Court made a general statement regarding the burden of proof rules in the EADA. While on the one hand finding proof that the two customers had subjected the woman to unwanted, sexual harassment that was troublesome, on the other hand the Court reiterated the misconceived conception of the reverse burden of proof rules embedded in the legislative history to the EADA and in its earlier decisions. It stated that: 'the burden of proof rule in section 37 is not an exception from the general standard of proof in civil cases. The standard of proof is, here as otherwise, that the most probable fact – after an overall assessment of the evidence – prevails.'[21]

Making this general statement, the Supreme Court case undermines one of the key elements in the equality approach to sexual harassment and is in direct conflict with the EU's Gender Equality Directive. This constitutes a step back.

Cases from the Discrimination Tribunal

The broader political and legal context of the 2019 reform

Since 2019, the Discrimination Tribunal has been authorised to enforce the prohibition against sexual harassment in the EADA. The proponents of the reform assumed that this change would enhance access to justice in sexual harassment cases.

The high number of rejected cases and the low number of successful cases, however, flies in the face of these assumptions. Between 2019 and 2021, the Tribunal received 49 complaints concerning sexual harassment whereof 13 are still under consideration.[22] The complainants were women, men, homosexuals, and transgender persons. Of the 36 cases that were decided, the Tribunal concluded a breach in two cases and non-breach in three cases.[23] Twelve cases ended without decision, ten cases where closed and eleven were rejected.

The low number of decided cases must be understood in the light of the legal and political context in which the 2019 reform took place. In 2017, the conservative Solberg government changed the organisation of the Equality Ombud and the Discrimination Tribunal. The aim was to make the enforcement system more cost-effective and efficient. To this end a one-tier, free of charge, written complaint procedure was introduced (EADOA Section 9). To speed up the process and get the number of cases down, the chairpersons of the Tribunal were granted competence to singlehandedly dismiss or close a case, thereby stopping further adjudication (EADOA

Section 10). A case can be dismissed if 'the conditions for processing the case are not met'. A case may be closed if 'the matter is trivial in nature' or if 'the submitted evidence fails to elucidate the case sufficiently'.

One step back: lack of legal information

A criticism of the new enforcement system is that it undermines access to justice in discrimination, harassment and sexual harassment cases (Hellum and Blaker Strand, 2022). The introduction of written proceedings constitutes a barrier for persons who lack knowledge of the law. Furthermore, complainants in discrimination and harassment cases are not entitled to legal aid. In practice, a large number of complainants are unaware of their right to seek advice from the Ombud (EADOA Section 5). In addition, the Tribunal Secretariat's duty to provide information to complainants is unclear.

The *Halloween Case* illustrates problems associated with the lack of clarity surrounding the Discrimination Tribunal's duty to provide information in combination with the Tribunal head's broad powers to reject and close cases.[24] In this case, the complainant argued that a fellow worker's comment about her attire was of a sexual nature, and as such was sexual harassment. The case was rejected by the Tribunal head because it was submitted before the change in the law that empowered the Tribunal to handle cases concerning sexual harassment came into force. The Tribunal, however, did have the power to assess whether the remarks constituted harassment on the basis of gender or gender identity. In the light of the blurred boundary between sexual harassment and gender-based harassment, the Tribunal should, in my view, have informed the complainant about the possibility of lodging a complaint of gender-based harassment.

One step forward: clarification of the 'troublesome' criteria

Critics of the Supreme Court decision feared that the lack of clarity as to what constitutes sexual harassment in one-off incidents would have a 'chilling' effect on the Tribunal's decisions in sexual harassment cases. Several of the cases decided by the Tribunal, however, help to clarify this question (Hellum, 2022).

In the *Pub Kiss Case*, the Tribunal, with reference to the unequal relationship between the parties, made clear that one-off incidents may be seen as 'unwanted' in situations where the recipient of the sexual attention has not explicitly said that it is unwanted.[25] In this case, A, a homosexual man, complained that he had been sexually harassed by his former boss, B. B had suddenly kissed him outside a pub on the way home from a work event. The Tribunal, with reference to the Supreme Court's statement that 'the attention must be of such a nature and seriousness that it suggests that, in an overall assessment, a reasonable person would understand that it is unwanted', concluded that the kiss came suddenly without any indication that A wanted it. In the light of A's feeling of humiliation, resulting in psychological problems, the Tribunal concluded that the incident was 'unwanted' and 'troublesome'.

The *Pub Kiss Case* represents a step forward in comparison to the *Boxer Shorts Case*, decided by the Tribunal shortly before the Supreme Court handed down its decision in the *Mechanic Case*.[26] In this case, a male supervisor came into the changing room and pulled down the boxer shorts of a male employee so that his private parts were laid bare. The Tribunal found that the event was 'unwanted' and in principle unacceptable. Since the supervisor had apologised and it was a one-off incident, that was not sexually motivated and took place in a work environment where a sexual tone was not unusual, the Tribunal concluded that the action was not serious enough to be seen as 'troublesome'. In its deliberations, the Tribunal overlooked that sexual harassment, which is a way of exercising power, does not require a sexual motivation.[27] Emphasising that the supervisor had later apologised, the Tribunal did not give due consideration to the imbalance in the power relationship between the parties. The Tribunal also overlooked that a sexualised environment does not constitute a factor that can excuse unacceptable behaviour (Rasmussen, Nielsen and Tvarnø, 2020).

In the *Health Worker Case*, a female employee complained about sexual harassment by a male supervisor on several occasions.[28] The Tribunal, unlike the Supreme Court, undertook a separate assessment of each incident. The Tribunal concluded that the first incident, where the supervisor, in front of other colleagues at the bar during a conference held at a hotel, asked whether it was time to go and have sex in the hotel room, constituted sexual harassment. It concluded that: 'This form of attention under such circumstances from a supervisor is clearly unwanted, even though the person who is harassed has not stated in advance that it is unwanted. For the same reason, the Tribunal is not in doubt that this was troublesome.' The Tribunal was also of the view that the second incident, where the supervisor touched the woman's tights at a bar after a summer party for employees, constituted 'unwanted' and 'troublesome' sexual attention.

One step back: the right to a remedy

To ensure effective enforcement of the prohibition, the Tribunal has the power to award compensation in cases concerning sexual harassment in the workplace. However, none of the victims in the cases described here claimed compensation. It should be noted that the Tribunal, according to the legislative history, is not obliged to inform the complainant about the right to claim compensation. This information gap clearly undermines the transformative potential of the equality approach to sexual harassment. To have a preventive effect, the prohibition must be accompanied by accessible and effective sanctions such as economic compensation.

Enforcement of institutional duties: a step forward

The Equality Ombud and the Tribunal have the power to deal with breaches of the institutional duties in the EADA. But how is the supervision and enforcement of these duties carried out in practice?

Under Section 5 of the EADOA, the Ombud is to exercise supervision over the duty of private and public sector employers and public authorities to promote equality and prevent sexual harassment and their duty to report on the measures that have been taken. To ensure accountability, the Ombud may, if public and private employers don't fulfil their reporting obligation, take the case to the Discrimination Tribunal. How the Ombud will balance its power to supervise and enforce the duty to prevent sexual harassment remains to be seen. The Ombud has so far published a guide for employers, service providers and educational institutions on preventing and dealing with sexual harassment in the workplace. No cases concerning the breach of the reporting duty have so far been brought before the Tribunal.

To ensure institutional accountability, the Discrimination Tribunal has the power to handle cases concerning breaches of the duty of employers, educational institutions and managers of organisations to take measures to prevent sexual harassment under Section 13 sixth paragraph of the EADA. Since the EADOA entered into force in 2018, the Tribunal has dealt with several complaints concerning breaches of these duties. Only one of these complaints has been successful.[29] In the *Fire and Rescue Service Case*, where the complainant was not successful in her claim that there was gender discrimination and gender/sexual harassment on an individual basis, the Tribunal concluded that the municipality had breached its duty to prevent and seek to prevent harassment.[30] The Tribunal found it proved that the employer had been notified a number of times of problems regarding sexual harassment and that no documentation had been presented that could substantiate that an investigation had been carried out into the actual conditions.

The Tribunal does not have power to handle claims concerning economic compensation for an employer's violation of the duty to prevent sexual harassment in Section 13 sixth paragraph of the EADA. So far, the courts have heard one such case. The Court of Appeal's judgment in the *Mechanic Case*, where the employer was ordered to compensate the woman who had been sexually harassed by two customers in the workshop where she was employed, was the first of its kind in Norway.[31] The Appeal Court upheld the District Court's judgment, where the workshop and the customers were seen as jointly liable for the woman's economic loss caused by the customers' sexual harassment.[32] The Appeal Court found that the employer, through its supervisors on the days in question, was to blame for not fulfilling the employer's duty to prevent sexual harassment. It concluded that the measures taken by the employer were inadequate and inappropriate and stated: 'The management had been aware of her psychological reaction to the harassment for several months, and should have respected this and worked systematically to improve her working conditions'.[33]

The Appeal Court thus concluded that the employer was at fault for the incidents of sexual harassment. The woman's economic loss of NOK 36,387 resulting from her quitting her job was seen as caused by both the customer and the employer. The judgment helps to clarify the individual's right to economic redress for a breach of the duty to prevent and seek to stop sexual harassment under Section 13 sixth paragraph of the EADA. By recognising the close connection between individual and institutional protections, it represents a step forward for the equality approach to sexual harassment.

Conclusion

The Norwegian case study shows the long and winding road whereby the Norwegian equality approach to sexual harassment has evolved. Insights on law reform, Supreme Court practice and cases from the Discrimination Tribunal describe ongoing tensions between different legal conceptions of sexual harassment.

On paper, the Gender Equality Act and the Equality and Anti-Discrimination Act see sexual harassment as both an individual and institutional issue. Both public authorities and private and public sector employers are obliged to take measures to prevent sexual harassment. These changes are the result of concerted efforts from women's rights activists and gender equality experts, as well as national and international accountability mechanisms.

The GEADA's definition of sexual harassment as 'unwanted' and 'troublesome' sexual attention was a breakthrough for the equality approach, pioneered by feminist jurisprudence in the 1970s and 1980s. For almost 20 years this understanding, which was rooted in the legal text and in the legislative history, existed in the shadow of other legal definitions and conceptions, such as the EU law's 'dual violations of equality and dignity' approach and the widely held legal view that sexual harassment had more in common with a breach of criminal law than of equality and non-discrimination law.

2020 was a breakthrough for the EADA's definition of sexual harassment. The #MeToo movement's making visible of the widespread incidence of sexual harassment paved the way for enforcement reform that recognised sexual harassment as a breach of equality and non-discrimination law. The Supreme Court's decision the same year made clear that Norwegian law's 'troublesome' criteria, unlike EU law, did not require the violation of a person's dignity. The Court's decision left a lot to be desired regarding the floor level of protection. Several of the cases decided by the Discrimination Tribunal, however, make it clear that one-off incidents that take place in the context of unequal power relationships may be seen as 'unwanted' and 'troublesome' even though the recipient of the sexual attention has not explicitly stated that it is unwanted.

These steps forward, however, have an uncertain future. Whether the courts will uphold the Tribunal's considerations regarding one off incidents and whether the Ombud's supervision and enforcement of private and public sector employers' duties to take measures to prevent sexual harassment will have the assumed effect remains to be seen.

There are also new setbacks. The Supreme Court's interpretation of the reverse burden of proof rule in the EADA is in conflict with Norway's EEA law obligation to ensure effective enforcement of the offended woman's right to equality. Another setback is the introduction of a new enforcement system resulting in high numbers of sexual harassment cases that are rejected or closed by the Discrimination Tribunal. These setbacks show how the equality approach remains an area of contention between different legal conceptions of how a woman's right to protection against discrimination, harassment and sexual harassment should be balanced against the rights of the offender.

Notes

[1] This chapter focuses on sexual harassment as an equal rights issue.
[2] The CEDAW Committee in General Recommendation No. 12 (1989) and General Recommendation No. 19 para 6 and para 18 (1992) included sexual harassment in its definition of gender violence as a form of discrimination against women.
[3] Article 69 of the EEA agreement, which is the cornerstone of relations between Norway and the EU, implies that the EU's gender equality directives are binding for Norway.
[4] C-303/06, S. Coleman v Attridge Law and Steve Law.
[5] Numhauser-Henning uses the term 'double equality and dignity harm' approach.
[6] Government Bill to the Odelsting No. 77 (2001–2002) point 9 p 108.
[7] Act 21 June 2019 No. 57 about changes in the Equality and Anti-Discrimination Ombud Act (etablering av et lavterskeltilbud for behandling av saker om seksuell trakassering og en styrking av aktivitets- og redegjørelsesplikten).
[8] Government Bill to the Odelsting No. 77 (2000–2001) p 72.
[9] Government Bill to the Odelsting No. 77 (2000–2001) p 152.
[10] Government Bill to the Odelsting No. 5 (2004–2005) pp 48–51.
[11] Government Bill to the Odelsting No. 5 (2004–2005) p 50.
[12] Government Bill to the Odelsting No. 5 (2004–2005) p 50.

13 Supplementary Report to the 8th Norwegian Report to the CEDAW Committee from the Equality and Anti-Discrimination Ombud, para 5.
14 CEDAW/C/NOR/CO/9, para 18b.
15 HR-2020-2476-A, *The Mechanic Case*. The Supreme Court applied Section 8 in the Gender Equality Act, which has been replaced by Section 13 in the EADA that upholds the *troublesome* criteria. The case is analysed in Hellum and Blaker Strand (2022) Chapter 8.
16 An interview with lawyer Tina Nordstrøm is found in the *Journal of the Norwegian Bar Association*: https://www.advokatbladet.no/advokat-jul/vi-mangler-tilstrekkelig-vern-av-mennesker-som-vil-ta-seksuell-trakassering-til-retten/156561.
17 HR-2020-2476-A, Premiss 35.
18 HR-2020-2476-A, Premiss 69.
19 HR-2020-2476-A, Premiss 63, 64.
20 HR-2020-2476-A, Premiss 87.
21 HR-2020-2476-A, Premiss 75 and Premiss 76.
22 As of 28 January 2022, The Discrimination Tribunal's website.
23 Breach: DIN 2020-169 and DIN 2020-191. Not Breach: DIN 2022-152, DIN 2022-118, DIN 2022-154.
24 DIN-2019-380 *Halloween Case*.
25 DIN 2021-169 *Pub Kiss Case*.
26 DIN 2020-118 *Boxer Shorts Case*.
27 Prop.81 L (2016–2017) punkt 18.2.2. s. 179 og kapittel 30 merknader til § 13, s. 320.
28 DIN 2020. *Health Worker Case*.
29 Not breach: DIN 2020-152 and DIN 2020-154. Breach: DIN 2028-20. *The Fire and Rescue Service Case*.
30 DIN 2028-20. *The Fire and Rescue Service Case*.
31 LH-2019-87696. This aspect of the *Mechanic Case* was not appealed to the Supreme Court.
32 This aspect of the Appeal Court judgment was not appealed to the Supreme Court.
33 This aspect of the Appeal Court judgment was not appealed to the Supreme Court, p 11.

References

Andreassen, S. (1997). Arbeidsmiljølovens vern mot uønsket seksuell oppmerksomhet. Ad Notam Forlag: Oslo.

Brantsæter, M.C. and Widerberg, K. (eds) (1992). Sex i arbeidet. Tiden Norsk Forlag A/S: Oslo.

Egeland, L., Hole, T. And Brucker, I. (2020). Seksuell trakassering i arbeidslivet. Gyldendal Akademisk: Oslo.

Equal Treatment Directive (2002/73/EC).

Gender Equality Directive (2006/54/EC).

Hellum, A. (2022). Kommentar til HR-2020-2476-A Mekaniker-saken og dens betydning for Diskrimineringsnemndas praksis i saker som gjelder seksuell trakassering». Juridica https://juridika.no/innsikt/kommentar-til-hr-2020-2476-a-mekaniker-saken.

Hellum, A. and Blaker Strand, V. (2022). Likestillings- og diskrimineringsrett, Gyldendal Juridisk: Oslo.

Hellum, A. and Ikdahl, I. (2019). Committee on the Elimination of Discrimination against Women. *Max Planck Encyclopedias of International Law*. Available from: https://opil.ouplaw.com/view/10.1093/law-mpei pro/e1329.013.1329/lawmpeipro-e1329?rskey=jDz5RQ&result= 1&prd=MPIL.

Hellum, A., Ikdahl, I., Blaker Strand, V. and Svensson, E.M. (2023) (forthcoming). *Nordic Equality and Anti-Discrimination Laws in the Throes of Change*. Abindon-on-Thames: Routledge.

McClimans, E.L. (2018). Plagsom uønsket seksuell oppmerksomhet – er vern for de få? *Kritisk juss*, vol. 46, nr. 2 s. 91–114.

MacKinnon, C.A. (1979). *Sexual Harassment of Working Women – A Case of Sex Discrimination*. Yale University Press: New Haven.

Numhauser-Henning, A, (2022). Sexual Harassment at Work –Discrimination versus Dignity Harm. A Comment in the Wake of the #metoo Movement. *Scandinavian Studies in Law*, Volume 68, *Equality*: Stockholm.

Numhauser-Henning, A. and Laulom, S. (2013). *Harassment Related to Sex and Sexual Harassment Law, 33 European Countries*, European Commission, Directorate-General for Justice: Brussels.

Petersen, H. (1988). Retsbeskyttelse af kvinders værdighed – seksuel chikane i komparativ og retsteoretisk belysning. Tidsskrift for rettsvitenskap årg. 101 nr. 3 s. 253–307.

Rasmussen, M., Nielsen, R. and Tvarnø, C. (2020). Gender Equality Law in Transition – Sexual Harassment is Discrimination – A Study of EU-law and Danish Case Law. Europarettslig Tidsskrift nr. 1. 2020.

15

IN THE GENTS

Mads Ananda Lodahl

Translated by Nielsine Nielsen and Paul Russell Garrett

Not long after the kids move out, Carsten and I move out of the house and into a smaller flat. It frees up a lot of time for us to do other things together, what with not having a big house to look after. It isn't long before we start missing our garden. After a couple of years in the flat, we manage to get an allotment garden outside of town.

The allotment cabin is fairly basic, but it has what we need: a kitchen, a bedroom and a front room, and it's big enough to have the kids over. Even with our first grandchild on the way. There's no toilet on the property, but the communal facilities further up Hollyhock Row have both toilets and showers. It's not too far.

Our garden has a lot of old fruit trees, a good variety of perennials, and herbs and berries, all framing the obligatory patch of grass, where Carsten and I can enjoy the sun and do crosswords.

Our allotment is part of an association, one of nearly four hundred neatly arranged plots in rows surrounding ours. There are narrow gravel paths that you can drive along, and all that separates one garden from the next is a hedge, so you're practically on top of each other. We can hear everything the neighbours say through the hedge, meaning they must be able to hear us as well.

On one side of our allotment, we have Tove and Anders, who keep everything trim and tidy (their garden has won awards). On the other side is one of the so-called 'ghost gardens', where everything is overgrown, and the cabin could do with some work because no one has been in there for years. We've signed all of our kids up to the waiting list, and in time we hope they'll get an allotment garden in our association. I like having family close by, but none of the kids made an offer on the ghost allotment when it went up for sale – and was sold – last winter. We haven't met our new neighbours yet, but I overheard Tove saying they were a young couple with kids.

Carsten pees in the hedge behind the shed when he has to go, but I always use the communal facilities up by the car park. It's an old red building with toilets for men at one end and for women at the other.

I'd heard from Tove that the renovations were due to start on the building, and as I approach the car park, I can see they've already begun. They're starting with the ladies, so in the meantime, everyone has to use the gents.

It's being completely gutted. They're putting in new sinks and cisterns, and they're even changing the pipes, apparently. The cubicles, made of red plywood, are being torn down and built from scratch, they're installing new flooring and giving everything a lick of paint. Once they're done with the ladies, everyone will be able to use the toilets and showers there while the gents is given the same treatment.

I get nervous when I step inside the gents, thinking I shouldn't be in here. The first thing I notice is the smell, and that the room has a different set-up. Ours has five cubicles and two showers, but in here, there are only two cubicles and two showers, leaving room for a urinal. I hurry into one of the cubicles and close and lock the door behind me. The little latch doesn't line up, so I have to wriggle it a little. I've never had that problem in our facilities. Makes me think the men might be a little less gentle with the lock, which is why it's not working properly.

Sometimes when I'm on the toilet, it can take me a while to do my business. Especially if I'm a little nervous. I hear someone enter the neighbouring cubicle and my body just stops. I hear him fart and pee at the same time.

It could be a woman, I think, and I'm calmed by the idea, but then he lets out a loud grunt, like he's been holding his breath and can finally let it all out, and I can tell it must be a man.

I can't finish as long as he's next to me, so I look around a bit while I wait. Sitting in the cubicle, you could just as well be in the ladies. Same size, same faded red walls. Then I spot something in the upper-right corner of the partition in front of me. Someone has written something with a black marker.

Bente from Hollyhock Row is a great lay, it says.

The text is plain to see from where I'm sitting. Underneath, in different writing, someone has written *Thanks for the tip* with a pen.

I read both messages a few times to make sure I'm reading them right. As far as I know, I'm the only Bente on Hollyhock Row. It has to be me. A strange, surreal feeling wells up inside me. It's disconcerting.

The guy next door finishes up. He flushes, opens the door and leaves without washing his hands. I wonder if he was the one who wrote it. Earlier. Did he time his visit to go at the same time as me? To gauge how I would react when I noticed the messages?

I start to wonder how long they've been there and who has seen them. Then I'm back to thinking about who wrote them. I haven't been with anyone other than Carsten since we met back in 1989. He's the only one who would know anything about that, and he wouldn't have written it. I know him well enough to be sure.

But he must have seen it. Why didn't he say anything? Why didn't he remove it? Maybe he did write it after all. No, I can't believe that. But surely he's seen it. Maybe he thinks I slept with someone in the association, who then wrote it.

I can't finish. Someone is in the next cubicle again. From the sound of it, more than one person. My whole body shuts down and I consider pulling up my trousers and leaving before I'm done.

"Come on love, let's get those trousers down."

A woman talking to a child. I hear peeing, and it must be the child. I relax a little and go in time with the child. It feels safe.

Bente from Hollyhock Row is a great lay, I read again.

It couldn't have been Carsten. It's not even his writing. Someone must have written this to upset me. Or because he wants to sleep with me. Maybe the kind of person who doesn't understand the word 'no'. I've been down that road before. The way he touched me. I was just out of college, my first real job, and then my boss had to get all handsy. That was before I met Carsten. He's never forced me to do anything.

But why didn't he get rid of it? Could it be he always uses the other cubicle and has never seen it? Not once?

When the mother and the child are gone, I'm finally done. I wipe, pull up my trousers and flush the toilet, but just as I'm about to unlatch the door, I hear someone again. At first, I don't recognise the metallic ringing, but then I realise it's someone using the urinal. I wait for him to finish. He washes his hands and leaves. Then I let myself out and walk, as fast as I can, away from the shared facilities towards the car park.

I should wash my hands when I get back to the allotment, I think to myself.

Summer Shade. That's the name of our allotment cabin. Sometimes we call it Summer Shade Hotel.

"Should we head out to Summer Shade Hotel", Carsten will ask with a smile when we wake up in the flat, the sun shining, and we have no plans. Then we'll pack up the car and head out here.

Thanks for the tip.

That's even worse than the original message, because now I know someone read it. It almost feels like a conspiracy, since more than one person is involved. Why didn't anyone come to my defence?

Why are you writing such nonsense? they might have written.

But this.

Thanks for the tip.

Like I'm being reviewed.

Why hasn't Carsten removed it? He must have seen it. Again I wonder how long it's been there. We've had the allotment for three years. Has it been there the whole time? Maybe Anders wrote it. We can hear everything he and Tove say, so maybe they heard Carsten and me making love. It's not Tove – I couldn't imagine that.

I picture Anders holding a marker, writing things about me on the wall of the toilet. It doesn't make any sense. He's older than us. It must have been some kids who wrote the messages, but why not write about one of the girls their age instead?

While I'm walking down the gravel path to our allotment, a car drives towards me. The road is narrow. I squeeze up against a hedge to let the car pass. A man is driving, and there's a woman in the passenger seat, probably his wife. They wave as they pass. With a smile on his lips, he touches the tip of his index finger to his forehead. I get a sinking feeling in my stomach when I realise he must have seen what's written about me in the gents. It's like getting punched in the gut. Maybe he was the one who wrote it.

Bente from Hollyhock Row is a great lay.

Bente from Hollyhock Row is a great lay.

Nobody could know anything about that. Why would they write that? Why would they do this to me? What reason could they possibly have? If only I knew who it was. Then I could ask them. Then I could give them a piece of my mind.

I could even go back there right now. I could write my own message on the wall next to the others.

You should be ashamed of yourselves!

Do you kiss your mother with that mouth?

No, that won't do.

Pricks!

Someone should just cross it out. Or paint over it. As if it was never there in the first place. I think we have some paint in the shed. I could go back right now and paint over it. I wish I could tear down the entire building, and I smile to myself when I remember the wall is going to be torn down soon and replaced by one without that stupid message.

When I get to our allotment, Carsten is there, chatting to another man. He's a few years older than our eldest son but quite a bit bigger. A bit rough-looking, to be honest, and I wonder if he might have written it.

"You want to trim them around midsummer and maybe again in August", Carsten says.

They're standing over by the ghost garden, talking about the hedge, so it's probably the new neighbour.

I wonder when they took over the allotment, and how long that message has been in the toilets. I've no way of knowing. I don't want to ask Carsten. How would I even tell him? Should I even tell him? I could ask him to paint over it. I just don't understand why he never told me.

They laugh, tug at the hedge a little, and talk about how it will grow thicker if they cut it back all the way. The new neighbour goes to introduce himself, but I head into the kitchen to wash my hands.

16

Conclusion: Re-imaginations and reflections for the future

Maja Lundqvist, Angelica Simonsson and Kajsa Widegren

We started out this edited collection with an ambition to problematise how knowledge production on sexual harassment has been shaped by certain historical and structural conditions. We argued that these conditions have not been productive for a comprehensive understanding of the issue of sexual harassment because the phenomenon is not as limited as previous discourses have portrayed it, nor is it sufficient to present it as a neatly packaged subject. We need not only to continue to collect stories of sexual harassment, as the #MeToo movement called on us to do, but also to collect stories about what happens next, and to unpack this phenomenon that we call 'sexual harassment'. One part of this is to let the concepts used in the different chapters guide the conceptual understanding in this conclusion as well. One effect of this is that the terms sexual harassment, violence, and sexual violence may well be used in somewhat inconsistent, overlapping, and divergent ways.

As a social imaginary, sexual harassment is most often constructed as a 'drama with two characters': the perpetrator and the victim. Sometimes there is a third actor, called the bystander. There is occasionally an administrator or a representative of the law standing in the background. The chapters of this book have underscored in a variety of ways that this understanding is far too limited. Therefore, in this concluding chapter, we want to try to bring together the different actors, voices and perspectives that the authors have placed on the stage of this drama. Here, we want to set the chapters in conversation with each other, because we believe that this will help us to broaden our understanding of sexual harassment. We have taken our cue from Paulina de los Reyes in Chapter 3, where she proposes a comprehensive approach. The doing of a comprehensive approach in our case is to set the different chapters in dialogue with each other, looking for common voices, but also for differences, the specificities of different contexts, the cutting-through of different intersecting power relations, and the use of new concepts, new imaginaries. Each chapter contributes new knowledge and engenders questions: theoretical, empirical and political. Relevant intersectional perspectives in particular nuance, challenge and develop our understanding of sexual harassment and notions of the Nordic region as structured on gender equality, transparency, and social and economic security. The accounts as well as the consequences and effects of sexual violence and harassment in this book are, so to speak, intersectional in themselves. They show how experiences, social positions and lives are always intertwined and affected by different positionalities at micro, meso and macro levels in society. A complex and diverse picture of experiences, and of the antecedents and consequences, of sexual violence and harassment emerges, helping us to blur the lines around this neatly packaged phenomenon. There is an urgent need for this.

The development of knowledge about sexual harassment in the context of the Nordic region was a starting point for this book. This focus on the Nordic region as a unity can of course be disputed. Norms will differ significantly in different parts of the Nordic countries and throughout the whole of the region. Indeed, can researchers and writers extract examples of best practice from this region, all ready for a smooth implementation in other regions or countries of the world, contributing to the quest for effective preventive measures against sexual harassment around the globe? We would say no to that question. Instead, we see the localisation to the Nordic region in this book as a reminder not to universalise sexual harassment. Thus, it is not specifically the Nordic region that is important here, but instead the need to be context-sensitive when trying to understand and grasp the particularities and magnitude of sexual harassment in any context. Local and regional understandings of gender equality, of citizenship, of women and men, for example, create specific conditions for the emergence, persistence and prevention of sexual harassment. In other regions and countries, other discourses on gender and violence will need to be scrutinised.

Since this book is a compilation of knowledge, we see some strains of thinking that we would like to develop in this concluding chapter, and we have therefore divided the chapter into four parts. First, the work that positions sexual harassment as an issue in relation to other forms of violence and harassment offers a long-awaited shift in the understanding of sexual harassment. It positions sexual harassment on a continuum of life and society, as well as on a continuum of violence and bodily transmissions of violence, across generations. Second, the book contributes core insights on the potential, as well as the limits, of the juridical system, targeting questions of possibilities for justice, restoration, and societal transformation. By problematising the limitations of the juridical understanding of sexual harassment, (in)justice within and outside of juridical systems are explored. Third, we focus on different aspects of the Nordic gender equality discourse, and how it obstructs both social and political change, reinforces Nordic exceptionalism and racism while also complicating individual interventions. Fourth, we close the chapter by offering a few lessons that we have learnt from the work on this book regarding prevention and recommendations. It ends with some reflections on what 'doing' can be in this context, and how re-imagining can be seen as an integral part of taking action.

Sexual harassment within continuums of violence, life and society

In the Introduction (Chapter 1), we borrowed Mary Douglas's thoughts on anomaly to try to describe the framing of sexual harassment as something out of place, as dirt and at the same time as something that points to an idea about an otherwise 'normal', clean and tidy everyday life. We want to underscore that the chapters in this book portray the complexity of sexual harassment; it is both an anomaly and normalised at the same time. The Nordic context, given its strong ideas about gender equality, modernity and non-violence, may also strengthen this ambivalent position of sexual harassment even more. Douglas explains: 'Uncleanness or dirt is that which must not be included if a pattern is to be maintained' (Douglas, 1984, p 50). Despite being singled out as dirty and out of place, for example in policy making, we can see clearly in Chapter 6 by Heta Mulari and Chapter 7 by Lea Skewes how the simultaneous everyday normalisation practices of sexual harassment function as a way to include the dirtiness without disrupting the pattern. Strong and clear signals in policy and procedures are not being reflected in practice. Instead, in practice sexual harassment and physical abuse are often portrayed as being part of the social fabric, of everyday procedure, structuring people's understandings of belonging while not receiving much attention. We also see this complexity represented in Sigbjørn Skåden's Chapter 8, in the intergenerational trauma of Sámi families and their inherited and justified distrust of the majority society's ability to identify injustices, and its institutional toolkit for solving social and legal issues in Sámi villages. In his chapter, Skåden asks questions about what an already vulnerable position does to additional vulnerabilities and for opportunities for redress. Similarly, in Chapter 3, de los Reyes illustrates this complexity when she highlights how the analysis of subordinate and vulnerable positions needs to include and broadly target norms about women's caring responsibilities and understandings of paid and unpaid work. This highlights the ambivalence and inadequacy of a narrative that portrays sexual harassment solely as dirt, or as easily identifiable stains on an otherwise clean social fabric; if we can't also smell the normalised dirtiness among us, we have little chance of dealing with it. The following paragraphs will discuss and highlight how the book variously situates sexual harassment as part of several continuums, how it is represented as both normalised and abnormal, and how a comprehensive approach is called for in order to identify, address and prevent it.

The need for a comprehensive approach

The chapters in this book move in and between macro, meso and micro levels of society, describing and problematising the boundaries for our understandings of sexual violence and harassment. All the chapters also discuss, in one way or another, the need for a more 'comprehensive approach', as de los Reyes calls it in Chapter 3, to the question of sexual violence and harassment. Important insights are offered when contributions do not single out and separate experiences of sexual harassment from other forms of violence and harassment, hence resisting the fragmentation so often affecting our thinking about and understandings of sexual violence. To understand sexual harassment as an integral part of the fabric of society, rather than as individual and delimited so-called 'unwelcome acts of a sexual nature', changes the possibilities for thinking about and preventing sexual harassment; it pushes the boundaries of our understandings of where the phenomenon begins and ends, which in turn pushes the boundaries of our understanding of the division of responsibility for it. When sexual harassment is seen instead as a phenomenon that involves the individual, organisational and structural levels in society, it becomes something else: neither monstrous nor normal, but rather something that is expected and that affects our overall ability to exist in a society together, with each other. The question of responsibility cannot then be placed solely on the level of the individual because the phenomenon transcends the relationships between a few individuals or, as previously noted, it transcends what has been seen as a drama with two characters.

As de los Reyes indicates in her chapter, by advocating the use of a comprehensive approach, incidents of workplace violence, including sexual violence and harassment, are not isolated acts, but 'expressions of structural and intertwined hierarchies of power that shape subordinate and vulnerable positions along lines of gender, class, sexuality and national belonging' (Chapter 3). De los Reyes conceptualises workplace violence as transcending traditional boundaries between paid and unpaid work, between the private and working life spheres, and between productive and reproductive work. She turns these perspectives around, shifting the question from the more common one of how experiences of intimate partner violence affect one's possibility to work in the public sphere, to how experiences of workplace violence affect one's capacity for a fulfilling private life, including performing reproductive and care work.

A comprehensive approach clearly shows how the continuums of violence, society and life are intertwined; life is lived in several arenas, but it is the same body that lives and labours, which of course has reciprocal consequences for these different arenas as well as for the worn-out body. In Chapter 4, Sofia Strid, Anne Laure Humbert and Jeff Hearn identify another kind of comprehensive approach, suggesting that we understand violence as autotelic, meaning that it has an end or purpose in itself. Their chapter deals with violence at the structural level, as an organising principle in a patriarchal system. Through understanding violence as a form of inequality, as power and privilege per se, Strid et al force us to think about the functioning of sexual violence and harassment in a society. They argue that, in some 'violating contexts', the use of violence might not even be needed in order to maintain oppressive and unequal relations. Again, this pushes the boundaries of our understanding of where the phenomenon begins and ends towards a more comprehensive approach, and it prompts us to think about who or what is responsible for it: where does it begin, where does it end, and who should bear the responsibility for it in various violent and threatening situations?

Normalising sexual violence and harassment

In this book, we have seen several examples of precariousness and sexual harassment as being part of the everyday fabric of institutions and people's lives, as being part of what constitutes local practices without causing any real outcry. In Chapter 7, Skewes presents experiences of sexism and sexual harassment as part of everyday life for the women at a university physics department. For them, it was a problem affecting their possibility of belonging and their right to belong on their own terms. At the same time, sexism and sexual harassment were expected and normalised as a consequence of them participating in a field dominated by men. The hallmark of normality is that it is something that happens without much fuss; it is taken for granted, it is anticipated, and it is not seen as out of place. This is the way norms function (Butler, 2011). Sexism and harassment appear in some of these texts as anticipated and endured repeatedly; these practices are normalised. However, harassment and sexism still have negative effects on those experiencing it, and it is only when the power to define the situation resides with those who are not experiencing it that it is accepted. Young women and non-binary persons in Helsinki learn from a very young age to be aware of, deal with and respond to adult men and their heterosexual gaze, as Mulari shows in Chapter 6. They are made aware that the public sphere is not for them, and they work to make it theirs. In the situations described in the chapters in this book, it is not possible for women and non-binary persons to be unaware of sexism and sexual harassment. Instead, there is a need for these groups to find individual and collective strategies and ways to handle experiences of sexism and sexual harassment. As Mulari shows, being in this kind of social setting requires anticipating, working around, and activating strategies for keeping one's body safe and carving out space by defining one's own place in it and defying assumed positionings.

Another way of discussing the normalisation of sexual violence and harassment that permeates these chapters is to look at what their existence normalises. The chapters give accounts of sexual violence and harassment as normalising unequal conditions and opportunities for some to live sustainable and fulfilling lives. The notion of a 'normal' subjectivity serves to mask exclusionary practices and violence. De los Reyes describes how workplace hierarchies are expected, are seen as supposedly normal, and how the repetition of microaggression is part of their maintenance (Chapter 3). Skewes shows how strong the male norm is in notions of the 'normal physics student/researcher', making it difficult for unequal conditions to appear *as* unequal, exclusionary, and contributory to harassment (Chapter 7). In Chapter 11, Silas Aliki reminds us of how possibility of calling the police or reporting without fearing for your own safety is assumed to be normal in discussions on prevention. And, as an undercurrent throughout the book, sexual violence and harassment seem to presuppose and reinforce heterosexuality and heteronormativity. By normalising gender inequality, sexual violence and harassment may well be understood as an organising principle in the Nordic region today, as Strid et al argue in Chapter 4.

When the book is read in its entirety, stories emerge that present sexual violence and harassment as an anomaly, as something monstrous and undesirable, and at the same time as something that is normalised to the point of being ignored. We argue that it is important to consider how these images of sexual harassment exist simultaneously, and how this might affect possibilities of making sense of lived experiences. This dual focus allows for greater awareness and helps distribute responsibility for prevention more widely.

Embodied experiences and encounters

We believe that the chapters in this anthology will help us to practise our ability to use a comprehensive approach in analysing sexual violence and harassment. This also includes blurring the line between past and present. De los Reyes introduces the concept of intergenerational transmission in her discussion of mothers' depleted bodies (Chapter 3). She shows how vulnerability and violence are continuously reproduced among women along generational lines, at the point of intersection between hierarchies of power and different spheres of private and working life. By placing the body at the centre of the analysis, she underscores the importance of seeing the body in all of this (the location of the reproductive body within historical structures and practices) and of seeing all this in the body (the location of historical structures and practices within the reproductive body).

This notion of intergenerational transmission is also present in other chapters in this book, though without using that particular term.

In Skåden's chapter (8), this question is in the foreground when the experiences and consequences of oppression, colonialism and violence on three generations of a Sámi family are explored. He asks what it means for a specific minority to be weighed down for generations, if there is an invisible line from generation to generation affecting their collective mentality as a result of practices of suppression and persecution. Skåden lets these questions connect to sexual violence and harassment, asking if and how there is a connection between being collectively oppressed and the formation of a culture of silence, where the oppressed within an oppressed collective have limited possibilities for bettering their situation by speaking up (Crenshaw, 2003). Mulari's chapter (6) bridges the different aspects of transmission by using the concept of encounters and discusses how previous encounters are always present, embodied, and affective. Here, Mulari illustrates the way that gendering, sexism and harassment are internalised in our bodies as lived memories and emotions, and that this is something that changes our ways of inhabiting our bodies. The concept of encounters is similar to the idea of intergenerational transmission, and it opens the way for an understanding of how these embodied memories are carried over generations, pointing to yet another boundary that is transgressed by experiences of violence. The idea of embodied memories reminds us that sexual violence and harassment are about physical bodies. The harm is done to bodies and to some bodies more than others. This becomes violently apparent in Chapter 5, in Mads Ananda Lodahl's short story 'On the freshers' trip', where a young transgender person's experience of sexual harassment is described. The main character says: 'I don't tell anyone what happened. I try to laugh when other people laugh. To drink when they drink.' Bodily harm, memories of it and anticipated harm affect how to move, dress, sound, and how to be; it affects subjectivity. It makes bodies sick, broken and depleted, and it makes them quiet.

Once again, a comprehensive approach is helpful in illustrating how communities to some extent consist of individuals who have inherited experiences of vulnerability and preparedness for vulnerability. We believe that there are possibilities for change if we allow invisible intergenerational lines to be recognised and blurred, and if we can manage to see how violent incidents are connected to each other, to their context, to the times when they occurred and their interconnectedness with the present, and to the effects that they have on the individual, their offspring and the community as a whole.

The ambiguities of the juridical system

For many countries, organisations, policy makers, politicians and researchers, the juridical framework has become central to our understanding of sexual harassment, with regard to definitions as well as to prevention and regulation. This can be described as juridification: 'a process whereby a situation or an issue takes on a legal or a stronger legal character' (Brännström, 2009, p 13). This makes it important to explore, discuss and think about the ambiguities of the juridical system with regard to sexual harassment as a phenomenon. One concrete example of juridification can be found in Chapter 11, where Aliki describes how criminal law is used as a pathway to gender equality, that men's violence against women should be solved by means of legislation. The chapters in this book accommodate several different perspectives on juridical frameworks and range from gender equality and anti-discrimination laws to criminal law, from acts of sexism to rape, and from restorative justice to shame to state violence. In the following, we will discuss and call attention to the options and limitations of the juridical system in dealing with sexual violence and harassment in a multitude of ways, posing questions on who the state is supposed to protect, victim-survivor needs, what the juridification of sexual harassment does, possibilities of speaking up, and the hands-on interpretations of the courts.

Counteracting restoration through juridification

Two well-known challenges of the use of the juridical system to deal with sexual violence and harassment also appear in the book. The first is that the juridical systems that we do have, under criminal law or anti-discrimination law, both see a low number of cases and, out of these few cases, a low number lead to some sort of conviction. Second, a conviction does not necessarily equal justice for victims. The juridical framework and its implementation demand a certain timeline, demand a clear situation, with a beginning and an end, forcing experiences of sexual violence and harassment to align with pre-conceived ideas, definitions, and responses. The idea and hope that the juridical system is able to achieve justice for victims of sexual violence and harassment does not seem to align with reality. While the different juridical systems clearly offer the possibility of some kind of redress, or at least some space for victims of sexual violence and harassment, its limitations are clear as well. When the perpetrator finally gets a restraining order, life slowly gets back to normal but when that restraining order is withdrawn before the set time, the uncertainty, anxiety, and fear returns, as Sumaya Jirde Ali describe in Chapter 13. This leads us to the need to discuss not only the juridical frameworks as such, but also to explore and discuss other ways of dealing with sexual violence and harassment. A lot of effort has been invested in amending and developing legal texts, policy, and practice, but the chapters in this book show that we are also in need of other imaginaries of sexual harassment, violence, and justice. In Chapter 12, Hildur Fjóla Antonsdóttir explores restorative justice as an alternative. Through letting her respondents' voices and thoughts take centre stage in her text, the challenges and possibilities of the idea of restorative justice with regard to sexual violence and harassment are made apparent, such as distrust of offenders, fear of unjust exposure and conflicting processes. In order to make restorative justice possible, Antonsdóttir reflects on the need for social transformation. She concludes that: 'According to participants, the necessary societal conditions entail support and understanding for survivors as well as creating both societal pressure and space for offenders to take responsibility for their actions but, at the same time, without justifying the violence.' Aliki also discusses social transformation in their text (Chapter 11). Through the concept of transformative justice, Aliki wishes to look beyond a repressive state and instead include the distribution of economic resources, social care and joint responsibility as a way forward in confronting and managing violence. Drawing on a range of empirical evidence, the complexity of issues of justice and redress is made abundantly clear in these chapters. For the respondents in Antonsdóttir's chapter (12), accountability (holding offenders to account and making them take responsibility for their actions) is emphasised as an important step in restorative justice for victims. Through her respondents, Antonsdóttir discusses an 'offender accountability process' as one way forward, making it possible to both meet the victim-survivor's need for offender accountability, and society's need for social transformation.

(In)equality and blind spots in juridical praxis

In Chapter 14, Anne Hellum describes how the Equality and Anti-Discrimination Act in Norway has evolved over time, and the different conflicts and tensions connected to this. The chapter includes a number of aspects of the equality and/or dignity approach often present in the development of juridical frameworks concerning sexual harassment, and Hellum calls for a careful consideration of the options and limitations of the equality and anti-discrimination approach as a means of combatting sexual harassment. She describes how the courts/tribunals in Norway work to try to determine if an act was 'troublesome', if it was of a 'sexual nature', and if it was 'unwanted'. The work that is being done by experts, judges and in the courtrooms is of importance, but it also highlights the complexity in defining and assessing acts of sexual violence and harassment, and how this rests on normative assumptions. For example, in the *Boxer Shorts Case* (where a male employee complained about sexual harassment by a male supervisor), the Tribunal concluded that the action was not serious enough to be seen as 'troublesome', exposing a lack of expertise in intersecting fields and failing to give due consideration to unequal power relations. In the *Health Worker Case*, meanwhile (where a female employee complained about sexual harassment by a male supervisor), the Tribunal found the behaviours to be 'unwanted' and 'troublesome', and hence constituting sexual harassment.

In Chapter 10, Silje Lundgren, Åsa Eldén, Dolores Calvo and Elin Bjarnegård introduced the concept of 'sextortion' to show how the juridical terms available fail to capture both the corruption and the sexual violence present in the cases discussed. They further show how an analytical framework of sextortion can help keep the focus on perpetrator responsibility and abuse of power, rendering the question of consent irrelevant. 'Sextortion occurs when a person with entrusted power abuses this power to obtain sexual favours in exchange for a service or a benefit that is within their power to grant or withhold', they write (Chapter 10). There are clear difficulties in handling inequality, and accountability and its consequences within the juridical framework where a situation with this kind of formal and apparent power hierarchy between victim and accused can still be understood as the victim consenting, with the consequence that the accused is acquitted. In the court's verdict, the victims' vulnerable positions as asylum seekers, migrants, non-heterosexual and young, in relation to the offender, made them complicit, and the abuse of power disappears from the argument and the conviction. Antonsdóttir (Chapter 12) also reflects on the power inequality that characterises cases of sexual violence and harassment, where the risk of exposure and of continuation of the violence has to be taken into consideration when discussing possible options for restorative justice.

The way in which the juridical understanding and handling of sexual violence and harassment cases is described in the chapters of this book shows, from different perspectives, the juridical system's weakness when it comes to being able to handle unequal power relations and how this affects victims of sexual violence and harassment.

The call to speak up – the right to remain silent

Juridification is related to reporting through the call to bear witness. 'Solving' problems through the legal system requires identifiable victims and identifiable perpetrators, as in the 'drama with two characters', mentioned previously. The person who is exposed to sexual violence and harassment is also the person who must speak about it, or speak up, otherwise there is no case and 'nothing' has occurred. The difficulties associated with this – the fear of retaliation, shaming and blaming – are well studied, not only in themselves, but as problems because they lead to underreporting. Again, victims are made responsible for their own victimisation. *They* need to report the assault in order for *us* to be able to do something about it.

But the difficulties of speaking up, the risks of it, correlate with the silencing context in which most acts of sexual harassment take place. In

Mulari's chapter (6), the teenagers who experienced sexualised encounters with strangers on a regular basis had become immune to them. They just expected them, and did not trust that they could get support from other people if they decided to resist or talk back. Speaking up, as an act in the world, must be followed by a reply. Speaking up without recognition will just confirm the violating acts, or as de los Reyes argues (Chapter 3), concrete events of violence or abuse, accompanied by a lack of recognition, can be perceived as revictimisation. When a situation, a phenomenon, is invoked by mentioning it, and this is then not acknowledged by the surrounding community but is instead met with silence, it is not only the situation, the phenomenon, but also the person who tried to draw attention to it that is recreated as irrelevant. This is further underscored in Chapter 13, where Ali describes how her initial reaction after being violated was to speak out, to run back into the room and tell the people there what had happened to her. She writes: 'By taking myself seriously, I had placed myself above the requirement of keeping up the great atmosphere.' To demand respect and acknowledgement for her experiences was apparently too much to ask for.

Calling out sexism and sexualising behaviour is a job for institutions, if we follow Skewes' analysis of the culture of silence around sexist behaviour in a physics department (Chapter 7). The silence around and normalisation of sexist and hostile behaviour need to be addressed and resisted, but it cannot be the responsibility of those who are already exposed to sexual harassment. The young men in Skewes' study can reflect on and joke about their own normative masculinity but, when it comes to making the connection between this, their overrepresentation in the study programme and privilege, and discrimination against women, many of them object, with reference to gender-essentialist explanations. An understanding of a distributed responsibility to identify, address and counter the reproduction of a sexist and gender-segregated work environment does not seem to be in place among these young men. Instead, the responsibility seems to be assumed to lie somewhere else; it is for someone else to point out, talk about and take care of.

In Antonsdóttir's chapter (12), the informants testify to the fear of their perpetrators. Even in an imagined secure space, the violence has already done something to its object, as one woman described: 'There is probably a lot that I would want to say but I just wouldn't want to talk to him … . I'm afraid of him… .' The violating acts have already made the possibility of an equal exchange of words, a dialogue, impossible. Ali describes it like this: 'In order to report a situation like this, you need to own it. And before you can own it, you must fight your own internal battle: to realise that your very being has been violated' (Chapter 13). How could a person speak up when the being, the very subjectivity that should form those words, and stand behind them, is already undermined? Ali describes how her objectification as the social retaliation for breaking the silence took the form of an erasure of her as a person: 'The conversation that followed took place as if I were not there. My gaze rushed back and forth between those who believed me and those who did not. Was this what I had initiated – a discussion?' Her experiences were now a talking piece.

Another risk of reporting is the repressing norm of speaking according to an intelligible discourse: speaking in a way to make yourself intelligible as a person. This is what the main character in Lodahl's short story 'On the freshers' trip' is trying to resist: 'I haven't told anyone either, until now, because then I would also have to tell people I'm trans, and I'm just one of those trans people who think it's a personal matter. Something I share with people I'm close to' (Chapter 5). The possibility of staying private is thus made impossible: victims are deprived of their right to privacy.

What is described here is the normative functions that strike back if you actually follow the exhortation to report, but do not give your account according to the discursive script expected (Butler, 2005). The victim must give an account of themselves according to an intelligible order. Taking oneself seriously deviates from that order. These are the paradoxes of speaking up. You must speak. You must speak in a manner that shows that you are the right type of victim. You must speak even if nobody responds to what you say. You must speak even if the violation of your being makes you feel that there is no 'I' who can speak.

Is it possible to stay silent and still have the right to justice, and how can one obtain justice in such cases? The book's last chapter, Lodahl's short story 'In the gents' (Chapter 15), describes the micro-sexism in everyday life. What kind of speaking up is actually possible for Bente? To paint over the insult, or to talk to her husband? To respond to the insult by writing on the wall herself, or to tear the building down? Or to stay silent?

Violence and the state

The Nordic model and the welfare state are discussed in several chapters in the book in connection with violence, gender equality and Nordic exceptionalism. But it is also relevant to touch on the welfare state with regard to justice and juridical systems. Discussions around knowledge-building and justice, within and outside of the juridical frameworks, have dimensions that need to be taken into consideration, for example with regard to who is protected, and who is supposed to be protected, by the juridical system and the state. This question relates to the state as a supposed protector of rights and of victims of crime, which one could say is an often taken-for-granted non-violent zero level (Žižek, 2008). In their chapter, Aliki problematises the starting point for such an understanding, showing how socio-economic differences, racism and migration status affect the possibilities for people in need of help and support to receive it. Aliki points out how not everyone can afford to have their perpetrators locked up, and how a police report entails a risk that both the notifier and the offender, as well as any children in common, will be expelled from the country, and that the current tightening of maintenance requirements entails a risk for family reunification if one partner is expelled. Their chapter paints a picture of how inequality increases along lines of sexuality, gender identification, ethnicity/race, and migration status when the welfare state becomes more of what they call a 'carceral state', and how people who are less dependent on the redistribution functions of the welfare state are those arguing for a stricter and harsher criminal justice system.

Another aspect of state repression, identification and national belonging affecting questions of justice surfaces when the history and presence of indigenous people in the Nordic are included in the understanding of the region; for example, the Sámi population. Skåden asks questions at the end of his chapter (8), about oppression and persecution across generations, and what it does to people, and people's trust and willingness to reach out to services built by their oppressors. Again, who is protected, and who is supposed to be protected, by the juridical system and the state? Skåden concludes: 'I do believe that when matters like the cases in Gouvdageaidnu and Divtasvuodna surface in a Sámi context these questions also need to be on the table. They are part of our map. If not imprinted in our flesh' (Chapter 8).

Nordic gender equality discourse

As previously discussed, sexual harassment is often silently anticipated and endured; everyday practices in the Nordic region still seem to be understood through the discourse of gender equality. Despite evidence of widespread everyday sexual harassment, society and its practices in the Nordic region is still understood as being at the forefront of the fight for gender equality. There seems to be a need to deconstruct the effects of national gender branding (Jezierska and Towns, 2018), of notions of what sexual harassment can be in the Nordic region. The presence of violence and anticipated violence in the allegedly gender-equal Nordic societies does something significant to our understanding of gender equality. 'Normal' Nordic gender equality thus appears to contain certain amounts of violence and anticipation of violence. If gender equality means the omnipresence of violence to some bodies, what then would the absence of (unequally distributed) violence mean for our conception of gender equality? The normalised omnipresence of violence in allegedly gender-equal Nordic societies obscures images of gender-equal societies where violence is absent, where violence is actually an anomaly and not a given. By disrupting the idea of the pervasiveness of gender equality in the Nordic countries, the contributions in this book give space and legitimacy to a wider variety of experiences and perspectives. The following paragraphs will elaborate on the gender equality discourse in the Nordic region and its interrelatedness with ideas about a women-friendly welfare state, about vulnerability and strong Nordic women and girls and national belonging, and about perpetrators.

A 'women-friendly welfare state'

Both de los Reyes and Strid et al discuss and challenge the Nordic gender equality discourse through problematising the idea of the Nordic 'women-friendly welfare state'. Strid et al (Chapter 4) argue that this particular idea does not foreground violence against women, and therefore must be revisited and revised. Through examining the differences between high rankings on gender equality indices and a high occurrence of violence against women in the Nordic region – the 'Nordic paradox' of gender equality – Strid et al conclude that so-called women-friendly welfare states have not been able to prevent or reduce violence against women and sexual harassment. De los Reyes (Chapter 3) challenges the idea, through showing how the divide between reproductive and productive work still persists in these 'women-friendly welfare states', how the reproductive burden still weighs heavily on women, and that the neoliberal organisation of labour, including traditionally gendered division of work, amplifies and relies on continuous differentiation of bodies along the lines of gender, class, national belonging and sexuality. She shows how, in normalised practices of working life, violence actually transcends all kinds of boundaries and has negative consequences on wellbeing and health far beyond the workplace. There is a need to include this knowledge when trying to understand both the welfare state and the existence of sexual violence and harassment in the region.

The notion of the gender-equal Nordic region as an obstacle

At a micro level, as seen in Mulari's chapter (6), the anticipation and self-image of being a strong, independent and equal woman in a sense can contribute to the silent normalisation of sexual harassment on public transportation in Helsinki. Mulari describes this Nordic gender equality discourse as a power-related set of public discourses defining acceptable and denied norms. She writes about how young femininity represented as a strong, independent Nordic girl has become an essential figuration for gender equality. You are, as Mulari writes, trusted to manage on your own. Being trusted to manage on your own does something to solidarity, a sense of community and trusting that someone else will step up and speak up if you are sexually harassed. Being trusted to manage on your own ignores the persistent (gender) inequality that also exists in the Nordic region, it builds on the idea that we are all on equal terms. That if a man twice your age comes and sits next to you, a 16-year-old girl, on an otherwise empty late-night bus, that this man is your equal. And that if you get scared, or if you move closer to the bus driver, or get off the bus at a different stop, or sigh with relief when another woman gets on the bus, that all of these strategies and emotions are about you, managing on your own. If the very definition of something normal is that it passes without recognition, then the silent endurance and avoidance of anticipated dangerous/abusive situations will no doubt underscore sexual harassment as unmarked practices (Brekhus, 1998), despite being carried out as actions in the name of strength, independence and equality. If normality is nurtured by silent anticipation and the unmarked, then every harassing practice or strategic avoidance move that goes by without public recognition of some kind will further embed sexual harassment as normal, or even mundane, in these local practices within the context of allegedly gender-equal societies. Thus, the image of gender equality can even be seen as producing a sense of responsibility in the harassed person to avoid harassment or at least avoid seeing harassing practices as practices of harassment. The image of the Nordic region as gender-equal seems to play a part in internalising processes of responsibility for avoiding dangerous situations among women in the region. The Nordic region, in this sense, seems to contribute to collective anticipations of gender equality, which in turn co-construct the understanding of local practices, including notions of masculinities, femininities and power. The figuration of 'the strong Nordic girl' also says something else about the gender equality discourse: namely, its difficulties in incorporating intersectional perspectives in the problem analysis. Can all young women and girls embody the figuration of 'a strong, Nordic girl'? If you are Black or wearing a hijab, are you still viewed/understood/read as 'a strong Nordic girl'? And if this position affects your strategies for safety, if the woman entering the late-night bus is a White woman, and your experiences of racism have taught you not to trust that you will get help or support from White women, then what are your options for managing on your own? What are the emotional and social boundaries that limit the available acts, or repertoire, of resistance strategies, or even the very possibility of acting at all, or talking about it?

Gender equality and national belonging

Sexual violence and harassment as a politicised issue in the Nordic region must be understood in the context of and ideas about Nordic exceptionalism. Lundgren et al (Chapter 10) show the risk associated with what they call Nordic exceptionalism in their chapter on sextortion. They discuss if and how ideas connected to Nordic exceptionalism, such as anti-corruption, might actually increase the risk of perpetrator impunity. Sexual violence and harassment tends to be othered, seen as something committed either by perpetrators with a background from somewhere else, or as something existing mainly within 'ethnic communities', hence with a background and culture understood as separate from the Nordic, othering sexual violence in line with a racist discourse. This is also a prerequisite for what Aliki describe as carceral feminism in Sweden, where demands for harsher punishments, expulsion and re-entry bans are made possible through this specific othering of sexual violence. In Lodahl's short story 'At the AGM' (Chapter 2), the main character tries to intervene in a hostile situation but gets told that: 'Danish girls can speak for themselves ... Not like where you're from'. Where sexual harassment functions as a means of male bonding, it demands the objectification of women, and it demands loyalty to a certain kind of masculinity, in this case a rather drunken Danish, White masculinity. The intersection of racism and sexism in that situation produces vulnerability by obstructing solidarity and resistance, which points to how structural inequality functions, and the limits and boundaries of the positions that are possible in an unequal world. Here, it is relevant to briefly reflect on the recent enthusiasm for bystander initiatives, and how the Nordic gender equality discourse may be a barrier to the implementation of such initiatives. The implementation of bystander initiatives might face specific difficulties within the Nordic gender equality discourse, where, at best, bystander interventions are seen as acts of solidarity, and where, at worst, they are seen as unnecessary or even as acts of sexism and disregard for women's independence and equal position in society, as shown in Lodahl's short story.

Research gaps: what about the offenders?

In her chapter (13), Ali writes: 'He appeared completely unaffected. How could an incident that affected me so much have so little effect on him?'

An identified knowledge gap in the research field on sexual harassment is about the perpetrators, the offenders, the ones sexually harassing, abusing and assaulting others. In one respect, the perpetrators are also absent in this book, but in another respect they are fully present. The perpetrators are there, using their entrusted power to sexually exploit persons in vulnerable positions; they are there as partners, fathers, employers, strangers, dates, peers and colleagues. They are there with their eyes, with their hands, with their bodies, with their words, with each other, with their power, with their jokes, with their money, with their institutions. They are simultaneously present and absent, and they are always someone else's responsibility to handle. The consequences of their acts are always their victims to carry. In Chapter 10, Lundgren et al describe how the perpetrators in the two cases discussed held positions that made them 'good Nordic men', perhaps contributing to them being understood as unlikely perpetrators, thus increasing the invisibility and impunity of their crimes.

We believe that there is a great need to reflect further on how, for example, positions that allow perpetration can travel across generations, and how this legacy of violence structures power relations. Also, we need to further discuss gender equality discourses and what it does to the invisibility of perpetrators in research and policy on sexual violence and harassment in the Nordic region.

The urge to do something

In Mulari's chapter, she writes about one girl who 'recalled a scary incident that had happened to her at the age of 12 or 13 where no one intervened or helped her out' (Chapter 6). And this is a pattern. Other informants say:

'They don't do anything.'

'They kind of said nothing to this person.'

'Well, they don't intervene.' (Chapter 6)

If we cannot rely on the Nordic gender equality discourse to handle the violating contexts that are analysed in this book, then what can we actually do? It is not surprising that sexual harassment researchers have been eager to position their results in contexts of 'doing something' – be it a checklist, updated legislation, a policy, or a list of recommendations. The urge to do something, that we discussed in the Introduction (Chapter 1), is understandable. We will end this concluding chapter with some lessons that we learned from working with this book, and that perhaps others can take with them as well.

Knowledge production and re-imaginations

We started out this book with the history of the theoretical concept of social imaginaries, which led to an account that would help position sexual harassment beyond the administrative handling of individual cases, repeated questions about its prevalence, and a juridification of it that in many senses has not helped actual victims of sexual violence and harassment. Understanding imaginaries as an intrinsic part of knowledge-building, inviting a multitude and variety of stories, voices, experiences and understandings into this knowledge-building process, makes possible imaginaries beyond the current situation. The need for gender and feminist research on sexual harassment, as well as on the juridical system and the organisation of work and welfare, is made visible throughout the book. The different ways of operationalising intersectionality and intersectional perspectives in each of the chapters have revealed the power dynamics at play in the Nordic region, historically and today. Changes in the Nordic welfare state, inequality, racism and colonialism, migration politics, everyday sexism, and violence together with solidarity, resistance and knowledge-building all make up the fabric of a society in great need of critical gender perspectives. In that sense, research can be seen as an action in itself, a movement that entails rearranging the way we think about ourselves and the world, but most of all as a way of trying to take into account the perspectives that are being represented.

Many of the problems pointed out are structural and material, built into the dismantling of the welfare state, the neoliberal construction of a precarious, women-dominated workforce and the covering-up of violence as autotelic, an organising principle for the Nordic societies in general. But many of the contexts that are analysed in this book can be described as part of a meso level, an institutional level. Institutions are structures as well, but they are lived structures. They cannot be maintained without actions, actions which are performed by us. The question of acting in different ways – to resist, intervene, instigate, speak up, or call out – is ever-present as subtext in these chapters. In order for those actions to move organisations in a different direction, we need to listen carefully for that subtext.

Micro-aggression is not micro in effect, since its modus operandi is repetition. For those who experience harassment, micro is not a question of size, but of visibility and responsibility: of getting close enough, listening carefully enough. We are all part of the contexts that we inhabit, be it a public toilet, a conference hotel, a train carriage, or a restaurant kitchen. Through interviews and observations, we can get access to situations that we have not been involved in ourselves, we can get a chance to see patterns that cannot be conveyed by the single, personal experience. Through fictional texts, we can get even closer to the micro details of sociality: a glance, a gesture, or the contradictory thoughts and feelings that run through the mind and body of a person being violated. They can reveal the ambiguities of the language that we are supposed to share, the possibility and impossibility of defending oneself, of looking for help, of intervening, of replying.

The practice of re-imagining sexual harassment turned out primarily to produce neither a new set of metaphors or images nor any new theoretical concepts, even if the book offers that as well. Instead, the importance of examining and exploring the social and cultural doing of sexual harassment emerges as the key: staying with re-imagining as practice.

Reflections for the future

We will end this chapter by trying to compile and share some concrete reflections resulting from our work on this book. Maybe our learnings will also make a difference for politicians, corporate executives, policy makers, administrators at HR departments and anti-discrimination agencies, researchers, activists and to all of us, usually categorised as bystanders.

The stories told in these chapters teach us that embracing and embodying a high degree of humility in relation to experiences of vulnerability and power relations is a prerequisite for change. Humility in this context means properly valuing and prioritising an understanding of vulnerability as it is presented by those who have experienced it themselves, and taking responsibility for effecting change on that basis. This means, in whatever position you are in, listening to the experiences of others, possibly outside of your own horizons of imagination and comprehension. In every position, be it professional or personal, there is a need for humble imagination beyond matrix-based perceptions of responsibilities.

The experiences described in this book show us how reporting requirements, formal management, and limitations in the definition and our understanding of the phenomenon 'sexual harassment' often make it difficult, if not impossible, to disclose experiences, and thus also make change more difficult. Consequently, case management systems often do not provide restitution for the victim but do give rise to retaliation or fear of retaliation.

In addition, we have learnt that accountability and responsibility are central in handling cases of sexual violence and harassment, and that this does not necessarily equal punishment and incarceration. It is about offenders being held accountable, but also given the possibility of taking responsibility for their actions. The surrounding society, be it the workplace, study environment, or social context, needs to have different options available for demanding accountability and responsibility, without at the same time excusing or diminishing the sexual violence or harassment. To build a society that can do this, we also need to be able to imagine a society strong enough to carry the burden of these experiences, offering redress, peace and space for victims.

There are no manuals of best practice that can be universally translated from one context to another, but instead local and regional norms and practices form the conditions that result in the prevalence of sexual harassment and the basis for its normalisation. There is a need to take the local context into account when trying to deconstruct the constituents of sexual harassment, regardless of which region is being analysed. Local knowledge, practices and habits are co-constructed with local norms about femininities, masculinities, intersecting power relations, material conditions, legislation and the law, and everyday norms. Precarious working conditions and sexual harassment are repeated within these structures. We believe that this is a valid starting point for everyone, regardless of their professional and personal position in society.

We have learnt that something else, something new, happens when applying a comprehensive approach, when incorporating and understanding sexual harassment as a continuum – not only of violence but of life, society and organisations – and that an intersectional lens is a prerequisite for doing this.

Furthermore, we have gained an understanding that a fundamental cornerstone for knowledge-building is the promotion of dialogue between actors such as activists, researchers, nongovernmental organisations, and other social actors. Listening to and hearing first-hand experiences is crucial, but so too is listening to those who listen: administrators, gender equality officers, HR staff. Also, let anyone be silent who wants to be silent.

The image of the Nordic region as gender-equal seems to be an obstacle to trying to reveal and emphasise the extent to which women, men and others in this region are exposed to sexual violence and harassment. In light of the analyses in the different chapters in this book, there seems to be a need for a review of the indicators in use for measuring and comparing the state of gender equality. The image of the Nordic region, maintained in part by rankings in international comparisons based on problematic measuring instruments, is in need of fine-grained scrutiny. The chapters in this book have prompted the need to look beyond glossy images of the region as a progressive haven for gender equality. The branding of the Nordic region as the most gender-equal in the world might in fact be counterproductive for social change and equality.

In one respect, we want to affirm the Nordic region and its history of cooperation between activists, nongovernmental organisations, researchers, and the political realm, which historically has had an impact on the development of social structures that have changed people's lives. This is a powerful tool that holds the potential for important ways of working towards the creation of a region that is better equipped to manage questions of sexual violence and harassment.

Part of the aim of this book has been to encourage dialogue across different disciplines and perspectives, and between different actors, in order to enable knowledge-building and create possibilities for new imaginaries of prevention. Prevention requires knowledge about what is to be prevented, and therefore we need to reflect upon the question of the legitimisation of knowledge about sexual harassment and let this focus enrich future discussion about the development of preventive measures. So, we encourage readers to stay with the text, read it, take it in. Social imaginaries have the power to describe, and thus create, the world, but only if we engage in those imaginaries, and learn from them. In this concluding chapter, we have explored what we, as editors and contributors to this book, have learnt during this process. Maybe you learned something different, maybe you disagreed, maybe you got frustrated? Maybe you recognised something, remembered something, or maybe you imagined something – something new.

References

Brännström, L. (2009) *Förrättsligande: En studie av rättens risker och möjligheter med fokus på patientens ställning. (Juridification: A Study of the Hazards and Potentials of Law, Focusing on the Legal Position of the Patient in Health Care).* PhD diss., Lund University.

Brekhus, W. (1998) 'A Sociology of the Unmarked: Redirecting Our Focus', *Sociological Theory,* 16.1: 34–51.

Butler, J. (2005) *Giving an Account of Oneself* (1st edn), New York: Fordham University Press.

Butler, J. (2011) *Bodies that Matter: On the Discursive Limits of 'Sex',* New York: Routledge.

Crenshaw, K. (2003) 'Mapping the margins: intersectionality, identity politics, and violence against women of color' *Stanford Law Review,* 43(6): 1241–299.

Douglas, M. (1984) *Purity and Danger: An Analysis of Concepts of Pollution and Taboo,* London: Ark Paperbacks.

Jezierska, K. and Towns, A. (2018) 'Taming Feminism? The Place of Gender Equality in the "Progressive Sweden" Brand', *Place Branding and Public Diplomacy,* 14(1): 55–63.

Žižek, S. (2008) *Violence: Six Sideways Reflections,* New York: Picador.

Index

References to figures appear in **bold** type; those in *italic* type refer to literary chapters and artistic works; references in roman type refer to academic chapters.

Printed and bound by CPI Group (UK) Ltd, Croydon, CR0 4YY

16/04/2025

14658341-0002